Visas and Walls

# Visas and Walls

Border Security
in the Age of Terrorism

Nazli Avdan

**PENN**

UNIVERSITY OF PENNSYLVANIA PRESS

PHILADELPHIA

Published by
University of Pennsylvania Press
Philadelphia, Pennsylvania 19104-4112
www.upenn.edu/pennpress

Printed in the United States of America
on acid-free paper

1  3  5  7  9  10  8  6  4  2

Library of Congress Cataloging-in-Publication Control
Number: 2018032185
ISBN 978-0-8122-5105-0

*For my family*

# CONTENTS

A book is a long-haul effort and demands time commitment. With good reason, then, each book has a personal tale behind it. As a migrant from Istanbul, Turkey, myself, I live my research, as some of my colleagues like to remind me. I have moved across the Atlantic Ocean four times, thrice to the United States and once from the United States to the United Kingdom. I encountered the processes, paperwork, complexity, and hurdles of both short-term and long-term migration. As I discuss at length in the book, in terms of pace and ease of mobility, migration trails behind trade and finance. For migrants, borders are salient, despite the most optimistic pronouncements of globalists on the irrelevance of borders. For migrants from some countries, borders matter even more.

As the following chapters elaborate, scholars have observed that mobility rights have expanded but disproportionately so, by favoring a subset of countries. My own traveling and migrating several times brought this observation into sharp relief for me. Of course, I am by no means unique in my migration experience. However, it was personal experience with unequal mobility rights that narrowed my interest in borders, migration, and security into a research question. At the same time, I noted that the experience of migrants sharply contrasts with globalization scholars' claims of a borderless world. Hence, although I focus on state-level policies in the book, my interest in the subjects I address arose from the perspective of the migrant.

This book is about transnational terrorism, globalization, and migration policies. While pundits and practitioners debate what migration reforms are politically feasible, necessary, security enhancing, and economically beneficial, I take an analytical approach to studying how these concerns interact to shape short-term migration policies. Rather than proposing what constitutes optimality, I examine variation in states' border- and migration-control policies. Some states have walls while others have completely open borders. Some have generous visa-waiver programs and others restrict short-term mobility. Equally important, some countries' citizens face steeper hurdles in migrating, or, put differently, some passports carry mobility privileges while others do not. What explains this variation? That is the question that motivated this book.

As this book goes to press, U.S. president Donald Trump has requested $33 billion for 316 miles of new fencing, enforcements for 407 miles of existing fence, surveillance and control technology, and training and recruitment of personnel. The fence is projected to cover 2,000 miles of the border with Mexico by 2027. The call has met withering criticism from political opponents while being hailed by supporters for enhancing security. Moreover, the proposed border wall figures as a bargaining chip in negotiations between Democrats and Republicans on immigration reform.

The United States is not a sui generis example of the politicization of migration. In Europe, the link between terrorism and migration has underpinned the rise of populism, xenophobia, and the far right. The vulnerability of migration systems figured into debates over Brexit. Migration and border policies often inspire fractious debate and polemic. This is with good reason because, like trade and financial flows, migration brings economic consequences and distributional costs to host societies. Yet unlike flows of goods and capital, flows of migrants trigger security fears, which typically coalesce around what it means to be a nation. Since September 11, and more so with the violent aftermath of the Arab Spring, transnational terrorism has loomed larger on the public agenda. Migration increasingly triggers fears over physical security. This has given rise to the frequently cited migration-security nexus. As such, human mobility now touches three facets of security: economic, cultural, and geopolitical.

The book casts light on a central dilemma countries face. After terrorist events, governments face mounting pressures to seal off their borders. At the same time, closing off borders carries economic penalties. How do states balance the twin objectives of economic maximization and security enhancement? This is the main issue the book addresses. It does not tackle long-term migration policies such as naturalization and citizenship rights and instead looks at how states monitor short-term mobility. I focus on visa policies and border barriers. These policies control migration before individuals have crossed borders. As I discuss in the following pages, states' migration policies are interconnected. States also differ in terms of what types of migration policies become salient and require policy reforms. Hence, my book constitutes the first step in uncovering the variations in terms of visa and border policies. It also calls for future research to examine how globalization and transnational threats shape other aspects of migration control.

====

# Globalization, Security, and Border Control

## The Question

Threats to state security are sometimes carried on the backs of individuals. And once they cross borders, these threats can wreak harm on destination countries. The Christmas market attack in Berlin in 2016 is a vivid example: a migrant to Germany carried out a terrorist assault against German citizens, on German soil. In December 2016, a Tunisian citizen, Anis Amri, drove a lorry into the Berlin Christmas market, killing twelve and wounding forty-eight (Eddy 2016). One of the deadliest incidents in German history, it brought the connection between migration and terrorism into sharp relief. The Islamic State (ISIS) claimed responsibility for the attack. Amri was linked to another militant, an Iraqi Salafist who had also made it into Germany. The Berlin attack highlighted the fact that migration could expose the country to infiltration by foreign militants. Amri had indeed crossed international borders several times, initially reaching Italy in 2012 and then Germany in 2015. Furthermore, he had gone through Germany's asylum system, obtaining papers to remain in the country. Not surprisingly, critics of Germany's welcoming refugee policies cast blame on Chancellor Angela Merkel, who had in the previous year opened the country's borders to half a million migrants.

A string of terrorist attacks in recent years has fueled the debate over terrorism and migration control. With each fatal attack on European soil, the migration-terrorism linkage has become more pronounced and states have been quicker to exhort policy stringency. Terrorist events have been publicized widely and the media has been quick to draw attention to target states' demands for tighter control over borders. After the Brussels attacks in March 2016, the Eurasia Group released a report noting, "Combined, these attacks will increase xenophobic and anti-immigration sentiment across the E.U., which has already been rising in light of the E.U.'s ongoing refugee crisis" (Erlanger 2016). The attacks gave ammunition to right-wing leaders in Europe to demand draconian policies. For example, after ISIS coordinated attacks in Paris, France's far right leader, Marie Le Pen, urged European states to abolish freedom of movement, a cherished pillar of the Schengen regime: "Without borders, neither protection nor security are possible" (Troinanovski and Walker 2015). After the March 22 attacks in Brussels, Mike Hookem, a member of the European Parliament from the UK Independence Party, declared that the "horrific act of terrorism shows that Schengen free movement and lax border controls are a threat to our security" (Erlanger 2016). The common thread in the responses to the attacks was that unmonitored flows of migrants are dangerous and that transnational terrorism warrants greater control over borders.

Clearly, for some European leaders, the knee-jerk reaction to these attacks was to emphasize the dangers of migration—terrorists gain access to European states' soil—and to then call for tighter border controls. The Christmas market attack vividly exemplifies the connection between transnational terrorism and border and migration policies. Border crossing was at stake in other attacks in Europe, and of course countries outside of Europe have suffered terrorist violence perpetrated by migrants. The Reina nightclub attack on January 1, 2017, in Istanbul, for example, was staged by an Uzbek national. One of the 2013 Boston marathon bombers was a Chechen, and the other was a naturalized American. Regardless of their immigrant status, the perpetrators had crossed borders and migrated to the United States. These events stirred latent fears over lax border control and the vulnerability of migration systems.

Increasingly in U.S. politics, migration and border control have occupied the headlines. The campaign trail to the November 2016 presidential election was littered with polemic and controversy over the need for harder borders. The Trump administration spelled a restrictionist bent in migration policies. Since taking office, Trump has barred travelers from select Muslim-majority countries, limited the number of refugees from certain countries, increased immigration arrests and deportations, and proposed a controversial bill aiming to drastically reduce legal migration (Baker 2017). In 2017, Trump reiterated his campaign pledge to build a border wall and to have Mexico pay for it. Shortly after that, he proposed tougher measures for screening green-card applicants (Kopan 2017). Trump often justifies his demands for a comprehensive tightening of migration and stepped-up border control with references to the terrorism-migration nexus.

We would thus conclude that the specter of terrorism will orient states toward harder borders. We might expect transnational terrorism to universally spur states to adopt tighter policies. Countries vary tremendously in how they control their borders. Some countries have walls; others are calling for walls. Some countries have open visa policies and others do not. What explains the variation in how states monitor their borders? This is the subject of my book. Do security concerns drive border closure? Speculation abounds on this question, but thus far scholars have not marshaled hard evidence to explain the complexities of this relationship. I argue that the answer to this question is not a straightforward yes. For one, not all terrorist events are fatal, and even when they are, they do not elicit the same reaction. For another, very rarely do countries enact wholesale border closure. Border closure is a misnomer because border control is multifaceted. Put succinctly, "immigration and border policy is much more nuanced than terms such as 'open' or 'closed' can capture" (Rudolph 2006, 27). Also, globalization further complicates the situation. On the one hand, countries need open borders for trade and free flow of workers. On the other hand, open borders have been heavily criticized for leaving countries open to terrorism.

Fortunately, states have multiple tools at their disposal with which to control borders. How politicians manipulate these various border controls is a careful balancing act between the state's economy and security. Two of these tools are border walls and visa policies.[1] What both instruments share in common is that they allow states to monitor migration upstream—that is, before individuals have crossed borders. In contrast, naturalization and citizenship policies control migration downstream—after individuals have crossed borders (Meyers 2000). Naturalization and citizenship policies deal with longer-term migration while visas and barriers regulate short-term migration. The scholarship on policies for short-term migration is rather thin (Mau et al. 2015). This scarcity of research is all the more glaring when we consider the connections between short-term and long-term migration policies (Koslowski 2009). Visa controls significantly influence longer-term migration patterns, including asylum applications and settlement practices (Czaika and Hobolth 2016).

Visa policies and border barriers differ on one significant component: visibility. Visa policies are formulated behind the veil of bureaucracy and are not directly observable by the public. A country's citizens are often unaware of which states their own government grants visa waivers to. In contrast, border barriers are readily observable by the public and are high profile. They afford symbolic value, independent of their objective effectiveness in forestalling illegal entry.[2] Andreas (2009) contends that high-profile enforcement initiatives are a form of security theater whereby governments demonstrate control without needing to prove the effectiveness of policies. Installing fences are about the spectacle of state authority through which governments signal that the state can defend its borders. Insofar as border instruments perform different functions, we cannot anticipate that states will stiffen policies across the board. Given these differences, the balance between economic and security incentives will depend on the functions that border instruments serve.

The trade-off between security and economic gain has come to light time and again after fatal transnational terrorist events. Politicians face mounting pressure to seal borders after attacks. After the Brussels attacks, for example, criticism turned to the Schengen system, which allows individuals to cross borders within the Schengen bloc of twenty-six countries without passport checks or immigration controls. Some commentators wondered if it should be scrapped and replaced with a tougher system. Despite pressure to seal off borders, politicians must also bear in mind economic security. Responding to calls to reinstate border checks within the Schengen zone, Ian Bremmer, Eurasia Group's president, stressed the possible ill effects of such a move: "There's going to be a lot of social instability that comes with that. It will tear at the fabric of what we think Europe is. It'll certainly hurt the economies." On the flip side, Bremmer further noted, "With Paris, suspending Schengen became a question of national security. Brussels fits into this latter category" (Wang 2016). Politicians are stuck between a rock and a hard place: they know that the economy depends on open borders, but this can create insecurity and increase the risk of terrorism. This leads to the second question that animates the book: How do states balance economic and security interests when crafting border-control policies?

My argument is three pillared. First, I distinguish between global and directed (or targeted) terrorist threats. Terrorism does not translate into blanket policy tightening because threats elsewhere and against others do not ignite fears as acutely as do threats on the state's own soil and against its own citizens. Second, economic interdependence offsets pressures toward tighter policies. States face the opportunity costs of diminished commerce resulting from tighter policies and fear backlash from partners. Liberal lobbies further stay the government's hand when it comes to tougher controls. Third, policy change is not uniform because different border-control instruments have varied functions. Take border barriers, for example. Walls assuage fears because they are overt manifestations of state power. They also do so by reassuring domestic audiences that the state can defend its borders. In comparison, visa restrictions may fly under the radar, unless the government enacts them with fanfare. If such differences exist by virtue of how a particular state chooses to control its borders, we cannot always expect terrorism to predict stiffer policies across the board.

## The Argument

Terrorist violence does not always result in harder borders. I argue that security incentives dominate policymaking when targeted attacks are the issue. In contrast, economic interdependence effectively tames fears over security when attacks are global. In the face of foreign attacks, economic interests hold sway over policymaking and make for open borders.

In order to unpack this argument, I emphasize that attacks do not trigger the same level of response across all states. Some attacks matter more than others. Much has been written about the discrepancy in the public response to international terrorist events that took place in 2015. Attacks on European soil received greater attention than did attacks in Kenya and Turkey. Whereas European countries lit up their national monuments in the colors of the flags of France and Belgium after the bombings in those countries, terrorist events elsewhere did not evoke the same level of outrage (Ahmed 2016). Commentators speculated that the discrepancy resulted from an empathy gap whereby people identified with victims they viewed as similar. This affinity functioned regardless of geographical distance. For instance, from the perspective of the United States, the London tube bombing on July 7, 2005, was more threatening than the Bali attacks in the same year because the latter incident was culturally distant to U.S. interests. The contrasting public responses to international events also clue us in on a simpler distinction: that between directed and diffuse threats. Violence that is geographically or culturally proximate strikes closer to us. More simple than that, however, attacks in our own backyard and against our compatriots strike closest to us. Terrorism is more likely to produce harder borders if the state's own interests are involved, that is, if its own nationals are hurt in attacks or if terrorists execute attacks on the state's own territory. Thus if threats strike close to home, they more readily effectuate policy change.

Terrorist events sow fear and are effective to the extent that they do so. In the absence of fear, violence would not elicit a response from targeted states. Fear affects whether and when governments respond and the shapes that responses take. Threat perception forges the implicit link between terrorist event and policy response (Rudolph 2006).[3] Along these lines, scholarship has shown that public perceptions of terrorist violence affect a range of policy outcomes (Huddy et al. 2002; Huddy et al. 2005). Public attitudes toward terrorism affect who comes to power in democracies and, more generally, reshape the political and social climate. Heightened threat perceptions generate support for right-wing parties, who may then enact more draconian policies. These perceptions also correlate with intolerance toward minorities, paving the way to restrictions on civil liberties and the rights of foreigners (Peffley, Hutchison, and Shamir 2015). If we apply these insights to border- and migration-control policies, several effects on policy stand out. First, heightened threat perceptions will translate into greater support for tougher border policies. Scholars have shown that fears and anxieties surrounding terrorism ratchet up support for harsher counterterrorism policies. This support is likely to accompany toughness on border and migration control, especially insofar as controlling borders is couched in counterterrorism terms. Second, electorates may bring to office candidates who are eager to toughen border control. In addition, a fearful public grants more leeway to politicians with a tougher agenda. How terrorism impacts threat perceptions thus affects the shape that border and migration policy takes.

Terrorist events heighten threat perception to differing degrees. Quite intuitively, we would expect terrorist violence occasioned on a country's own soil to matter more than events that transpire abroad. We might also expect threats to be more salient if a country's own nationals are hurt. To assess these expectations, I differentiate between global and targeted (or directed) threats. Targeted threats directly imperil state interests by victimizing its nationals and endangering territorial integrity. Attacks on the state's soil showcase that violent non-state actors can not only cross borders unnoticed but also mobilize and launch attacks within its territory. Transnational terrorist events that transpire on other countries' soil but hurt the state's own nationals also incentivize policy stringency. Terrorist incidents executed on a country's territory or that involve its citizens, even when they occur abroad, strike at the core of state sovereignty.

Table 1 synthesizes these insights, posing threat perception as an intermediary link between the terrorist threat and policy impact. Assaults that

Table 1. Terrorist Events, Threat Perception, and Policy Impact

| Venue | Victims | Threat Perception | Policy Impact |
|---|---|---|---|
| Global terrorism | Foreign victims | Low | Muted |
| | Compatriots | Moderate to high | Moderate |
| Targeted terrorism | Foreign victims | Moderate to high | Moderate |
| | Compatriots | High | Acute |

victimize citizens and/or transpire on the state's own territory are both targeted against state interests and expected to have a more pronounced impact on policies. Global attacks are defined as events that transpire abroad and do not involve the state's own citizens. Such attacks are diffuse and remote; they do not stoke anxiety as cogently as do targeted terrorist events. We also expect attacks abroad to have a moderate impact on policies insofar as personal proximity trumps geographical distance. Incidents within the state's borders sometimes only involve foreigners, but these events are likely to impel tighter policies simply because of physical proximity. Contrarily, foreign attacks that victimize others' nationals are geographically and personally remote.

Why doesn't terrorism always produce harder borders and tougher migration polices? After all, terrorism is designed to strike fear into the hearts of an audience broader than the immediate victims (Hoffman 1998). By extension, transnational terrorism terrorizes not just the victims or even the targeted populace but the global audience. We might then anticipate that countries gradually toughen policies as they witness bombs go off on other shores. The answer is simple. The effects of global terrorism—violence on other shores and against other peoples—are modest relative to directed terrorism. This makes room for economic concerns to dominate policy. Globalized states selectively guard their borders. They prefer open border policies, as long as threats remain remote.

Sealing off borders may enhance security, but it is costly. Consider visas, for example. Governments use visa requirements to monitor flows and deter unwanted travelers. The flip side, however, is that visa restrictions impose burdens on legitimate business and dampen tourism (Neumayer 2011). The Cato Institute, a libertarian think tank, estimated that visas dampen bilateral trade and foreign direct investment (FDI) by 25 percent. The same study also added that the United States would stand to gain $90–123 billion in annual tourist spending if it eliminated all travel visas ("Europe's Response to the Paris Attacks Is Different This Time" 2015). Consider border fences. The Secure Fence Act of 2006 authorized 700 miles of fence to be built along the U.S. border with Mexico. Customs and Border Protection (CBP) spent over $2.4 billion between 2006 and 2009 on 670 miles of the U.S.-Mexico fence. The United States spent $341 million in 2017 just to maintain the existing fence. And in September 2017, President Trump asked Congress to allocate an additional $1.6 billion toward building a 1,900-mile wall (Nixon 2017).

Costs are not restricted to the actual price tag on the border instrument. Stringent border controls "place governments on a collision course with easy trade, which is central to sustained expansion and integration of the global economy" (Flynn 2000, 58). Stringent controls run counter to liberal principles that are integral to reaping the benefits from benign flows. After 9/11, for example, the United States pushed forward illiberal measures that limited the rights of foreigners and immigrants (Flynn 2003). The Patriot Act is a case in point. These measures were controversial not only because they defied the tenets of liberalism but also because of their deleterious economic effects. Illiberal measures may impede desirable migration flows by undercutting incentives to migrate or by pushing existing migrants to exit the country (Czaika and Haas 2013). Stiffer policies are also not feasible long term because of downstream and lasting economic losses. Shortly after the 9/11 attacks, the United States toughened its border-control efforts. As a direct consequence of border closure, cross-border traffic in the area covered by the North American Free Trade Agreement (NAFTA) slowed to a crawl in the weeks following the September 11 tragedy. The United States faced immediate economic losses from its border crackdown. These losses resulted directly from the logistical hurdles of border closure. There are also downstream and lasting economic repercussions. Such measures can put a dent in cross-border exchange by temporarily relocating trade. They can also anger commercial partners and hurt diplomatic ties and even elicit overt backlash from trade partners. In sum, at the dyadic level, we expect economic interdependence to render states reluctant to close their borders.

## Globalization and Borders

The foregoing discussion underscores that globalization engenders open borders. Globalists take the argument further, however, by proclaiming that globalization will wipe out international borders (Ohmae 1990, 18). Some scholars even claim that cross-border mobility signifies the retrenchment of state powers and the weakening of territorial authority (Sassen 1998; Strange 1997). While globalists' assertions of a borderless world seem exaggerated, there is some evidence of freer movement across borders. There is support for both sides of the debate on the costs and benefits of maintaining borders in a globalizing world. Since World War II, more and more states' citizens enjoy visa-free travel. Mau et al. (2015) refer to the visa-waiver programs as the global mobility regime. The global mobility regime is certainly expanding, but it's also lopsided in privileging a select number of countries. While only 20 percent of the world's population benefited from visa-free travel in 1968, in 2010, that number surpassed 35 percent. Global migration has also risen considerably, reaching 244 million migrants in 2015, a 41 percent increase from 2000. These numbers seem impressive. Nevertheless, the world's population grew at a faster rate than that of the migrant population. Hence, the global migrant pool as a ratio of the world's population is still modest. In fact, the ratio has remained fairly steady since the 1960s, hovering at around 3 percent (Czaika and Haas 2015).

Trade and financial flows have grown more rapidly than labor flows. States' policies partially explain the lag: we know that even economically liberal states retain restrictions on legal migration (Hollifield 1992, 516). Moreover, when states have loosened controls, they have done so selectively. Mobility rights have increased for a subset of countries—primarily citizens of advanced Western democracies (Mau et al. 2015; Neumayer 2006). Western democracies tend to have disproportionate passport power in terms of the number of countries their citizens can travel to without a visa. When it comes to their migration policies, however, Western states are not the most open. For instance, the United Kingdom, Germany, and Canada rank among the top three countries in terms of passport power; however, these same countries are not among the most liberal in terms of their visa policies toward other countries.[4] The limited scope of the global mobility regime means that aside from a select subset, countries still encounter steep visa hurdles. In other words, borders continue very much to matter where human mobility is concerned: "Anyone who thinks differently should try landing at a Sydney airport without an entry visa or go to France and apply for a job without a work permit" (Freeman 1998, 93).

Perhaps more vivid evidence against globalists' prognostications of a world without borders is the recent trend toward fencing borders. Since the fall of the "iron curtain," new border barriers have cropped up, and they have done so at an accelerated pace. From 1945 until 2013, states built sixty-two new fences, and they built forty-eight of them after the end of the Cold War. More recently, the war in Syria and resulting outpouring of refugees into Europe have spurred EU member states to fortify their borders (Batchelor 2015). As a result, non-EU citizens now face tougher hurdles to enter the European Union. This has led to concern that European consensus on the freedom of movement is beginning to show cracks. While terrorism is not the sole reason why states erect border barriers, fears over security in general certainly serve as a politically expedient justification for building walls and fences. President Trump, for example, lists a host of security threats including crime, narcotrafficking, and illegal migration in pushing for the construction of a wall along the border with Mexico. Yet, in most cases, politicians sincerely believe in the necessity of a fence as well as in the effectiveness of a barrier in blunting the terrorist threat. Democratic leaders tout fences as security enhancing and necessary for the protection of the country against external threats. In no other context is the security link more pronounced as when politicians can point to terrorism as a concrete and formidable threat and the border wall as a panacea against that threat (Jones 2012a, 2012b). For example, Israeli prime minister Benjamin Netanyahu stressed concerns about ISIS infiltration of Jordan when trumpeting a new fence along Israel's border with Jordan. Netanyahu underscored that the wall is necessary, noting, "We must be able to stop the terrorism and fundamentalism that can reach us from the east at the Jordan line and not in the suburbs of Tel Aviv" ("Netanyahu" 2014).

In sum, globalists' claims that we are headed toward a borderless world do not find much support. Borders may matter less for some types of flows, but for people, they continue very much to matter. We may speculate that non-state threats, or the "globalization of informal violence," is the culprit (Keohane 2002). Globalization has negative externalities such that the transport and communication technologies that facilitate benign flows empower threatening actors as well. Globalization increases states' vulnerability to non-state threats. Just as goods and money are now able to traverse larger distances in a shorter amount of time, so are individuals. If threats are carried on the backs of individuals, then more remote threats have the potential to traverse greater distances to reach target states. With globalization, perforated borders stand to endanger states' security. Non-state actors can wield large-scale violence, previously the preserve of states' militaries. These actors can surmount the gap in capabilities they face vis-à-vis states through surprise, secrecy, and shock. The growing menace of non-state actors demands that we rethink our assumptions about geographical space as barriers. Coincident with the rise of non-state threats, globalization also makes possible dangerous alliances, for example, as evidenced by the crime and terrorism nexus (Dishman 2005). As non-state groups forge links across borders, they are further able to capitalize on globalization.

Thus it is not surprising that states lean toward restrictionism when it comes to human mobility. The preceding discussion leads us to expect that border controls are here to stay, even among liberal states. These trends may only lend circumstantial evidence on the domineering influence of security fears, however. In order to gain granular traction on how states balance economic and security objectives, we need to narrow the analytical focus by examining the impact of a specific type of security challenge: transnational terrorism. The impact of economic objectives may remain unclear, as I argue, if we look at states' overall economic openness. Although the European Union has been castigated as "fortress Europe" (Finotelli and Sciortino 2013), economic liberalism is its mainstay. Hence, it is misleading to expect economic liberalism as a philosophy, or economic openness as grand strategy, to directly influence migration- and border-control policies. To better capture the effect of economic incentives, we need to look at ties between states and analyze how these ties in turn affect policies toward commercial partners. This perspective takes inspiration from economic interdependence theory in arguing that economic ties affect how states seek security.

## Existing Explanations of Migration and Border Policies

Previous studies have not adequately analyzed the trade-offs between trade and security with borders while also accounting for the differences in policy options for border control. My work is the first to do both of these things at the same time and evaluate hypotheses based on this framework on a grand scale. Migration policy remains woefully undertheorized in international relations (IR) scholarship. Where theoretical accounts exist, the bulk of the literature studies migration *flows* rather than *policies*. When scholars have turned attention to migration policies, they have analyzed the policies of single countries rather than adopting a comprehensive framework. Existing work employs a case study design, engages in discourse analysis, or is normative in orientation. Discourse analysis provides an incomplete picture insofar as there is a gap between rhetoric and practice. The prevailing approaches to migration policy form a comparativist lens, highlighting its domestic underpinnings. A cursory survey of the literature shows that economic and cultural arguments dominate scholarship.

Comparative political economy informs us that firms generally support open migration policies while labor does not. Domestic coalitions on both sides form in response to the fiscal and distributional economic effects of migration. A popular perspective draws on the Heckscher-Ohlin framework to argue that the owners of scarce resources stand to lose from open policies and thus will trumpet protectionism (Hiscox 2006; Scheve and Slaughter 2001). A related perspective refines the factor endowment model to maintain that owners of mobile resources will advocate economic openness. At the center of both perspectives is the view that commerce bifurcates society, simultaneously creating protectionist and liberal stakeholders (Hollifield 2000). Liberal lobbies anticipate revenue loss in the event of retaliation by trade and financial partners. Accordingly, winners from economic liberalization champion sustained liberalization and open-border policies. Migration policy may be conceived as client politics whereby the openness of migration policy depends on the relative strength of these lobbies (Freeman 2001). Liberal lobbies have an organizational advantage because the benefits of open migration are concentrated, but the costs are diffuse. In contrast, opposition to migration is omnipresent, yet poorly organized. Additionally, to the extent that trade and migration are complementary (Rudolph 2008), we would expect pro-trade lobbies to join forces with those in favor of open migration policies. As such, anti-immigration lobbies find it more difficult to mobilize and pressure the state to maintain protectionism (Freeman 1995). Insofar as liberal lobbies carry the day, we would expect the domestic-level mechanisms to support the state-level argument.

The economic perspective is strictly premised on labor market effects of migration and ignores that unlike other factors of production, labor comes with sociopolitical consequences (Zolberg 1987). This insight has inspired a separate strain of comparative literature, which draws on the cultural effects of migration to explain policies. Migration may stoke cultural insecurities by undermining societal cohesion and challenging the boundaries of what defines a nation (Teitelbaum and Weiner 1995; Waever et al. 1993). Particularly if migrants carry starkly different normative templates, their codes of conduct, belief systems, and self-identities may clash with the host state's way of life (Collier 2013). Homogeneous host societies find accommodating cultural diversity particularly challenging, also because for these countries, the concept of nationhood is ethnic rather than civic. Such societies are hermetic, inflexible, and predisposed to opposing cultural diversity. In contrast, settler states built on significant waves of immigration at historical junctures—such as Canada, the United States, the United Kingdom, New Zealand, and Australia—base citizenship on civic principles and hence have an easier time reckoning with dissimilar migration (Brubaker 1992). The cultural perspective thus expects countries to pursue restrictive policies in an effort to preserve a coherent sense of nationhood or, more generally, to buoy cultural security. It also maintains that states that are more ethnically homogeneous and states that lack a tradition of migration are inclined toward stricter migration and border controls.

Arguments drawing on comparative politics to explain why states pursue open or closed migration and border-control policies illuminate the domestic underpinnings of policies. However, they cannot tell us much about how interstate dynamics affect migration policies. For example, we know from comparative political economy which actors forge pro- and antimigration lobbies. But we do not know if these actors compel governments to attune liberalization toward economic partners. This is where theories about bilateral trade and commercial dependence have merit. From a comparative economic perspective, closed migration policies are rooted in the domestic economic consequences of labor flows. This perspective does not shed light on how economic factors interact with other facets of state grand strategy. As part of its grand strategy, a state conjointly seeks economic, geopolitical, and cultural security (Rudolph 2005). The cultural perspective tells us that nativist lobbies exploit ethnocentric sentiment to fuel cultural insecurities and galvanize people against open migration policies. But we know less about whether the economic ties between states temper domestic cultural insecurities. Moreover, the subfield of IR has rich scholarship on territoriality and borders and a wealth of theories to draw upon in tying interstate dynamics to migration policies. Yet it has not adequately leveraged this literature (Gavrilis 2008a; Rudolph 2003). IR scholars' oversight is surprising in light of the fact that international migration has assumed center stage in policy debates in the past few years. As Adamson stresses, "International scholars and policy makers are finding it increasingly difficult to ignore the relationship between migration and security in a highly interconnected world defined by globalization processes" (2006, 165–167). Hence, the topic of migration control provides fertile ground for theorizing from the international relations lens.

There are a handful of scholars who have recognized the scholarly void and taken a comprehensive perspective. Rudolph (2003) argues that trading states' migration policies tend to be more liberal given external geopolitical threats, as was the case during both world wars. The relationship reverses in the absence of external threats, where the absence of a common enemy means states can afford tougher policies. Rudolph's work offers one perspective on when economic interests matter the most: when geopolitical threats compel states to value economic security and trigger a rally effect, thereby overriding concerns over cultural insecurity. Peters (2017) offers another perspective. She argues that globalization initially predicted open migration policies because of strong pro-migration lobbies. Deindustrialization and offshore mobility of firms shrank the pro-immigration lobby. She maintains that these factors are why globalized states now pursue strict migration policies. Both perspectives highlight that material considerations matter. For Peters, the current wave of globalization fails to exert a liberalizing force on migration policies because the domestic pro-migration lobby shrank as states moved production offshore and technological development blunted the demand for foreign labor. For Rudolph, globalization may fail to produce open policies in times of relative peace—absent an external common aggressor. In this scenario, threat perceptions turn inward and host states become preoccupied with cultural rather than economic insecurity.

Rudolph and Peters show that globalizing has varied effects on states' migration policies. But neither work tells us much about how non-state threats—and informal violence wielded by these actors—influence migration-control policies. My argument points to a different reason why economic incentives may have limited impact on open-migration policies. Economic models stipulate that states engage in cost-benefit analysis when deciding how open borders should be. Fears affect policy through an appeal to emotion rather than strict cost-benefit analysis. This suggests that states deviate from strict cost-benefit analysis when policies then reflect these fears (Friedman

2011; Mueller 2005). Coupled with weak lobbies, emotional decision making should further winnow support for open migration.

## Theoretical Anchor

My book speaks to debates about the role of borders and territoriality in states' pursuit of sovereignty. Territoriality and borders occupy a venerable and important role in IR scholarship; this lends a solid theoretical foundation when generating empirical implications about borders. Nonetheless, when IR scholars have studied borders, they have done so by looking at the role of borders in conflict (Huth 1996) or cooperation (Simmons 2005). Conflict scholars examine why states clash over the location of borders. Cooperation scholars explore how borders can function as effective institutions facilitating cross-border trade. Neither perspective tells us much about how states manage their borders. Common to both perspectives is that territorial demarcation is a given. Agnew refers to the unquestioning acceptance of demarcation as the "territorial trap," noting that mainstream IR "assumes implicitly that a state is a fixed territorial entity operating much the same over time and irrespective of its place within the global geopolitical order" (1994, 54). The territorial trap handicaps our understanding of how states manage borders in the face of non-state threats. An important consequence of globalized informal violence is the emerging role of borders as perimeters of defense against intrusion by non-state threats. While scholars underscore that non-state actors can exact considerable damage (Keohane 2002; Salehyan 2008b), scant attention has been paid to whether these concerns do in fact alter how states manage their borders. By looking at transnational terrorism, I shift attention to how states manage their borders in the face of such threats. This book also asks scholars to reconsider territoriality in international relations.

The territorial trap is underpinned by realism's contention that sovereignty is predicated on territorial exclusion. As an early voice in classical realism, Morgenthau defined sovereignty as "supreme legal authority of the nation to give and enforce law" (Morgenthau 1978, 4). Eighteenth- and nineteenth-century geopolitical thinking mirrors realist thinking and stresses that geography plays a pivotal role in state security (Starr 2006). Within its borders, the state monopolizes the legitimate use of force. Borders delimit the bounds of states' policing and lawmaking authority. In a similar spirit, the modern state has appropriated the legitimate means of movement (Torpey 2000a; Torpey 2000b). Dating back to the turn of the twentieth century, the passport is a relatively new invention. In previous centuries, individuals could traverse boundaries unencumbered by the need for documentation. The passport and the visa regime allow the modern state to monitor movement across its borders (Salter 2003). The realist perspective contrasts sharply with liberalism on the role of borders. Liberals view borders primarily as institutions that regulate and facilitate cross-border exchange (Simmons 2005). Whereas realists emphasize territorial sovereignty, liberals stress managing and monitoring flows across borders, or what Krasner (1999) has dubbed interdependence sovereignty. Territorial sovereignty requires the exclusion of external actors; in contrast, interdependence sovereignty turns on "the ability of public authorities to control transborder movements" (Krasner 1999, 9).

The book's analysis also sheds light on a second debate between globalists and security scholars. To summarize the debate, the material benefits of transnational exchange in an increasingly globalized economy have led many observers to anticipate the erosion of state territorial control and ultimately the obsolescence of state borders. The security externalities of globalization, however, point to the opposite expectation: harder borders. To date, no one has attempted to reconcile these propositions. This debate remains unresolved also because it ultimately rests on an empirical question of how globalization affects border politics. The book addresses this controversy by expanding economic interdependence theory beyond its conventional boundaries, which are limited to questions of conflict and cooperation. An extensive scholarship addresses how economic incentives can restrain states from using militarized force (Oneal and Russett 1997; Oneal and Russett 1999; Russett and Oneal 2001). We know much less about how economic ties influence how states seek security when faced with nontraditional threats.

Border and migration control is an ideal testing ground for studying how economic and security incentives influence policies because this is one policy domain where both types of incentives intersect (Rudolph 2005). In contrast, for example, other policy domains may be about maximizing primarily one objective. Trade policy concerns economic security. Counterterrorism is about physical security. Migration and border control are about both in that states simultaneously pursue economic and security objectives in their grand strategies.

Globalization scholars assert that commerce inspires policy liberalization because economic interests override security incentives in state grand strategy (Rosecrance 1986). Some might go even further to say that globalization imposes a golden straitjacket on states, rendering unilateral policies infeasible (Friedman 1999). This perspective is limited, however, because it does not account for economic ties between pairs of states but rather expects trading states to have open borders. This limitation underwrites the enduring clash between the expectations of globalization and security scholars. Economic interdependence theory suggests that economic ties between states constrain policies. The constraining effect grows with the relative strength and salience of such ties. I propose a similar argument and maintain that asymmetric interdependence in particular creates a push for softer policies toward trade partners. To illustrate, Canada and Mexico are disproportionately dependent on commerce with the United States; bilateral trade comprises a higher proportion of overall trade and of gross domestic product (GDP) for both states than it does for the United States. This asymmetric dependence compelled Canada and Mexico to oppose a border clampdown in the wake of 9/11. Commerce also creates stakeholders that advocate for open borders. Transnational firms and commercial interests were vocal in opposing the thickening of borders within NAFTA.

These debates anchor the broader implications of the book's three inter-related findings. First, I show that states harden borders against origin countries whose nationals have conducted attacks against their own interests in the past. This is a targeted rather than universal policy response; in other words, states targeted in terrorist attacks do not exhibit a blanket response but tighten up policies against only a subset of countries. Second, trade and capital ties render states less eager to harden borders against the citizens of commercial partners, regardless of previous attacks. Third, the identity of victims matters in conditioning states' policy choices. States factor in attacks against other similar countries and treat these events as striking closer to their own interests. This effect is evident in the European Union whereby attacks on the European continent compel states to tighten up their border- and migration-control policies, regardless of whether their own citizens were hurt in such attacks. These findings yield support for both sides of the debate. I argue that borders continue to matter, but they take on the role of a shield against transnational threats rather than traditional, military threats. The argument refines realist insights on borders as a hard shell against the militaries of other states. My argument also upholds the liberal perspective, however, by showing that economic ties soften policies and reduce the likelihood of fortified borders.

I show how the insights from economic interdependence encompass state behavior beyond the decision to engage in militarized disputes. The book demonstrates that parallel to their effects on conflict behavior, material incentives shape how states cope with transnational terrorism. The insights in this book would thus appeal to scholars interested in how security and economics intersect. The empirical results should cause students of economic interdependence theory to be cautiously optimistic: as long as violence does not transpire in the state's own backyard, commerce prohibits policy tightening. However, even distant terrorist events that harm the citizens of the state inspire policy tightening. In other words, they are regarded as occurring in the proverbial backyard.

# CHAPTER 1

## Harder Borders in a New Security Climate

Faced with the exigencies of globalization, states walk a tightrope when balancing security fears against economic incentives. Globalization promises economic gains from factor mobility. Economic interdependence also reshapes the way that states formulate grand strategy. Unilateral policies can have pitfalls, resulting in short-term and long-term repercussions. Given interconnected policies, states must anticipate other states' policy shifts. At the same time, globalization imposes formidable exigencies. The processes that facilitate factor mobility also embolden and empower violent non-state threats, making undetected entry across borders more feasible. Globalization also has an underbelly: "every sector of the licit economy has its illicit counterpart" (Andreas 2004, 644). Naim (2005) contends that "the dark trades, driven by the same globalizing forces responsible for the surge in international commerce over the last two decades, now threaten the smooth functioning of the legitimate world." What renders illicit flows particularly challenging is their clandestine nature: by evading the state's gaze, smuggling and trafficking networks stand to weaken state authority. Clandestine actors foment anxiety over the retreat of state power (Sassen 1996; Strange 1996). Although these anxieties may be exaggerated, clandestine transnational actors impede the state's bid to exclusive territorial control.[1] Economically open states prioritize effective border management insofar as border instability detracts from economic exchange (Simmons 2005) and stable borders require effective control over transboundary movement (Newman 2000). Far from erasing borders, globalization has served to bolster the importance of border control (Naim 2005; Newman 2006).

In this security climate, it should come as no surprise that policymakers propose harder borders as a panacea against transnational threats. The new security climate also focuses on individuals as threats, even if origin governments are not hostile. As a consequence of this shift in focus, controlling human mobility is essential to maintaining security. Uncontrolled borders are vulnerable to different types of transnational threats, and inter-linkages among organized crime and terrorist groups make border management all the more demanding (Shelley 2006). In this context, borders emerge as ramparts of defense against non-state threats (Biersteker 2002). Countries retool existing border management systems to adapt to the new focus on counterterrorism (Andreas and Nadelman 2006). For instance, while pre-inspection at airports had been implemented as a check on illegal immigration in the 1990s, the United States expanded its scope within the context of the global war on terror. Similarly, terrorism made a comeback on the European continent after 2001. The Madrid and London incidents animated a flurry of measures labeled as antiterrorism directives.

Discerning borders ward off threats and, at the same time, bridge economic flows. To accomplish this, they permit benign flows while weeding out malign flows. Discerning border policies are also politically appealing as a means of handling globalized violence. Terrorists rely on secrecy and surprise, which magnifies the psychological malaise that results from terrorist violence. Bolstering interdependence sovereignty—control over transborder flows—goes some way toward managing the psychological repercussions of transnational terrorism. The new security milieu has augmented the importance of border control by showing that porous borders are likely to serve as a conduit for transnational violence. Keohane expands on this: "Geographical space, which has been seen as a natural barrier and a locus for human barriers, now must be seen as a carrier as well" (2002, 32).

The contemporary foreign policy context has thus broadened the conceptualization of security to encompass transnational threats. In traditional IR terms, security is "defined in political military terms as the protection of the boundaries and integrity of the state" (Doty 1998, 73). The new security paradigm blurs the strict distinction between the domestic and international insofar as a military logic is applied to coping with atypical threats. Writing after 9/11, Kraska elaborated on this, noting "the traditional distinctions between military/police, war/law enforcement, and internal/external security are rapidly blurring" (2001, 501). As I outline below, the militarization of borders whereby states deploy specialized and sophisticated technology fits within this trend. From a broader theoretical standpoint, this alters how sovereignty is practiced. Traditionally, states reserved policing efforts to the domestic realm and military operations to balancing against external threats (Clausewitz et al. 2006). The new focus on asymmetric trends breaks this distinction down, with the result that borders reassert the privilege of the state (Rosiere and Jones 2012).

Do security incentives make for harder borders? I answer this question by focusing on transnational terrorism to capture the contemporary security dimension. Policy tightening can take several forms. Tougher policies commence with forging a link between different types of undesirable flows. The United States accomplished this in the wake of 9/11 by rebranding law enforcement efforts as antiterrorism measures, which served to stress the link between illegal migration, organized crime, and terrorism (Andreas and Nadelman 2006; Andreas and Richard 2001). At the same time, states harness existing measures by making entry requirements tougher. Higher rates of visa denials, the requirement of in-person interviews and more extensive paperwork to apply for visas, and wider surveillance exemplify this trend. States also establish tighter controls through an extraterritorial shift of border controls whereby the state's territorial reach expands outward (Bigo 2000). This culminates in an enlarged border zone (Bigo 2011). The recalibration of policies shifts part of the burden of control to other actors, such as other states as well as third parties such as airlines, travel agencies, and other private companies with authority to monitor travelers. The 9/11 Commission endorsed such a shift, arguing that "the US government cannot meets its obligations to the American people to prevent the entry of terrorists without a major effort to collaborate with other governments" (National Commission on Terrorist Attacks upon the United States 2002, 390). This shift is exemplified by prescreening checks, airline sanctions, and stricter requirements for upstream policies of control that by definition screen passengers abroad. In other words, harder borders expand the scope of who is monitored and bring more actors into the fold, thereby enlarging the scope of actors responsible for monitoring.

Harder borders also manifest through visible, on-site policies that we would typically associate with border closure: physical barricades, cameras installed at border ports, and deployment of paramilitary personnel, or at the more aggressive extreme, minefields. Part and parcel of this process is a movement away from policing to a militarized approach to border control (Donaldson 2005). This transition transforms borders from sites of law enforcement and policing to sites of military operations aiming to prevent violent non-state actors from obtaining access to the state's territory (Lutterbeck 2004). Such high-profile border instruments are more amenable to serving ceremonial functions. Insofar as these instruments affirm the state's ability to protect, high-profile, highly visible policies mollify trepidation over non-state violence. On one level, high-profile policies have a demonstrative purpose (Andreas 2009). These policies are rooted in political motives; rather than deterring access, these measures communicate moral resolve and display authority.

On another level, however, technological development and sophistication have advanced high-profile policies. Some examples of more sophisticated technology include unmanned aerial vehicles (drones), ground-penetrating radar (GPR) to detect underground tunnels, and new motion and heat sensors as part of a virtual fence (Elden 2013). These instruments also permit a smart borders approach to border control, which increasingly obviates the need for human personnel while also expanding the breadth and depth of the security zone. This pattern goes hand in hand with the militarization of borders insofar as the newer and more advanced technologies deployed are purchased from military suppliers and the tactics of monitoring cross over from the military realm (Jones and Johnson 2016). Not surprisingly, as a consequence of increased sophistication, border control requires an expanded budget. Bigo (2014) defines the European Union's approach to border control as one of policing and monitoring, in contrast to the militarized approach of the United States. The past decade and a half has seen the European Union move closer to the U.S. model. As a result of this trend, Frontex, the European Union's border-monitoring agency, saw its budget rise fifteenfold (Frontex 2014).

To recap, highly visible border policies can simultaneously demonstrate military strength and fulfill symbolic roles. Rather than debordering, globalization has resulted in a rebordering, a process that rearticulates sovereign power.[2] In addition, "the old model of security at discrete crossing points and dispersed monitoring of spaces in-between has been replaced with a model that strives for 'total awareness' and 'effective control' over the entire border zone" (Jones and Johnson 2016, 194). As extraterritorial policies have been gaining currency, the state has witnessed a shift in not just how but where it exerts territorial sovereignty.

At first blush, we might expect a perfect correlation and an automatic connection between the threat of terrorism and harder borders. In fact, this expectation seemingly bears fruit after significant transnational terrorist attacks, with commentators predicting tighter border controls and expressing fears that the events harken back to the immediate aftermath of 9/11. After a terrorist attack in Ottawa in October 2014, Canada's former deputy prime minister John Manley forecasted a clampdown on border controls, stating: "If it is in fact related to religious extremism, then I think we will see an increased ramping up of U.S. paranoia about the border and Canada being a source of potential risk for the United States" ("Ottawa Shooting" 2014). After the November 2015 terrorist attacks in Paris, France drew up proposals for more rigorous security checks, calling for "immediate, reinforced, systematic and coordinated controls" on the external borders of the Schengen Area. Pundits became alarmed that EU citizens would endure significantly higher logistical travel costs, including longer wait times, and systematic checks on identification documents. The United Kingdom, an EU member not part of the Schengen Area, criticized the proposals on the grounds that its citizens would bear the brunt of the burden.

Moreover, states that border volatile regions encounter pressure from the international community to shore up border controls. After the ISIS staged the Paris attacks, the United States and EU countries called for Turkey to crack down on its perforated border with Syria. Then U.S. defense secretary Ashton B. Carter stated about Turkey, "The single most important contribution that their geography makes necessary is the control of their own border" (Arango 2015). Thus the connection between terrorist events and harder borders is not unfounded. Nevertheless, such an automatic linkage misses the fact that policy instruments serve different functions. In other words, border strategies differ in how they allow states to express territorial sovereignty. Consequently, it would be misleading to expect uniform policy change.

Border management strategies vary according to the nature of the terrorist threat. More precisely, restrictive policies are more likely if terrorist events are salient. Violence that hits closer to home and is easily observable by the public is more likely to spur policy tightening because such events are more likely to push policymakers to take action. In other words, events that directly imperil state interests more acutely galvanize public anxieties, stoking fears over loss of control. Direct threats inflate the emblematic role that border control can play in tamping public anxiety. Previous scholarship has not shed much light on these distinct pathways insofar as it assumes an unqualified linkage between terrorism and border closure. By distinguishing terrorist events by venue of attack and nationality of victims, I argue that the impact of terrorism on border management is contingent upon whether threats are direct or global.

We might also expect material incentives to counter policy tightening. September 11's deleterious effects on economic exchange within the NAFTA area left a lasting impression. In the immediate aftermath of 9/11, the United States introduced harsher border measures (Andreas 2003b). As a result, traffic across the U.S. borders with Canada and Mexico slowed to a trickle. As Andreas and Nadelman (2006) stress, this was not the first time that a crackdown by the United States halted cross-border traffic in North America; Operation Intercept, an anti–drug trafficking endeavor, three decades earlier had virtually shut down the border with Mexico. What was more significant about the post-9/11 case, however, was that it occurred in the context of economic interdependence, institutionalized and propelled through NAFTA. There are more recent examples where policymakers voiced alarm that terrorist attacks and their aftermath would throttle trade. The aforementioned Ottawa shooting, for example, triggered fears that border checks and red tape would stymie U.S.-Canada trade. Likewise, these fears surfaced in the wake of the June 2015 attacks in Tunisia as well as after the November 2015 Paris assaults (Bensemra 2016). The fears were not unwarranted: Tunisia witnessed a significant decrease in tourism inflows during the rest of 2015 (Kim 2015).

Economic interdependence and openness raise the costs of draconian border policies. Their effects on state behavior, however, are not uniform. The costs are expected to be lopsided insofar as states are asymmetrically interdependent (Gelpi and Grieco 2008). Consider the disproportionate effects of 9/11 within NAFTA, for example (Andreas 2009, 164). The economic costs of border delays for Canada were much higher than for the United States. Bilateral trade for Canada comprises 87 percent of its total trade. By comparison, for the United States, the figure stands at 25 percent. The asymmetric commercial relationship can be expressed in terms of trade to GDP ratio. Forty percent of Canada's GDP comes from (is tied to) its U.S.-bound exports. In sharp contrast, only 2.5 percent of U.S. GDP comes from its exports to Canada.

States strive for a balance between borders that remain open to economic exchange but yet are impregnable to penetration by undesirables. The balance also hinges on whether threats are diffuse or targeted. Before delving into the interplay between security and objectives, we need to spell out why transnational terrorism should predict tighter controls and hardened borders.

## Transnational Terrorism

Terrorism is the "anxiety-inspiring method of repeated violent action, employed by (semi)clandestine individual, group, or state actors, for idiosyncratic, criminal, or political reasons, whereby . . . the direct targets of violence are not the main targets" (Schmid and Jongman 1988, 28). The audience of terrorist violence is broader than the immediate targets of attacks. In other words, the victims are not always the intended targets of the terrorist actors but individuals who are simply at the wrong place at the wrong time (Sanchez-Cuenca and Calle 2009).[3] The latter aspect is why the repercussions of terrorist events transcend the physical damage and carnage caused by the incidents. By intimidating an audience greater than the victims of attacks, and by promising further violence to come, terrorist actors aim to intimidate and force policy change from target governments (Pape 2006).

In terms of military capabilities, terrorism is the strategy of the weak (Hoffman 1998). Terrorist groups, even when they solidify territorial control and draw on a global pool of recruits, cannot amass military capabilities that match those of state actors. They make use of transnational organizations to leverage borders to their advantage. They foment uncertainty over when and where attacks might occur through the stealth element. They explicitly seek to catch states unaware in order to cast doubt on their ability to protect. They do so by making use of individuals to transport violence across states. The degree of damage inflicted can be on par with that of state actors (Salehyan 2008b). By doing so, they highlight states' strategic vulnerability in the face of non-state threats. Gearson writes that the September 11 militants "utilized the long-established terrorist approach of careful planning, simple tactics, and operational surprise, to effect the most stunning terrorist 'spectacular' in history" (2002, 7).

Transnational terrorism takes advantage of the processes of globalization. It also shares the stealth element in common with other types of non-state threats—or clandestine transnational actors (CTAs). CTAs include relatively harmless actors such as undocumented immigrants or refugees, more harmful actors such as smugglers and human traffickers, and more imminent security threats such as insurgents and terrorists. Border strategies are increasingly geared toward inhibiting access to such actors. As such, the theoretical connection between transnational terrorism and border control leverages insights about borders as preventive barriers against atypical threats (Andreas 2003a; Jones and Johnson 2016). Harder borders impede the movement of CTAs across borders by raising the costs of entry and increasing the likelihood of apprehension by state agents (Hassner and Wittenberg 2015). These policies aim to deny such actors access to territory. Terrorism, however, is on the dangerous end of the continuum of CTAs. Organized crime, for instance, may prey upon and detract from the legal economy, but terrorism is distinct in that it can cost lives, damage property and infrastructure, and even degrade the health of the country's economy (Enders and Sandler 2006b).

I contend that three interrelated features of transnational terrorism are important for understanding why transnational terrorist events prompt tighter border policies: (1) nonhierarchical spread, (2) stealth, and (3) psychological import. I flesh out each component in the sections that follow and then discuss why directed and global terrorist events have distinctive effects on the state's responses to violence.

## Nonhierarchical Spread

Transnational terrorism, by definition, involves crossing borders. As the preceding discussion illustrated, when a transnational terrorist event transpires, either the perpetrators or victims cross frontiers (Li 2005). In addition, transnational terrorist groups are nonhierarchically networked across multiple states and sometimes multiple regions (Enders and Su 2007). Groups can mobilize, recruit, and train in bases spread across several countries. Even if a terrorist group is initially limited to a specific region, it can evolve over time to develop offshoots or branches elsewhere. A noteworthy example is ISIS, which the international community initially hoped would remain confined to the Levant. After the Paris attacks, attention turned to the group's external operations branch in Europe (Callimachi, Rubin, and Fourquet 2016).

To be sure, transnational networking does not diminish the inhibitory impact of distance (Gelpi and Avdan 2015). Although transnational terrorism calls to mind the September 11 attacks, in actuality, terrorism is a relatively short-gun phenomenon. Terrorist groups tend to cluster in specific hot spots of high-volume activity (Braithwaite and Li 2007). Nonetheless, even if terrorist operatives are not mobile across borders, and even if organizations do not possess bases of operation in multiple countries, there are other ways in which terrorism can traverse borders. In general, terrorist violence features spatial dependency (Sageman 2004). Even when the tangible assets behind violence (arms, personnel, funds) do not travel across countries, the intangibles that support violence—tactics, ideas, and knowledge—can diffuse across borders. The form that violence takes can spread to other countries as homegrown groups mimic and adopt foreign groups' tactics (Midlarsky, Crenshaw, and Yoshida 1980). For example, Hamas borrowed the suicide vest from the Tamil Tigers in Sri Lanka (Horowitz 2010). The decision to go transnational—rather than remain tied to a specific piece of territory—can signal group resolve and capabilities. To the extent that transnational spread permits more interlinkages among groups, transnationalization can also raise group lethality. Not surprisingly, then, ISIS's ostensible decision to go global by waging a campaign in the West compounded anxiety over the group's growing reach. Pundits speculated as to whether the attacks on the European continent signaled a tactical shift in the ISIS's operations, in part to counterbalance its territorial losses in Iraq and Syria (Hegghammer and Nesser 2015). Furthermore, loyalties may also traverse borders, facilitating transnational recruitment (Piazza 2006). Finally, funding and weapons are also smuggled across borders, a dynamic that gains speed and currency with the emerging organized crime-terrorism nexus (Dishman 2005). In sum, transnational terrorism defies and circumvents state borders in a number of ways, most starkly because groups establish bases across frontiers but also through transnational financing, emulation of foreign groups' tactics, and transnational mobilization and recruitment.

In contrast, the state's power is hierarchically organized within its own territory. Scholarship maintains that borders are more constraining on states' armed forces than on transnational actors (Naim 2005; Salehyan 2006; Staniland 2006). Salehyan (2006) places the state's agents at the far end of a continuum of global mobility. The moral opprobrium on territorial conquest, buttressed by the normative consensus on territorial sanctity, means that in theory at least states cannot easily move troops across neighboring territories (Zacher 2001). International borders constrain different types of flows unequally: capital and then goods occupy the relatively mobile end of the spectrum, whereas the state's security forces are at the other end. "In sum, the state is limited by its boundaries—the capacity to wield force. . . . is largely constrained by sovereign borders" (Salehyan 2006, 31). This limitation partly stems from the transaction costs involved in efficient collaboration among states. States confront hurdles when cooperating against atypical threats. To begin with, states cannot agree on a common list of designated terrorist groups (Sandler, Arce, and Enders 2009). They also are not effective at coordinating antiterrorism efforts. In contrast, terrorist organizations sometimes strategically pool their resources together to offset their relative military weakness (Hoffman 1998). They are effective at networking: forming alliances with each other, learning new techniques and modes of attack, and even going so far as to train together even in the absence of ideological commonalities. Terrorist groups excel at developing cross-border connections and are in fact found to be, on average, more centrally connected than criminal networks (Helfstein and Solomon 2014).[4]

Transnational actors are able to capitalize on the disproportionate constraining effect of borders (Shelley 2006). Smugglers, for example, take advantage of price differentials across borders (Carter and Poast 2015), in addition to being able to relocate operations to skirt state monitoring. Transnational terrorists can similarly reap the benefits of mobility across borders by relocating and regrouping if dislodged from state territories. Terrorists' ability to network across countries makes it difficult to detect and identify them, which in turn facilitates clandestine entry into states' territories. To surmount the asymmetrical limitations on state power projection capabilities, states may turn to defensive measures focused on preventing access to territory. Fortifying borders may emerge as a more attractive and feasible strategy when compared to risky endeavors such as air campaigns or ground incursions into neighboring territories (Staniland 2006).[5] Arguably, however, technological innovations make a state's power projection across borders more feasible.[6] Drones, for example, can augment monitoring and surveillance regimes. Newer technologies overcome the normative constraint to some extent by permitting states to project power without actual boots on the ground. These technologies, however, are certainly not impervious to criticism.[7] In addition, territorial integrity is closely linked to border fixity: as territorial conquest has become uncommon as a form of power maximization, states' borders have become more and more fixed (Atzili 2006).

## The Stealth Element

The spread of transnational terrorism makes it difficult for states to mount a counterresponse, and the stealth element deepens states' disadvantage in the face of non-state threats. Terrorist groups can leverage information asymmetries to gain an edge against militarily advantaged states. As a consequence, ""an information society" such as that of the contemporary United States would be at an informational disadvantage with respect to networks of individuals whose communications seem to occur largely through handwritten messages and face-to-face contacts" (Keohane 2002, 34). Militants can defy border control, escape law enforcement, and circumvent state surveillance. Contrary to popular perception, however, clandestine territorial access does not always mean that militants slip undetected across borders. It can also transpire when terrorist groups exploit legal channels of territorial access. In fact, fears that terrorists would exploit the refugee regime were at the heart of some European states' calls for stringency. Surreptitious entry reifies the idea of loss of control over borders and erodes sovereignty (Sassen 2006). Insofar as terrorist actors are hard to detect, conventional notions of defense do not apply to counterterrorism (Cronin 2002; Paul 2005).

Additionally, terrorist events inflict psychological costs on targets because they carry shock value. By exploiting uncertainty over the when and where of violence, terrorist actors are in effect able to gain symbolic power over state actors (Juergensmeyer 1997). This was true of several surprise attacks against democracies: Madrid in 2004, London in 2005, Paris in 2015, Ankara in 2015 and 2016, and Brussels in 2016. These events drove home the message that despite surveillance systems, the governments had failed to insulate citizens from these attacks. Even where societies were on high alert and anticipated transnational terrorist violence, the unpredictability of these events underscored the feebleness of the security establishment.[8] For example, in the wake of the Brussels attack, commentators stated that while Belgium had been identified as a likely target by ISIS, and worries had been expressed over its status as a cradle of radicalization, the attacks quickly drove attention to the failures of the state's security apparatus (Ivanovic 2016).

Thus, on one level, the stealth element exacerbates anxieties that even militarily powerful states are at the mercy of transnational militants. We imagine that militants mask their true aims at border crossings and carry out their nefarious plans once they attain territorial access. On another level, however, there is also uncertainty over whether legal travelers are prospective recruits. The *National Strategy for Combating Terrorism* warned about terrorism's global reach, that is, its capacity to have transnational and global appeal (United States 2011). Universalist non-secular ideologies, central to the contemporary wave of terrorism, permit groups to broadcast their message to broader, abstract, and often transnationally constructed communities, which they purport to represent and on whose behalf they commit violence (Rapoport 2001). This lends another layer of uncertainty insofar as religion can be utilized as a transnational recruitment mechanism (Juergensmeyer 2003; Lacqueur 1999). The globalization of recruitment also makes detecting and ferreting out operatives more difficult. Foreign fighters, for example, can mask their true intentions when crossing borders.

The stealth element contributes to fears over migration as a conduit for terrorism flows (Bove and Bohmelt 2015). Migration can function as an avenue for transnational terrorism to the degree that it feeds the social and kinship networks that underpin radicalization and recruitment. This possibility focuses on radicalization after migrants have already gained access. A report by the Nixon Center voices these fears: "Migration and terrorism are linked; not because all immigrants are terrorists, but because all, or nearly all, terrorists in the West have been immigrants" (Leiken 2004, 6). The Hamburg Cell, a group of expatriate students that formed around a jihadi radical who had illegally immigrated to Germany, orchestrated the 9/11 attacks. Radicalization is a multistep process (Sageman 2004), whereby host-country context can interact with active recruitment machinations by terrorist groups to produce extremism on host-country soil. States also fear that operatives may hide among the general populace and activate sleeper cells within the host (Dishman 2005). The prospect of infiltration makes it possible that foreign violent actors can lodge themselves within the state, in effect allowing them to repudiate borders and gain a foothold in destination states.

## Psychological Impact

The desire to instill and disseminate fear lies at the core of terrorist violence. Fear is what links the motivation to use violence to an anticipated policy outcome (Braithwaite 2013). Fear is the pivot point of terrorist violence and, consequently, public perception is the true target of terrorist assaults. Terrorists use violence to manipulate the expectations of an audience that expands beyond the immediate victims. They intimidate through the promise of future violence to come. The public has a double role as the audience of terrorist violence and the impetus for policy change (Friedland and Merari 1985). By spreading fear, terrorist actors also seek to undermine the government's competence in the public's eye (Bueno de Mesquita (2005).

Public fears stimulate policy change insofar as political leaders believe tougher policies will alleviate these fears. For public attitudes to have policy impact, leaders should also factor in these fears. Typically, because democratic leaders are office seeking, they are cost-sensitive and more responsive to these fears. Management of fear is especially important given empirical patterns of terrorism: terrorism is a rare event (Mueller 2006). Risk assessment becomes more inaccurate in the face of high-consequence rare events (Kunreuther 2002). Transnational terrorists embody this phenomenon: terrorist actors capitalize on unpredictability to create a sense of helplessness. Mueller stresses that "the costs of terrorism commonly come much more from hasty, ill-considered, and over-wrought reactions, or overreactions, to it than from anything the terrorists have done" (2005, 222). Precisely because these threats are hard to anticipate, ameliorating fear goes a long way toward effective counterterrorism (Friedman 2011; Khalil 2006).

Scholarship from psychology is insightful in terms of understanding how the public responds to terrorist violence. Persistent terrorism generates a range of ill effects. Moreover, these effects are enduring: terrorism not only dampens public morale but negatively (and perhaps irrevocably) alters the psychosocial fabric of democratic societies (Peffley, Hutchison, and Shamir 2015). We also know that terrorism evokes fear and anger and that these emotional responses are tied to different types of policy demands (Huddy et al. 2005). Fear demands caution whereas anger demands retribution. Attitudes toward terrorism have implications for a range of policy outcomes. Policy change is more likely in the face of terrorism because the political milieu shifts to the right, whereby the public gravitates increasingly toward illiberal and authoritarian attitudes. Chronic terrorism leads to limitations on minority rights (Merolla and Zechmeister 2009). Terrorism rewrites public attitudes by sapping forbearance in societies, thus posing a danger to democratic governance (Peffley, Hutchison, and Shamir 2015). The literature thus conveys that terrorism has direct and indirect effects on policies. More directly, violence can animate specific antiterrorism measures. Indirectly, it shapes public attitudes toward policies and thereby enlarges the scope for policy-making. The public becomes more intolerant of minorities and more willing to support hard-line policies such as increased surveillance, enhanced interrogation tactics, and restricted civil liberties and minority rights (Peffley, Hutchison, and Shamir 2015; Piazza 2015).

So far, scholarship has sidestepped the question of how public attitudes toward violence affect migration and border control. The political attitudes that inspire toughness in antiterrorism may do the same for migration and border control. Widespread authoritarianism and illiberalism should generate a political environment supportive of migration restrictions and border crackdowns. If heightened fears bring in strongman leaders and right-wing governments, this should also bolster policy stringency. Chronic terrorism also foments generalized feelings of insecurity, which are linked not to particular incidents or perpetrators but to beliefs that the state and society are vulnerable (Joslyn and Haider-Markel 2007). Even when threats do not emanate from outside the state or are unrelated to terrorism, leaders can animate latent feelings of insecurity in order to push forward hard-line agendas. The death of a border agent in Texas in November 2017 reanimated the Trump administration's calls for the border wall (Bever, Hawkins, and Miroff 2017). The incident is unrelated to terrorism, but it can still be leveraged to push the wall forward because of extant fears of outside threats.

There are two insights from previous research about public attitudes toward terrorism that I argue connect fears to policy change. The first concerns the distinction between selfish and communal fears, which mirrors the well-known distinction economists draw between pocketbook concerns and macroconcerns over the national economy. Joslyn and Haider-Markel (2007) show that sociotropic fears rather than personal fears connect more closely to policy demands. Perceptions that the community and the way of life are endangered are more powerful drivers of policy change than personal fears that one's life is in danger. The second insight is that terrorist threats are prone to othering and, at the extreme, scapegoating those outside of the community (Piazza 2015). Violence stirs resentment, creates demand for punitive measures, and exacerbates ethnocentrism (Feldman and Stenner 1997). The perception that threats emanate from outside the community justifies stringency in migration and border control. Moreover, the link between terrorism and border policies relies on the perception that threats arise from outside the state. Threat perception functions through the prism of nationhood, which turns on a hard distinction between the nation as a community and foreigners as others.

Taken together, the psychological effects of terrorist violence link terrorist events to harder borders insofar as border policies serve a reassurance function. They are symbolic because they permit the state to demonstrate its commitment to protecting the citizenry. Public anxiety can prompt tighter policies through a corollary mechanism: widespread anxieties furnish policymakers with greater latitude in pushing forward more draconian policies. Part of this process hinges on the exploitation of fear (Altheide 2006; Mueller 2006). Fears can instigate novel policies or, alternatively, rekindle stalled policy endeavors that favor more rigorous border control. For example, in the case of India and Israel, border security projects that had stagnated as a result of domestic opposition gained renewed steam as a direct consequence of a series of terrorist incidents: after the Second Intifada in the case of Israel and after a series of bombings following the 2008 Mumbai attacks in India's case.

Nevertheless, hypervigilance is not always about manipulating fear. Given uncertainty about the timing and location of terrorist events, it pays to be overly cautious (Friedman 2011). Policymakers would rather be overcautious than communicate optimism and be proven wrong. As Gelpi and Avdan note, "Policy makers are willing to tolerate large numbers of false-positive predictions of a terrorist threat in order to avoid a single instance of a false-negative prediction that results in a terrorist attack" (2015, 18). After all, it is far more costly for states—and for the political careers of decision makers—to be overprepared for terrorist events that do not come to pass (false positives) than to fail to be prepared for incidents that do occur. After the attacks in Brussels in March 2016, the Belgian government was denounced for precisely this type of error in judgment.

## Targeted and Global Threats

The policy response to terrorist events is determined by how close to home the assaults occur. Incidents that directly target the state's interests tie into tighter policies in a more straightforward manner. Direct experience can take two forms: transnational terrorist incidents conducted within the state's borders and events that transpire abroad but victimize the state's own nationals.[9] To illustrate, on March 19, 2016, a suicide attack took place in Istanbul, killing four foreigners and injuring thirty-six more. Among the victims were nationals of the United States and Israel. From the perspective of the United States and Israel, the attack occurred abroad but involved direct experience with terrorism in the sense that these states' own citizens were maimed or killed. From Turkey's perspective, however, despite not leading to any Turkish fatalities, this incident would still be classified as direct experience with terrorism because it occurred on Turkish territory (Mickolus et al. 2007).[10] To provide a contrasting example, on October 10, 2015, Turkey suffered an attack on its own soil, in the capital city of Ankara, of an unprecedented nature. The victims were Turkish nationals. From Turkey's perspective, the Ankara incident fits under both forms of direct experience: on its own territory and involving its own citizens. In practice, these two types of incidents overlap to a great extent: thus the majority of assaults that occur within the state's borders also involve its own nationals.[11] While these incidents may overlap in practice, it is possible to differentiate between two types of avenues of impact: targeted incidents that I dub the territorial effect and compatriots' effect.[12]

I propose two complementary mechanisms to support this expectation. First, targeted terrorism plays into the hands of policymakers that champion policy stringency. In effect, targeted terrorism sets in motion the process of securitization, whereby a particular issue area is redefined and repackaged as an existential threat (Buzan, Ole, and Wilde 1998). Through this process, policymakers emphasize the external roots of terrorism and the dangers of permeable borders. Securitization repackages international terrorism as a grave and pressing danger, on an equal footing with military threats (Huysmans 2006). Direct threats expand the scope of policy options that are politically palatable. As a consequence, controversial policies that might have been a hard sell are easier to justify. To illustrate, in response to 9/11, liberal democracies adopted tough legislation dealing with immigrants and foreigners and expanded the rights of the executive to survey and assemble information (Epifanio 2011). Some of these measures might have been politically unpopular, without the threat of transnational terrorism, because they cut into the procedural and privacy rights of not just foreigners but also citizens. However, the sense of urgency generated by attacks on these countries' own territories—9/11, 4/11 (Madrid), and 7/7 (London)—downplayed the influence of liberal reservations.

Second, targeted events have a more pronounced impact on public fears and anxieties. To the extent that border control aims to quell these fears, we should expect incidents that trigger alarm to connect more closely to harder borders. Psychologists connect fear to a demand for caution and defense (Huddy et al. 2005). Tighter controls align with a defensive perspective and borders are viewed as a protective shield against external threats (Staniland 2006). Researchers also document a significant shift in public attitudes as a

consequence of terrorism, such that people are more willing to tolerate pain-
ful measures, including restrictions on civil liberties (Davis and Silver
2004). Accordingly, the public will be more likely to welcome and even em-
brace draconian policies that run counter to liberal norms. Harder borders
depart from liberal principles of freedom of movement. Absent direct attacks,
the public may not support them. An ancillary line of research finds that
transnational terrorism realigns the political environment by making the
public more likely to elect right-wing, hawkish political leaders (Huddy et al.
2005; Lahav 2004). It is plausible that hard-line leaders are more likely to
trumpet tougher border controls.

## Territorial Effect

Transnational terrorist incidents that transpire on the state's own territory
are likely to heighten negative attitudes toward terrorist violence more than
terrorist events that transpire abroad. Physically proximate events are more
salient. An extensive line of research shows that those proximate to areas suf-
fering from prolific levels of terrorism exhibit higher levels of anxiety and
fear and that these emotions endure (Allouche and Lind 2010). Analogously,
proximate violence is more vivid in memory (Lowenstein et al. 2001). Empirical studies of public attitudes show that Americans exhibited symptoms
akin to post-traumatic stress disorder (PTSD) in response to 9/11 and, further, that these symptoms were more acute among those who lived in New
York's metropolitan areas (Schuster et al. 2001). Violence that takes place on
one's own soil will also be more jarring and therefore enduring in collective
memory. Numerous studies, conducted in countries that bore witness to
major terrorist events—Spain, the United Kingdom, and the United States—
corroborate this insight (Allouche and Lind 2010; Braithwaite 2013; Romanov,
Zussman, and Zussman 2010).

## Compatriots' Effect

Incidents that victimize the state's citizens are a form of direct experience
with terrorism. I contend that even when assaults occur in other countries,
the involvement of the state's own nationals will generate a stronger policy

response. Such events are simply publicly more visible; the death of a country's citizens invites longer and more expansive media coverage. People are more likely to be cognizant of these events. Such attacks may be physically distant but are personally proximate. Personal proximity centers on shared communal traits, in this instance defined by citizenship. People come to believe they may be next in line. Such events also pose a danger to citizens' broader community and way of life (Huddy et al. 2002). Assaults that victimize the state's own citizens are likely to elicit a stronger outcry because the public can readily empathize with fellow citizens. Parallel to attacks on the country's soil, these events create room for tougher policies and play into the hands of hard-line policymakers who espouse a tougher approach to border control.

## Trading Security for Economic Gain

Smart borders demand that states pursue selective policies instead of a blanket clampdown. Border closure targets specific source states and takes into account the past history of attacks. In contrast to global threats that are diffuse, incidents that are traceable to source countries permit selective border closure. A selective strategy is more appealing to economically open states that cannot afford wholesale border closure. Naim (2005) argues that selective border policies are necessary for coping with the exigencies of globalization. He maintains that such policies are necessary for "a government that is mandated to control an increasing number of cross-border activities, on all borders" (Naim 2006). Precisely because states are limited in their ability to identify and track down clandestine transnational actors, we expect them to craft policies that minimize territorial breach by potential threats. However, smart borders do not simply screen undesirables. They also sustain borders open to benign flows. Therefore, permeable borders necessitate that, to some degree, states must trade security for economic gain.

Economic interdependence scholarship helps illustrate how states balance economic goals with security objectives. A rich body of knowledge in international relations maintains that trade and capital ties shape states' conflict behavior (Doyle 1997; Mansfield and Pevehouse 2000; Mansfield and Pollins 2003; Polachek 1980; Viner 1951). Extrapolating from this, I argue that commercial ties influence states' security-seeking behavior vis-à-vis transnational threats. Economic and security interests intersect when it comes to controlling borders. The argument builds on the work of liberal scholars who argue that trading states are more reluctant to use militarized force (Domke 1988; Rosecrance 1996; Rosecrance 1986). Mirroring this contention is the idea that commerce and territorial conquest accomplish the same objectives, so that material incentives eclipse security interests in state grand strategy. A more nuanced argument is rooted in the logic of opportunity costs whereby bilateral economic ties are central to the pacifying effect of trade (Oneal and Russett 1997; Oneal and Russett 1999; Russett and Oneal 2001). Specifically, states shy away from engaging in militarized disputes against commercial partners. Opportunity costs are an important reason why states are reluctant to take up arms against economic partners. States anticipate backlash from partners; the prospect of economic loss from disruption or diminution of trade in turn restrains the use of force.

Neoclassical economics would tell us that economic openness predicts open borders. Empirical patterns, however, fail to sustain this expectation. To stress an earlier point, migration scholars argue that trading states continue to pursue relatively closed migration and border policies (Cornelius et al. 2004; Hollifield 2000). The neoclassical argument may miss the mark insofar as it ties economic openness to liberal migration policies without heeding how bilateral ties affect states' policies. In order to overcome this theoretical shortcoming, I contend that general openness to economic flows may not necessarily entail open borders; instead, economic interdependence with a commercial partner will predict more liberal policies toward the partner. Specifically, asymmetric dependence on commercial partners will inhibit draconian policies against their citizens. Two distinct lines of argumentation support this proposition. Hardened borders and restrictive policies are hostile signals. States view visa restrictions, for example, as punitive sanctions, and the imposition of visa requirements may trigger retaliation from dyadic counterparts. A more extreme example is border barricades: these impediments aggravate neighbors even in the absence of territorial disputes (Donaldson 2005). To the extent that neighbor states perceive barriers to be adversarial signals, tighter policies bear opportunity costs. If these costs restrain states' conflict involvement, we can expect similar restraints to act upon states' border-control policies.

A somewhat less well-known strain of economic interdependence scholarship is grounded in sociological liberalism (Viner 1951). Scholars writing in this tradition argue that economic exchange hinges on communication and contact between states, which in turn enhance trust (Fordham and

Kleinberg 2010). Through commerce, states gain knowledge about each other's customs and practices. Harder borders are antithetical to liberal precepts and collide with the norms of a free market society (Flynn 2003). As such, economically integrated states should be guided by shared liberal tenets. At the same time, greater trust entails that states downplay security fears from economic partners.

The state-level arguments can only take us so far. After all, there are highly interdependent states, such as U.S.-China and U.S.-Mexico, that do not have liberal migration and border policies with regard to each other. In other words, state-level arguments are limited because migration control is not high politics and is thus on a different footing compared to the decision to use militarized force. There is, in addition, a societal layer to how interdependence connects with more open borders. Economic ties create vested interests in maintaining open borders. Tighter policies hinder personal contact and interaction, which are crucial to international economic exchange. Stakeholders are thus likely to oppose policy tightening due to the costs on face-to-face contact with business partners. Fervent proponents of trade and capital liberalization have historically trumpeted open migration policies (Hollifield 1992; Hollifield and Zuk 1998). Insofar as trade and migration are complementary, we expect pro-trade lobbies to champion looser migration policies (Rudolph 2008).

## Looking Ahead

To recapitulate, border control fulfills two functions. The first one is demonstrative and premised on showing the state's territorial authority. The second one centers on effectiveness and necessitates screening out and denying access to threats. Border instruments are differentiated according to how well they can perform these functions. The theory of border control makes three overarching claims with empirical implications. First, fears over security lead to policy restrictiveness. The book concentrates on terrorism as a crucial manifestation of security concerns in the contemporary policy climate. The second claim adds nuance to the first by arguing that threat perception varies according to whether violence is directed toward state interests. The third claim is grounded in economic interdependence theory and suggests that trade and capital ties make for more open borders. They do so, directly, through the opportunity costs generated by harder borders. They also do so by modulating the impact of concerns over terrorism. While the theory developed in this chapter applies broadly to border control, the empirical chapters develop hypotheses on specific instruments of control and test the implications of the theory separately on these instruments. Looking ahead, Chapter 2 formulates hypotheses on visa restrictions. Chapter 3 focuses on visa requirements and visa rejection rates. Chapter 4 shifts the focus to border barriers in the twentieth and twenty-first centuries.

### CHAPTER 2

# Terrorism, Trade, and Visa Restrictions

## Visas and Border Control

In the previous chapter, I argued that border closure will be more likely in the face of transnational terrorism, especially when attacks are directed against a state's territory and citizens. Economic ties will offset the impact of security concerns and make for open borders. This chapter will explore the observable implications of the theoretical framework for visa restrictions.

Visa restrictions comprise an important, albeit understudied, component of migration and border control. A visa is defined as a "document issued in the country of origin (or residence) of the individual by the authorities of the state to which he or she wishes to go" (Guild 2009, 118). If a state has imposed a visa requirement against an origin state, the citizens of the origin state need to apply for a visa to legally gain entry. Visas thus constitute an upstream form of control, in the sense that they regulate and monitor migrants before they have gained entrance to the destination state. Travelers apply for permission to legally enter destination states' territories at consulates and embassies abroad. The upstream aspect of visa controls permits states to push border controls outward, beyond physical borders, both into cyberspace and into foreign space (Bigo 2011). At the same time, governments enlist third parties, for example, obliging private agents such as transport companies, in monitoring travel. Legal entry often requires varying degrees of documentation, depending on the host, origin state, and visa category (Hobolth 2013). Importantly, the visa does not guarantee admittance but merely allows travelers to legally ask for permission to enter destination states' territories. This grants border officials some discretion when monitoring border crossings.

However, sometimes states also utilize visa controls at border ports as an on-site mechanism of control over border crossings. Sometimes referred to as the "sticker visa," this policy instrument does not require that travelers obtain legal permission to enter destination state territories beforehand. Hence, the visa at the border does not embody the screening goal that the more common upstream visa requirement serves (Neumayer 2006). Instead, the visa-at-the-border generates revenue by requiring a nominal fee from border crossings, similar to the toll on an interstate highway in the United States. As such, the analyses herein focus on the upstream visa instrument.

The Universal Declaration of Human Rights stipulates a right of exit and entry to one's own country (Article 13) but not a right to enter foreign space. States have the prerogative to arbitrate who gains access to their territories. Visas and border controls are important tools for states to exercise control. They are also historically intertwined with the emergence of the modern territorial state. With the development of standing armies, the state took over the legitimate means of coercion. Concomitantly and similarly, the modern state has monopolized the legitimate means of mobility, restricting entry and exit across international frontiers (Torpey 2000a). Identity cards and codes, and eventually the passport, were essential for documenting membership and developing mechanisms to distinguish among them for administrative purposes. Visa restrictions are, relatively speaking, a modern invention. Together with the passport, visas and biometric identity documents uphold the mobility regime (Huysmans 2006).

Visas monitor short-term mobility. In the empirical analysis that follows, we will address visa controls as they pertain to short-term territorial access. The next chapter also examines visa applications for different categories of short-term migration, including work, study, business, and tourism. Importantly, however, visa policies impact other dimensions of migration control. For example, states tighten visa policies in order to ward off prospective asylum seekers (Finotelli and Sciortino 2013). For precisely this reason, migration scholars consider the visa regime an important component of the state's overall asylum and refugee-control regime (Czaika and Hobolth 2016). Visa restrictions thus dissuade prospective asylum seekers and divert them to states with softer border-control policies.

Visas also are essential for reducing illegal migration. Contrary to popular belief about migrants slipping across borders unnoticed, visa violations are one of the primary ways in which people gain illegal access to advanced democracies (Jordan and Düvell 2002; Torpey 1998). According to the Department of Homeland Security, for example, in 2015, of the 10.9 million illegal migrants in the United States, 40 percent gained access via visa transgression

(Attanasio 2016). Neumayer (2006) contends that visa overstay is one of the primary causes of irregular migration into Europe, where clandestine border crossings have been traditionally less frequent than along the U.S.-Mexico border. In general, stricter visa regimes compel migrants to seek irregular ways of gaining access to and staying in destination states. Czaika and Hobolth (2016) find a 4–7 percent jump in the irregular migration rate into the European Union following a 10 percent spike in the visa rejection rate.

States use visas to regulate entry into destination state territories.[1] Visa restrictions perform a screening function, acting as "the first line of defense" against the entry of undesirables (Torpey 1998, 252), which include prospective undocumented migrants as well as security risks. States design visa regimes to lower the ex ante probability of migrants transgressing the terms of the visa. To do this, they must be able to weed out individuals most likely to overstay and thereby transition into illegal status. For this reason, for instance, origin states that generate a high volume of undocumented migration typically confront a higher likelihood of visa requirements from advanced democracies (Neumayer 2006). Visas also have a preselection function. Czaika and Haas (2013) argue that, in general, migration control aims to distinguish between desirable and unwelcome migrants. Through selective controls, states target the composition of flows, usually in terms of skill but sometimes in terms of ethnicity and religion. Similarly, visa controls allow governments to encourage the mobility of some while inhibiting and deterring the mobility of others.

Boehmer and Peña (2012) conceptualize border openness as a continuum, reflected in the amount of documentation the destination state requires for legal entry. Fully open borders allow passage with minimal documentation; the Schengen zone has heretofore permitted citizens of Schengen member countries to travel without a passport. In other instances, states may have a separate category of origin states from which they demand only an identity card in lieu of a passport to gain entry. The requirement of a passport to gain admittance indicates a stricter approach. To illustrate, in 2009, the United States introduced the requirement that individuals carry a passport to enter from Canada, a development that signified the tightening of border controls in NAFTA. Visa requirements are a more restrictive requirement, representing a step toward border closure. Not surprisingly, there are no cases where states impose a visa for travel without a passport.

The global visa regime has become more permissive over time. However, this liberalization has proceeded in an uneven fashion (Mau et al. 2015; Neumayer 2006). While the citizens of advanced Western democracies gained visa-free travel privileges to a greater number of countries, the rest of the world's citizens encountered new restrictions. In other words, visa policies are not necessary reciprocal. Where reciprocity applies, it is restricted to a smaller set of advanced democracies. What we do not yet know is whether and how transnational terrorism contributed to this bifurcation in the global visa system.

## Empirical Implications of the Theory

This section develops a set of testable propositions concerning bilateral visa restrictions that serve as the basis of the empirical analysis. The first set of hypotheses ties transnational terrorism to visa policies. Under what conditions does terrorism impel stricter visa policies? First, we can envisage a global effect. By design, visa requirements are a tool for defending against security risks. Nevertheless, there are several ways that visa policies can be used more or less discriminately. We expect states to capitalize on the preselection, screening, and deterrent roles of visa controls to regulate territorial access. Prospective migrants who are exempt from visa requirements are deemed nonthreatening and those facing restrictions undergo additional scrutiny and background checks (Neumayer 2006).

The previous chapter argued that states confront an endemic type of uncertainty with respect to transnational terrorist groups. Asymmetric informational disadvantages make it more difficult for states to detect and ferret out transnational militants. Through clandestine access, terrorist actors can flout states' surveillance technologies. Terrorist groups make up in secrecy and surprise what they lack in military power. By organizing across states, they place states at an operational disadvantage. Hence, uncertainty over the where and when of terrorist violence reinforces the importance of visa controls. If visa policies are the first line of defense against potential threats, as Torpey (1998) surmises, then states should capitalize on visa controls to address this type of uncertainty.

### Hypothesis 1: Global Effect

*States will enact restrictive visa policies against origin states whose nationals have perpetrated incidents of transnational terrorism.*

One possible response is to restrict mobility from terror-exporting origin states. If we conceptualize transnational terrorism as a flow of violence, then states whose nationals have been involved in a high volume of incidents worldwide are significant exporters of terrorism (Muller 2010). I label this policy response the *global effect* of transnational terrorism. Namely, destination countries are attentive to whether the nationals of an origin state have frequently executed transnational terrorist events. This expectation is consonant with the notion that in the current security climate, states respond to individuals as threats (Salehyan 2008a). States may place restrictions on certain countries even if there is no animosity toward their home governments. From a slightly different perspective, the rogue-state framework that gained currency post-9/11 labels specific countries as pariahs because of their purported support of terrorism (Caprioli and Trumbore 2005). The international community may cast blame upon terror-rich states for turning a blind eye to their nationals' involvement in worldwide terror.[2]

The contagion of terrorist violence across borders magnifies the global effect on policies. Transnational terrorist events may spill over into neighboring states even if the grievances are homegrown (Braithwaite and Li 2007). Alternatively, terrorist groups strategically target softer targets (Enders and Sandler 2006). Hence, proximate states' more stringent policies may redirect terrorist violence toward states with more permissive conditions for violence. Thus events in other states inspire heightened perceived probability of future violence. Even if the state in question is not targeted in attacks, violence in other countries increases the perceived security risks of human mobility. In sum, we expect states to tighten visa policies in response to attacks elsewhere.

### Hypothesis 2: Targeted Effect

*States whose citizens or territory have been harmed in incidents of terrorism will enact restrictive visa policies against origin states whose nationals were associated with these incidents.*

The global effect is selective in the sense that states tailor policies to specific countries, imposing restrictions on terror-rich origin states. That is, it does not imply a wholesale response whereby attacks abroad drive destination states to enact more stringent policies against all sending states. However, it is somewhat less discriminate in that it means stricter policies against origin states, regardless of whether the destination state has been directly harmed by these attacks. We can imagine a more selective type of policy whereby states respond to attacks by origin-country nationals only if their national security interests were involved in these attacks. Incidents that harm the state's citizens, or take place on the territory of the state, directly threaten its national security. I refer to this as the *targeted effect* of terrorism.

Targeted events also more directly activate the fear-management aspect of border controls. Friedman (2011) argues that responding to terrorism is mostly about managing perceived vulnerability to attacks. Targeted assaults generate a sense of vulnerability, propelling states to calibrate policies according to the possible harm rather than to precise risk. However, Andreas (2009) contends that policy stringency is, to an extent, an outgrowth of public demand. Regardless of the objective efficacy of policies, restricting territorial access to outsiders also fulfills domestic demand. Policymakers also utilize draconian measures to symbolically assert their commitment and ability to insulate the citizenry from external threats.

The symbolic aspect is muted when it comes to visa controls because the public is not always cognizant of visa restrictions. The government may make much ado about imposing visas on terror-exporting states, but even then the visa requirement is physically not salient. That said, insofar as attacks on the country's soil or involving its citizens elevate threat perception, they inspire the public to demand that the government take action.

Furthermore, targeted attacks compound the securitization of human mobility, which pivots on countries reframing migration as a threat to physical integrity (Lavenex 2001). Terrorist events on the state's own soil directly allow securitization of short-term mobility. Targeted attacks muster public backing of harder policies by creating widespread fears of being victimized. In addition, they agitate the public into demanding tighter policies. In effect, the public push allows governments to put aside the objective efficacy of policies. Additionally, terrorist events tend to cluster together spatially and temporally (Braithwaite and Li 2007; Gelpi and Avdan 2015). Put simply, unlike lightning, terrorist events do strike the same locale twice. Hence, it is logical to expect states that have suffered violence at the hands of origin-country citizens to selectively curb human mobility from these states.

*Hypothesis 3: Economic Interdependence*

*Economically interdependent states will be less likely to pursue restrictive visa policies with respect to their economic partners' citizens.*

At the heart of the theoretical framework is the argument that economic ties make for more liberal policies. They do so through direct and indirect effects; that is, by affecting migration policies and by conditioning the impact of terrorism. Insofar as stiffer visa policies degrade economic exchange, we'd expect opportunity costs to matter in states' decision making. That is, anticipating revenue from economic exchange to shrink, states will be less willing to implement stringent policies. Reduced travel is a detriment to economic exchange to the extent that trade and foreign direct investment rest on face-to-face contact. The same characteristics of visa controls that augment security can inhibit travel. Visa restrictions raise the costs of travel as a result of the wait time, paperwork, fees, and uncertainty involved in the application process. Not surprisingly, visa requirements may discourage prospective travelers. In addition, tougher visa policies significantly dampen tourism. Neumayer (2010) demonstrates that, on average, visa controls decrease travel between pairs of states by 52–63 percent.

We may contend that tourism-dependent destination countries are more likely than other states to hesitate to impose restrictions.[3] However, this misses the strong positive correlation between travel and commerce. As O'Bryne notes, "Freedom of travel is freedom to trade" (2001, 409). Visa requirements function akin to non-tariff barriers to trade because while goods and capital can circulate, the producers of goods and owners of capital cannot. We can further unpack the wisdom behind these words if we consider that even in the electronic age, the physical presence of investors encourages the establishment and preservation of business interlinkages. Neumayer (2011) reports the reductive impact of visa restrictions on the flow of goods and capital. He argues that primarily by hampering personal contact across borders, visa restrictions significantly lower bilateral trade and foreign direct investment (FDI). He finds that visa restrictions result in a drop of 21–32 percent in bilateral trade and a moderately higher drop of 33–38 percent in bilateral FDI.

Neumayer's (2011) findings point to the direct negative correlation between restrictive visa policies and economic transactions. Stricter visa policies can erode the dyad's economic relationship through an alternative mechanism: to the degree that draconian policies are viewed by the commercial partner as an antagonistic signal, we might expect a backlash. After all, restrictions on mobility are antithetical to liberal tenets and collide with shared norms between trade partners (Flynn 2003). Consequently, restrictions might anger economic partners. To illustrate, in response to the European Union's controversial proposal to impose visa restrictions on the citizens of the United States and Canada, critics were quick to voice concern over the breakdown of transatlantic relations (Kanter 2016). Additionally, the commercial partner may retaliate by enacting tougher legislation, further stifling economic revenue. Neumayer's (2010) empirical analysis validates this intuition, showing that reciprocal visa restrictions reduce capital flows between states by 6–12 percent more than unilateral visa requirements.

Reprisals can also manifest as weaker economic ties, either because investors become reticent to continue doing business in the partner state or because the state revokes economic privileges. Key domestic actors in the origin state may also feel slighted by stiff policies. By inhibiting face-to-face communication and contact, restrictive policies will undercut mutual affinity. Turkey's response to severe visa requirements by Schengen states is a case in point (Kirişçi 2007).[4] Pro-trade lobbies and business in Turkey have time and again castigated the European Union for tough visa legislation that contravenes the spirit (and, to some extent, the legal framework) of the European Customs Union. These concerns prompt commercial lobbies at home to champion liberal visa policies toward economic partners. In sum, states will consider the opportunity costs of reduction in trade and capital investment when devising visa policies. Policymakers will also be attuned to vested interests favoring liberal policies.

### Hypothesis 4: Conditioning Effect

*Economic ties will decrease the impact of transnational terrorism on visa policies.*

Economic interlinkages also impose indirect effects by modulating the impact of security imperatives. Material incentives carry more weight than security imperatives in trading states' grand strategy (Rosecrance 1986; Rudolph 2003). Societal actors that stand to lose from tighter policies may boost the salience of material concerns in the state's calculus. For example, trade lobbies and multinational corporations have admonished the U.S. government for tough policies that stymie and slow down trade (Yu 2010). Trade groups in particular raise the concern that visa restrictions risk rechanneling business to economic competitors of the United States, such as Brazil, China, and India. Even when the visa is granted, it might have a cooling-down effect and divert foreign business abroad, thus weakening a country's competitive edge over its economic rivals. Domestic coalitions with internationalist preferences may forge cross-national bonds, facilitating economic interdependence and prosperity (Solingen 1998). These ties in turn significantly shape foreign policy attitudes, both among political elites and at the public level (Fordham and Kleinberg 2009). Economic exchange inculcates mutual trust, which in turn should temper fears associated with economic partners' citizens. Hence, we expect economic interests to downplay the impact of transnational terrorism: the positive impact of transnational terrorism on policy stringency declines with the strength of economic ties.

## Measuring the Concepts

The hypotheses pertain to visa policies in general. This chapter focuses on visa restrictions; the subsequent chapter proceeds to visa rejection rates and documentation requirements. The dependent variable (DV) employed in the analyses that follow is coded 1 if the destination state has a visa requirement in place for the citizens of the origin state and 0 otherwise. The data cover 189 member states of the United Nations and 18 nonmember political territories.[5] This yields information on bilateral visa restrictions for 36,300 directed dyads. Directed-dyad design allows each state to appear once as destination (recipient) and once as origin (sending) state. That is, the data differentiate between a visa in force by state A against state B and vice versa. The directed-dyad design is appropriate for this study because visa reciprocity is not guaranteed. To illustrate, 32 percent of states do not reciprocate visa *waivers*; reciprocity is more common among Western democracies and the Organisation for Economic Co-operation and Development (OECD) member states. Put another way, 68 percent of states do reciprocate *policies*, but this figure also includes reciprocating by imposing visa restrictions (close to 25 percent).

The data on visa restrictions are cross-sectional and allow me to interrogate variation across pairs of states (dyads). Ideally we would track visa restrictions over time.[6] However, as Neumayer (2006, 2010, 2011) has noted, assembling such a data set would be a prohibitively costly and time-consuming endeavor. I utilize Mau et al.'s (2015) data set on visa waivers for 2010, coded from the International Aviation Travel Association's (IATA) *Travel Information Manual (TIM)*, which provides authoritative information on states' visa policies (IATA 2010). The main analysis focuses on visa restrictions for 2010. Mau and coauthors' coding registers 1 if the destination state extends visa-waiver privileges to the origin state and 0 if visas are not in place. A visa waiver is defined as visa freedom if individuals can travel to the destination state without an application procedure before departure. Visa waivers usually allow a stay of ninety days, which is also standard for a short-term visa. I reversed this variable so that 1 represents a visa restriction by state A for citizens of state B and 0 otherwise. Mau and coauthors' data set excludes small island states (Tuvalu), territories that lacked international recognition of statehood as of 2010 (Kosovo), and very small states (Andorra). I filled in these cases from Project Visa, a website that provides information on visa-free travel privileges between countries.[7]

Neumayer (2006) used the 2004 edition of TIM to code visa restrictions for 2004 to create a more comprehensive data set that also covers small island states and nonindependent territories. I used the data in Avdan 2014a, which examines the impact of terrorism and trade on visa restrictions. Here, I refer to these data to compare visa restrictions across these two time points. Although visa policies evolve slowly, the comparison of 2010 with 2004 does show change over time, mainly toward liberalization. For example, the 2010 data show 783 new directed-dyad pairs that have visa-free travel; given the total number of directed-dyad pairs (36,300), this figure reflects 2.15 percent of the sample of countries that have liberalized their visa policies. Nevertheless, to ensure that the discrepancy was not an artifact of different coding procedures by the researchers, I consulted alternate sources on incongruent cases. Specifically, where visa policies as of 2010 conflicted with those of 2004, I cross-checked the cases with Project Visa. To illustrate, in 2005 and 2010, Turkey lifted visa requirements for a number of countries in the Middle East, including Jordan and Lebanon; the variables for 2004 and 2010 would thus differ, taking the values of 1 and 0, respectively. The updated 2010 data are thus fairly recent and reflect these changes in countries' visa policies.

### Independent Variables

The first set of hypotheses concentrates on the impact of transnational terrorism. The data for transnational terrorism are sourced from International Terrorism: Attributes of Terrorist Events (ITERATE). The ITERATE data cover transnational terrorist events for 1968–2011 and provide information on event characteristics (Mickolus et al. 2012). Unlike other comprehensive databases on terrorism, such as the Global Terrorism Database (GTD), ITERATE focuses exclusively on transnational terrorism. A key advantage of ITERATE is that data harness information from international as well as domestic media outlets, which is particularly important when accounting for terrorist violence in countries with state-controlled media. According to ITERATE, terrorism is defined as "the use, or threat of use, of anxiety-inducing, extra-normal violence for political purposes by any individual or group, whether acting for or in opposition to established governmental authority, when such action is intended to influence the attitudes and behavior of a target group wider than the immediate victims" (ibid., 2). By definition, the database excludes crimes or violence committed by state agents. ITERATE also excludes violence that occurs during civil or interstate war. For instance, violence conducted by guerilla groups would not be included unless it is aimed at civilians.

Transnational terrorist events are those that cross borders through the nationality or foreign ties of perpetrators, institutional or human victims, location, the dynamics of resolution, or repercussions. Hence, domestic events are excluded from the overall count of terrorist events. To illustrate, in July 2011, Anders Breivik, a Norwegian citizen, committed a terrorist assault in Oslo. The attack does not make it into the ITERATE database because it does not qualify as a transnational incident. The victims of the attack and the perpetrator were all Norwegian citizens, and the incident took place on Norwegian soil. In contrast, consider the Boston marathon bombing of April 2013. While one of the perpetrators was a naturalized American citizen, the other was a foreign citizen. In addition, the victims included both American citizens and citizens of other countries; one of the three people who were killed was a Chinese national. The incident thus qualifies as transnational and would make it into ITERATE by virtue of the nationalities of the perpetrators and victims.[8] Incidents carried out by the state's own citizens—so-called homegrown events—can also be transnational if they involve foreign victims. The London tube bombing in July 2005 provides an illustration. Although the event was considered homegrown because British nationals staged the attacks, citizens of other countries were also victimized. In short, ITERATE includes incidents in which either the victims or perpetrators of attacks have crossed borders and incidents in which both victims and perpetrators have crossed borders.

To assess the first set of hypotheses, I create separate global and targeted counts of transnational terrorism. The global count aggregates the total number of incidents committed by the nationals of the origin country anywhere in the world. The measures sum incidents from 2000 until 2009. This operationalization allows for a check on potential reverse causality: the dependent variable registers visas implemented in 2010 and the sums are therefore lagged by one year. To capture targeted terrorism, I utilize two measures. The first records incidents by origin nationals against destination nationals. The second records incidents by origin nationals on destination territory. These two indicators also correspond to the nationality- and location-based indicators widely used by terrorism scholars to create directed-dyadic measures of transnational terrorism (Young and Findley 2011). The San Bernardino attack in December 2015 would be reported as a targeted incident, executed by a Pakistani national, and transpiring on U.S. soil and involving U.S. victims. The March 2015 bombing in Istanbul, which killed and injured American citizens, also fits the targeted operationalization: although occurring abroad, it would be counted in the nationality-based targeted measure of transnational terrorism, with the United States as the target state. Similarly, the June 2015 attack in Tunisia has Britain as the target state because it victimized British citizens. One of the assailants was a Tunisian student. Therefore, if the targeted count were extended to include 2015, this incident would count as a directed-dyadic incident by Tunisia against the United Kingdom.

To keep the operationalization of variables consistent, the targeted counts aggregate incidents from 2000 until 2009. In sensitivity analyses, I reevaluate models using measures that include the years 1990–2009. A further coding decision is worth mentioning. ITERATE records up to three nationalities for perpetrators and victims. My measures account for all three nationalities, but the results are not altered if only the first nationality is accounted for.[9] Finally, targets of attacks may not necessarily be the victims of attacks; it might be impossible to tell who the intended victims were. For instance, Americans and Israelis were victimized in the Istanbul bombing in March 2015, but we do not know if the ISIS explicitly sought to target Americans and Israelis in this case. This issue plagues the wider spectrum of empirical studies of transnational terrorism (Young and Findley 2011). However, for my purposes, what matters is if the state's interests (citizens or territory) are directly involved, regardless of the actual aims of terrorist operatives. Hence, there is no reason to expect the issue to systematically affect inferences from multivariate analysis.

Table 2. Summary Statistics for Transnational Terrorism Indicators

| Variable | Mean | Std. Dev. | Min. | Max. |
|---|---|---|---|---|
| GLOBAL TERRORISM | | | | |
| Global terrorism, post-1990 sum | 14.71 | 33.29 | 0 | 257 |
| Global terrorism, post-2000 sum | 4.38 | 12.03 | 0 | 92 |
| Fatal incidents, post-1990 sum | 3.84 | 9.34 | 0 | 69 |
| Fatal incidents, post-2000 sum | 1.68 | 5.18 | 0 | 38 |
| TARGETED TERRORISM | | | | |
| Targeted terrorism, post-1990 sum (by nationality of victims) | 0.10 | 1.21 | 0 | 78 |
| Targeted terrorism, post-2000 sum (by nationality of victims) | 0.03 | 0.58 | 0 | 44 |
| Targeted terrorism, post-1990 sum (by event venue) | 0.09 | 2.31 | 0 | 220 |
| Targeted terrorism, post-2000 sum (by event venue) | 0.02 | 0.67 | 0 | 63 |
| Fatal incidents, post-1990 sum (by nationality of victims) | 0.03 | 0.50 | 0 | 45 |
| Fatal incidents, post-2000 sum (by nationality of victims) | 0.02 | 0.30 | 0 | 26 |
| Fatal incidents, post-1990 sum (by event venue) | 0.02 | 0.54 | 0 | 41 |
| Fatal incidents, post-2000 sum (by event venue) | 0.01 | 0.31 | 0 | 33 |

*Note*: The summary statistics include the West Bank and Gaza (Palestine), which is not included in the statistical analysis. The sums do not, however, include anonymous attacks.

Table 2 depicts summary statistics for the number of incidents of transnational terrorism. The summary statistics do not include anonymous attacks where ITERATE reports the nationalities of perpetrators as uncertain or unknown. It also omits incidents whose victims are anonymous.[10] The global incident counts range from 0 to 257 (1990–2009) and from 0 to 92 global incidents (2000–2009). Global fatal incidents vary between 0 and 69 (1990–2009) and 0 and 38 (2000–2009). These patterns are congruent with overall patterns of transnational terrorism over time. Since the end of the Cold War, while the volume of transnational terrorism has declined, fatal incidents, both as raw counts and as a proportion of the aggregate count, have risen (Enders and Sandler 2005). In terms of targeted counts, these have maxima of

78 (1990–2009) and 44 (2000–2009). Let's take a look at the countries that generate the greatest number of incidents globally in terms of the nationality of perpetrators.[11] The top 95th percentile of the global post-1999 count consists of Afghanistan, Colombia, Iraq, Jordan, Nigeria, Pakistan, and Palestine (the West Bank and Gaza).[12] In terms of the most terrorism-ridden dyads, by the nationality-based coding, Israel-Palestine, U.S.-Palestine, U.S.-Pakistan, U.S.-Saudi Arabia, and U.S.-Iraq are at the top. The first three dyads here also experience the most fatal incidents. In terms of targeted terrorism post-2000, the United States occupies the top position, followed by the United Kingdom and Israel.

## Economic Interdependence

Hypotheses 3 and 4 focus on the impact of economic interdependence. To tap into trade interdependence, I create measures that reflect directed dependence. That is, rather than averaging bilateral trade values by dyad, I compute state A's (the destination state's) trade dependence on state B (the origin state). This coding aligns with the theoretical intuition that the destination state's dependence on economic exchange with the origin state will affect its policies. Thus, directed trade is distinct from both general trade exposure and average bilateral trade. Two operationalization decisions permit me to account for potential reverse causality—the possibility that visa restrictions impact levels of dyadic trade: first, I take the one period lag of the trade indicators; second, in other models, I utilize the average of values over the 2005–2009 time period.[13] Following previous scholarship, I formulate two specifications of trade dependence. The first I label trade salience: this indicator represents the sum of imports from and exports to state A to B as a ratio of state A's total trade value. Trade salience represents the bilateral trade value as a proportion of the destination state's commercial portfolio (Mansfield and Pollins 2003). The second indicator expresses the total trade value as a share of the destination country's GDP. This operationalization taps into the possibility that the impact of trade dependence may be contingent upon the size of the state's economy (Russett and Oneal 2001). I derive the export and import values from the Correlates of War (COW) trade data (Barbieri and Keshk 2012; Barbieri, Keshk, and Pollins 2009). Version 3 has been extended to include 2009. COW trade data have a dyadic and a monadic version; I make use of the former to create the directed-dyadic trade measures and the latter for the country's total trade. GDP data originate from the World Bank's World Development Indicators (WDI) (WDI 2015).

To capture capital flows, I create a directed capital interdependence indicator that measures FDI divided by the recipient state's total GDP. Data on dyadic FDI are taken from the OECD's statistical database (OECD 2009). I complemented missing data from Neumayer's (2011) replication data. (Neumayer purchased bilateral FDI data from the United Nations' UNCTAD database.) FDI data are stock foreign investment data. I then perform two transformations. To guard against sensitivity to yearly fluctuations, I average FDI over 2005–2009 and then take the natural log of the values. The latter ensures the results are not influenced by outlier values. Given that the DV captures visa policies for 2010, using the average values also allows me to model the lagged effect of capital dependence. As sensitivity checks, I also deploy overall FDI, incorporated from the World Bank's WDI.

### Control Variables

Next, there are two subcategories of control variables included in the models. The first set pertains to the push-and-pull factors of migration. These variables assess host and sending state macroeconomic and institutional traits that drive human mobility (Cornelius et al. 2004). The second set gauges dyadic attributes, pertaining to the relationship between sending and receiving states. For the sake of brevity, Table 3 enumerates the list of variables and respective data sources. A few require elaboration here. In terms of the first set, I expect migrants to be drawn to democratic states with extensive liberal liberties. Accordingly, I include the revised Polity score for regime type from the Polity IV Project (Marshall and Jaggers 2013). I use Norris's (2009) comprehensive democracy data set version 3 to bring in the Freedom House (FH) civil liberties score. I transform the FH score into a dummy equal to 1 for liberal states and 0 otherwise. I expect negative institutional conditions in origin states to affect emigration. Toward that end, I also control for origin-country democracy score. Conflict in the origin state may be positively related to migrant outflows; accordingly, I utilize the armed conflict intensity measure from the UCDP/PRIO database, coded 2 if the origin state has seen conflict producing at least 1,000 battle deaths, 1 if it has seen lower-scale conflict with at least 25 battle deaths, and 0 in the absence of conflict (Gleditsch et al. 2002; Strand, Wilhelmsen, and Gleditsch 2004).

Distance affects migration patterns much as it affects trade and financial flows (Fitzgerald, Leblang, and Teets 2014). Hence two distance measures, distance between capitals and contiguity, are included. The first originates from Simmons's (2005) data; contiguity is drawn from the COW Direct Contiguity version 3.1 (Stinnett et al. 2002). Consistent with the work of Neumayer (2006) and Avdan (2014a), the models include a battery of shared dyadic traits that tap into links between recipient and sending states: colonial and linguistic ties. These are time-invariant dummies, originating from a variety of source databases that I take from Avdan's replication data (Avdan 2014a). The inclusion of these dummies also controls for pull dynamics whereby migrants gravitate toward destination countries with a common language or colonial history. The ratio of destination to origin state GDP per capita controls for wealth differentials; we expect migrants to flow from poorer to richer states. Also included is (logged) migrant stock in destination states. Migrant networks function as another pull factor (Fitzgerald, Leblang, and Teets 2014); the same time, traditional emigration states may be more liberal in their visa policies.[14]

To account for conflict and cooperation dynamics within the dyad, I also inject dummy variables, coded 1 for the existence of an alliance tie and a militarized dispute (MID) within the past decade. These are coded from the COW Alliance data version 4.1 (COW 2015 Douglas 2009) and COW MID data version 4.0 (Palmer et al. 2015). These indicators are lagged, representing values for 2009 in source data. All other time-variant control variables are the mean of the 2005–2009 period; exceptions to this rule are listed in Table 3. This is consonant with the operationalization of other temporally variant regressors and permits for a check against yearly perturbations in data; it also allows for the lagged effect of independent variables. Finally, I also control for the EU membership of the destination state. EU harmonization means that we should account for interdependence among member states' policies; for example, member states have a common list of third-party countries whose citizens are required to have a visa (Huysmans 2006).[15] Visa-free mobility within the European Union has also been pivotal to deeper integration, suggesting that EU membership may simultaneously influence visa freedom and economic ties. To account for this, I include dummies for whether the destination and sending states are members of the EU-27, which reflects the European Union's enlargement as of 2007.[16]

The dependent variable, visa restrictions, is binary, which necessitates the use of a nonlinear estimator such as probit or logit (Greene 1997). The analysis

Table 3. Variable Descriptions and Sources

**Control Variables**

| *Migration Push-and-Pull Factors* | *Description of Indicator* | *Data Source* |
|---|---|---|
| Origin's regime type | Polity IV score, –10 to 10, ordinal scale | Polity IV (Marshall and Jaggers 2013) |
| Origin liberal state | 1 if home liberal state, 0 otherwise, 2006–2009 median | Norris 2009 |
| Origin's civil liberties | 2 to 14 ordinal scale, denotes increasing restriction; dummy below 6 for liberal state. | Norris 2009 |
| Origin's GNI per capita | Gross national income per capita, logged, in PPP | WDI 2015 |
| Armed political conflict in origin country | 0 to 3 scale for increasing levels of civil unrest; 2009 values | UCDP/PRIO Armed Conflict Database (Gleditsch et al. 2002) |
| Recipient's migrant stock | Logged number of migrants from origin country | WDI 2015 |
| Recipient's GDP per capita | Gross domestic product, logged, in PPP | WDI 2015 |
| Recipient's civil liberties | 2 to 14 ordinal scale, denotes increasing freedom; 2006–2009 median | Norris 2009 |
| Recipient's regime type | Polity IV score, –10 to 10, ordinal scale, 2006–2009 median | Polity IV (Marshall and Jaggers 2013) |
| Recipient's tourism revenue | International tourism receipts as % of home GDP | WDI 2015 |
| DYADIC ATTRIBUTES | | |
| Differences in wealth (GDP per capita differences) | Differences in net GDP in PPP | World Bank (WDI), accessed in 2016 |
| Logged distance | Logged distance between capitals in dyad | Simmons 2005 |

(continued)

Table 3 (continued)

### Control Variables

| Migration Push-and-Pull Factors | Description of Indicator | Data Source |
|---|---|---|
| DYADIC ATTRIBUTES | | |
| Dyadic conflict (MID) | 1 if militarized interstate dispute existed in 2009 | Correlates of War Project MID version 4.0 (Palmer et al. 2015) |
| Alliance tie | 1 if origin and home joined any type of alliance pact within past 5 years, 0 otherwise | Correlates of War Project; Alliance Data version 4.1 (Palmer et al. 2015) |
| Common language | 1 if home and origin share the same language | Avdan 2014a |
| Colonial link | 1 if home and origin belong to same civilization | Avdan 2014a |
| SUPPLEMENTARY CHECKS | | |
| Shared civilization | 0 otherwise Modified measure of Huntington's civilization tie 1 if home and origin belong to same civilization 0 otherwise | Avdan 2014a |
| IGO sum | Sum of joint intergovernmental organization, coded for past decade | Avdan 2014a |
| Contiguity (modified direct contiguity score) | Modified direct contiguity score | COW Direct Contiguity Data 2007 |
| Bilateral log migrant stock | Values for 2010 | WDI 2015 |

uses logistic regression, but probit generates equal inferences. Logistic regression employs maximum likelihood estimation (MLE) after linear transformation of the dependent variable into the natural log odds of visa restrictions. In this way, the logistic regression estimates the probability that the recipient state imposes visa restrictions on the origin country. I employ Huber-White robust standard errors clustered by recipient state. This modeling choice accounts for the possibility that destination countries may be uniquely liberal or stringent in visa policies.

## Analysis

Table 4 presents the statistical tests for hypotheses 1–4. The first model demonstrates the impact of global terrorism while the second and third models focus on targeted terrorism, using the aforementioned measures based on nationality of victims and venue of attack. Models 4 and 5 focus only on fatal global and targeted attacks, defined as incidents with at least one death. In terms of overall model fit, all models produce significant global Chi statistics (Wald test significant at the 0.000 level). The mean variance inflation factor (VIF) is 1.36 with all values well below 5.0, which demonstrates that multicollinearity is not a cause for concern. Across the board, transnational terrorism exerts a positive impact on the probability of visa restrictions, lending support to hypotheses 1 and 2. The coefficient on targeted terrorism in model 3, however, falls short of conventional levels of statistical significance. This indicator counts attacks within destination state by origin nationals. Sensitivity checks show that when incidents are aggregated from 1990 on, the effect is marginally significant ($p < .10$). This finding does not necessarily contravene hypothesis 2, however, if we keep in mind that terrorism is a short-gun phenomenon. Incidents on destination territory by foreign nationals are thus rarer and fewer. When such incidents accumulate over time, however, the hypothesized positive impact obtains. Notably, the substantive significance of coefficients on targeted terrorism is higher than that on global terrorism. Turning to fatal incidents, we appraise a slightly higher magnitude in impact. Importantly, the same pattern holds whereby fatal targeted incidents exercise a stronger influence on the probability of visa restrictions than do global incidents.

The models include trade salience, operationalized as bilateral trade to total trade value of the recipient state. This variable ranges from 0 to 81, with a mean of .58 and standard deviation of 2.75, indicating considerable variability in levels of trade salience. Consistent with hypothesis 3, trade salience significantly reduces the propensity to observe visa requirements. Considering control variables, the push-and-pull factors perform as expected and all, except for recipient's tourism revenue and recipient's democracy score, are statistically significant. In brief, the lack of democracy and experience with civil war correspond to a higher likelihood of visa restrictions. Liberal states are less likely to impose visas. Not surprisingly, a positive GDP per capita ratio—meaning a higher wealth differential within the dyad—significantly heightens the probability of visas. As expected, EU destination states are less likely to enact visa restrictions and EU origin states are less likely to face restrictions. Geographic proximity, colonial history, and cultural similarity matter: states are less likely to impose visas against distant and linguistically similar origins but more likely to do so against former colonies. Echoing the insights of Boehmer and Peña (2012), interstate dynamics also matter: thus peaceful relations (lack of past militarized disputes) and alliance ties result in visa liberalization.

Next, Table 5 analyzes the impact of economic interdependence from a different angle. Models 6–8 employ the bilateral trade to destination GDP ratio as an alternate measure of trade dependence; to safeguard against influential outliers, this measure is logged and varies between .10 and .88. Models 9–11 bring in the (logged) bilateral FDI stock as a measure of capital interdependence; values of this indicator range from .698 to 13.8. The OECD source data that provide the bilateral FDI stock values are limited in the number of states they encompass; hence as a result of missing data on this measure, the sample size is reduced to a little under 4,000 observations. Mirroring Table 4, the models examine the effects of global and targeted terrorism separately. For the sake of brevity, I limit the discussion of the results to the main effects. In line with hypotheses 1 and 2, the coefficients on the terrorism measures are positive and significant. In congruence with the patterns depicted in the previous table, transnational targeted attacks impose a more cogent positive impact on the likelihood of visa restrictions compared to global incidents. While the impact does not attain statistical significance in model 8, in model 11, targeted attacks within recipient territory also significantly heighten the probability that states demand visas. We also witness that the coefficients on targeted attacks within territory are larger in magnitude than those on global attacks. These results bolster confidence in the first two hypotheses. Hypothesis 3 also receives support, as

Table 4. Transnational Terrorism, Trade Salience, and Visa Restrictions

|  | All Incidents | | | Fatal Incidents | |
|---|---|---|---|---|---|
| Variable | Model 1 | Model 2 | Model 3 | Model 4 | Model 5 |
| Global terrorism | 0.024***<br>(0.00) |  |  |  |  |
| Targeted terrorism (by victims) |  | 0.349**<br>(0.12) |  |  |  |
| Targeted terrorism (by location) |  |  | 0.184<br>(0.16) |  |  |
| Global fatal terrorism |  |  |  | 0.084***<br>(0.01) |  |
| Targeted fatal terrorism |  |  |  |  | 0.374*<br>(0.15) |
| Bilateral trade salience | −0.035***<br>(0.01) | −0.032***<br>(0.01) | −0.040***<br>(0.01) | −0.032***<br>(0.01) | −0.03***<br>(0.01) |
| Recipient to origin GDP per capita ratio | 2.158***<br>(0.48) | 2.125***<br>(0.47) | 2.089***<br>(0.47) | 2.134***<br>(0.47) | 2.138***<br>(0.48) |
| Recipient's democracy | −0.045<br>(0.03) | −0.046<br>(0.03) | −0.043<br>(0.03) | −0.045<br>(0.03) | −0.045<br>(0.03) |
| Origin's democracy | −0.085***<br>(0.01) | −0.088***<br>(0.01) | −0.078***<br>(0.01) | −0.083***<br>(0.01) | −0.089***<br>(0.01) |
| Civil conflict in origin (UCDP/PRIO) | 0.418***<br>(0.07) | 0.618***<br>(0.08) | 0.717***<br>(0.09) | 0.433***<br>(0.08) | 0.632***<br>(0.09) |
| Recipient liberal state | −1.190**<br>(0.38) | −1.189**<br>(0.38) | −0.976*<br>(0.38) | −1.188**<br>(0.38) | −1.188**<br>(0.38) |
| Recipient's tourism revenue | −0.012<br>(0.01) | −0.011<br>(0.01) | −0.009<br>(0.01) | −0.012<br>(0.01) | −0.011<br>(0.01) |
| Recipient migrant stock | −0.071*<br>(0.03) | −0.071*<br>(0.03) | −0.088**<br>(0.03) | −0.071*<br>(0.03) | −0.068*<br>(0.03) |

(continued)

Table 4 (continued)

|  | All Incidents | | | Fatal Incidents | |
|---|---|---|---|---|---|
| Variable | Model 1 | Model 2 | Model 3 | Model 4 | Model 5 |
| Colonial link | 1.702*** (0.42) | 1.676*** (0.42) | 1.623*** (0.41) | 1.667*** (0.41) | 1.677*** (0.42) |
| Common language | −1.280*** (0.18) | −1.276*** (0.17) | −1.297*** (0.19) | −1.271*** (0.18) | −1.272*** (0.17) |
| Dyadic alliance | −1.645*** (0.31) | −1.633*** (0.30) | −1.541*** (0.29) | −1.629*** (0.31) | −1.619*** (0.30) |
| Militarized interstate dispute | 0.834+ (0.43) | 0.742+ (0.40) | 1.016* (0.41) | 0.000 (.) | 0.766+ (0.40) |
| Dyadic distance (logged) | 0.509*** (0.10) | 0.522*** (0.10) | 0.381*** (0.10) | 0.517*** (0.10) | 0.524*** (0.10) |
| Recipient EU member | −0.756*** (0.19) | −0.746*** (0.19) | −0.928*** (0.21) | −0.751*** (0.19) | −0.747*** (0.19) |
| Origin EU member | −0.766*** (0.10) | −0.732*** (0.10) | −0.657*** (0.08) | −0.777*** (0.10) | −0.728*** (0.10) |
| Constant | −0.530 (0.59) | −0.489 (0.58) | 0.133 (0.58) | −0.562 (0.59) | −0.523 (0.59) |
| Chi statistic | 255.521 | 252.433 | 269.016 | 242.157 | 253.082 |
| Wald test | 0.000 | 0.000 | 0.000 | 0.000 | 0.000 |
| Number of cases | 18,940 | 18,940 | 18,940 | 18,940 | 18,940 |

*Notes:* Cells contain regression coefficients with standard errors (SEs) underneath in parentheses. The SEs are robust and clustered by destination state. Main effects in **bold.**

+$p < .10$
*$p < .05$
**$p < .01$
***$p < .001$

**Table 5. Results with Alternate Measures of Economic Dependence**

| Variable | Trade Dependence | | | Capital Dependence | | |
|---|---|---|---|---|---|---|
| | Model 6 | Model 7 | Model 8 | Model 9 | Model 10 | Model 11 |
| Global terrorism | 0.033*** (0.00) | | | 0.027*** (0.01) | | |
| Targeted terrorism (by victims) | | 0.335** (0.12) | | | 0.386** (0.15) | |
| Targeted terrorism (by venue) | | | 0.110 (0.07) | | | 0.229* (0.09) |
| Bilateral trade/GDP | −4.400*** (0.77) | −4.150*** (0.75) | −4.140*** (0.75) | | | |
| Bilateral FDI (logged) | | | | −0.159*** (0.04) | −0.157*** (0.04) | −0.155*** (0.04) |
| Recipient to origin GDP per capita ratio | 1.564** (0.49) | 1.566** (0.49) | 1.595** (0.49) | 3.502*** (0.93) | 3.432*** (0.93) | 3.537*** (0.93) |
| Recipient's democracy | −0.039 (0.03) | −0.039 (0.03) | −0.039 (0.03) | −0.059 (0.05) | −0.062 (0.05) | −0.061 (0.05) |
| Origin's democracy | −0.088*** (0.01) | −0.093*** (0.01) | −0.093*** (0.01) | −0.113*** (0.02) | −0.118*** (0.02) | −0.120*** (0.02) |
| Civil conflict in origin | 0.497*** (0.08) | 0.768*** (0.09) | 0.783*** (0.09) | 0.947*** (0.15) | 1.124*** (0.16) | 1.151*** (0.16) |
| Recipient liberal state | −1.199*** (0.33) | −1.205*** (0.33) | −1.206*** (0.33) | −1.462** (0.48) | −1.454** (0.48) | −1.462** (0.48) |
| Recipient's tourism revenue | −0.012 (0.01) | −0.011 (0.01) | −0.011 (0.01) | −0.011 (0.02) | −0.010 (0.02) | −0.010 (0.02) |
| Recipient migrant stock | 0.002 (0.03) | 0.000 (0.03) | 0.004 (0.03) | 0.045 (0.04) | 0.041 (0.04) | |

*(continued)*

Table 5 (continued)

| Variable | Trade Dependence | | | Capital Dependence | | |
|---|---|---|---|---|---|---|
| | Model 6 | Model 7 | Model 8 | Model 9 | Model 10 | Model 11 |
| Colonial link | 1.629*** | 1.620*** | 1.641*** | 2.233*** | 2.229*** | 0.045 |
| | (0.40) | (0.40) | (0.40) | (0.48) | (0.48) | (0.04) |
| Common language | −1.198*** | −1.189*** | −1.187*** | −1.267*** | −1.245*** | 2.204*** |
| | (0.18) | (0.18) | (0.18) | (0.37) | (0.36) | (0.48) |
| Dyadic alliance | −1.592*** | −1.569*** | −1.550*** | −0.500 | −0.532 | −1.229*** |
| | (0.31) | (0.30) | (0.30) | (0.44) | (0.44) | (0.36) |
| Militarized interstate dispute | 0.810+ | 0.776* | 0.763+ | 2.100*** | 1.944*** | −0.528 |
| | (0.42) | (0.39) | (0.40) | (0.47) | (0.48) | (0.44) |
| Dyadic distance (logged) | 0.474*** | 0.496*** | 0.501*** | 0.440*** | 0.437*** | 1.864*** |
| | (0.09) | (0.09) | (0.09) | (0.12) | (0.12) | (0.48) |
| Recipient EU member | −0.448* | −0.452* | −0.459** | −0.747** | −0.716** | 0.453*** |
| | (0.18) | (0.18) | (0.18) | (0.26) | (0.26) | (0.12) |
| Origin EU member | −0.519*** | −0.476*** | −0.471*** | −0.548*** | −0.510** | −0.741** |
| | (0.09) | (0.09) | (0.09) | (0.16) | (0.16) | (0.26) |
| Constant | 2.446** | 2.301** | 2.232** | −2.086+ | −1.921+ | −0.495** |
| | (0.86) | (0.84) | (0.85) | (1.12) | (1.10) | (0.16) |
| Chi statistic | 326.520 | 321.805 | 325.877 | 190.220 | 185.899 | 185.348 |
| Wald test | 0.000 | 0.000 | 0.000 | 0.000 | 0.000 | 0.000 |
| Number of cases | 16,284 | 16,284 | 16,284 | 3,965 | 3,965 | |

*Notes:* Coefficients with robust clustered standard errors (by recipient) in parentheses underneath. Main effects in **bold**.

+*p* < .10
*\*p* < .05
*\*\*p* < .01
*\*\*\*p* < .001

evidenced by the positive and significant coefficients on trade and capital interdependence.

Hypothesis 4 advanced a contingent relationship whereby economic interdependence tempers the impact of terrorism. Table 6 examines this proposition by including interactive terms. Models 12 and 13 include variables that interact trade salience with global and targeted terrorism, respectively. The final two models report findings with an interaction term for trade to GDP ratio with global and targeted terrorism. The positive coefficients on global terrorism demonstrate that at low levels of trade interdependence, global incidents augment the probability of visa controls. Let's consider the lowest possible levels of trade salience, in model 12. If we set trade salience to its minimum (0), the coefficient on global attacks is positive and significant. As levels of trade salience rise, however, this impact is modest, as the negative coefficient on the interaction term shows. In model 14, the coefficient on the trade to GDP measure is positive, albeit insignificant. The minimum value for (logged) trade to GDP is 0.17; at this value, the linear combination of coefficients produces a positive albeit insignificant coefficient. However, in both models, the Wald test of joint significance reveals that the coefficients on global terrorism and the interaction terms with trade are jointly significant ($p < .001$).

These results tell us that the impact of global terrorism is rather limited and is effectively mitigated by economic interdependence. The higher magnitude of coefficients on targeted terrorism is informative. However, the pattern is the same: with the exception of model 13, the consistently negative and significant coefficients on trade ties corroborate hypothesis 3. To substantiate, using the coefficients produced in model 12, for a dyad enjoying average levels of economic interdependence, increasing global terrorism from 0 to its maximum of 92 increases the predicted probability of visas from a little over 79 percent to 98 percent. Strikingly, however, it takes only 4 incidents directed against destination nationals for nearly the same spike in the predicted probability of visa restrictions.

Additionally, I reconsider the effect of transnational terrorism given regime type. The regime type may moderate the relationship between terrorism and visa policies. A core claim among security scholars is that democracies are more vulnerable to terrorism for a variety of reasons (Chenoweth 2010; Gelpi and Avdan 2015). They are constrained in their antiterrorism efforts and have more expansive civil liberties that may be subject to exploitation by violent groups (Li 2005). Democratic leaders are casualty sensitive (Pape 2006). They are also office seeking and take stock of audience costs. Hence democracies may be more sensitive to the costs of terrorism. Andreas's (2003b) argument about symbolic politics informs us that politicians use border policies to assuage public anxieties over clandestine infiltration. Democratic governments are more likely to leverage symbolic politics in order to allay fears and modify public opinion favorably toward the leadership. We may surmise then that democracy compounds the policy consequences of transnational terrorism. The main models controlled for regime type by incorporating the Polity IV score. However, these insights suggest an interactive dynamic. To assess the veracity of these insights, I separately examine the effects of global and directed terrorism for democracies (Polity score equal to or greater than 6), anocracies (Polity score between −6 and 6), and autocracies (Polity score less than or equal to −6).[17] If the argument is correct, we should see that the positive effects of terrorism on the probability of visa restrictions increase across levels of democracy. Table 7 presents six models: models 16–17 employ the directed terrorism indicator and models 18–21 look at global terrorism.

The patterns corroborate the intuition that regime type modifies policy impact. Unsurprisingly, directed attacks have the most pronounced impact in democracies. Directed violence galvanizes the public to a greater degree than do attacks elsewhere. Democratic leaders are sensitive to these public anxieties. Global terrorism produces a tamer response from the public and hence democratic leaders may lack the incentive to implement tougher migration-control policies. For democracies, the positive coefficient on targeted terrorism is of substantively higher magnitude than the coefficient on targeted terrorism for nondemocracies. For democracies, the coefficient on targeted terrorism is 0.43 and significant at the 0.01 level. In contrast, for anocracies (Polity IV score greater than −6 and less than 6), the coefficient is still negative and is no longer statistically significant. For autocracies the coefficient is positive (0.21) but does not attain significance.

Global terrorism yields a muted impact compared to directed terrorism, consistent with the previous results. Interestingly, however, global terrorism's impact is positive across regime types but declines in substantive value. In contrast, attacks that hurt the country's interests matter the most for democracies. Considering full democracies, the coefficient on global terrorism is 0.03, and significant at the 0.001 level. For anocracies, the coefficient diminishes to 0.01 and falls just below the 0.05 level of significance. Interestingly,

Table 6. Economic Ties and Transnational Terrorism: Interaction Effects

| Variable | Trade Salience | | Trade to Destination GDP | |
|---|---|---|---|---|
| | Model 12 | Model 13 | Model 14 | Model 15 |
| Global terrorism | 0.029*** (0.00) | | 0.030 (0.03) | |
| Targeted terrorism (by victims) | | 0.430** (0.16) | | 2.338+ (1.25) |
| Bilateral trade salience | −0.007 (0.01) | −0.030*** (0.01) | | |
| (ln) Trade to GDP | | | −4.413*** (0.77) | −4.123*** (0.75) |
| Trade salience × global terrorism | −0.004*** (0.00) | | | |
| Trade salience × targeted terrorism | | −0.075 (0.05) | | |
| Trade/GDP × global terrorism | | | 0.004 (0.05) | |
| Trade/GDP × targeted terrorism | | | | −2.647+ (1.56) |
| Recipient to origin GDP per capita ratio | 2.173*** (0.48) | 2.125*** (0.47) | 1.563** (0.49) | 1.559** (0.49) |
| Recipient's democracy | −0.045 (0.03) | −0.046 (0.03) | −0.039 (0.03) | −0.039 (0.03) |
| Origin's democracy | −0.085*** (0.01) | −0.088*** (0.01) | −0.088*** (0.01) | −0.093*** (0.01) |
| Civil conflict in origin | 0.418*** (0.07) | 0.615*** (0.08) | 0.497*** (0.08) | 0.767*** (0.09) |
| Recipient liberal state | −1.191** (0.38) | −1.187** (0.38) | −1.199*** (0.33) | −1.203*** (0.33) |
| Recipient's tourism revenue | −0.012 (0.01) | −0.011 (0.01) | −0.012 (0.01) | −0.011 (0.01) |
| Recipient migrant stock | −0.073* (0.03) | −0.071* (0.03) | 0.002 (0.03) | −0.000 (0.03) |
| Colonial link | 1.710*** (0.42) | 1.686*** (0.42) | 1.628*** (0.40) | 1.626*** (0.40) |
| Common language | −1.279*** (0.18) | −1.278*** (0.17) | −1.198*** (0.18) | −1.192*** (0.18) |

(continued)

Table 6 (continued)

| Variable | Trade Salience | | Trade to Destination GDP | |
|---|---|---|---|---|
| | Model 12 | Model 13 | Model 14 | Model 15 |
| Dyadic alliance | −1.632*** | −1.634*** | −1.593*** | −1.573*** |
| | (0.30) | (0.30) | (0.31) | (0.30) |
| Militarized interstate dispute | 0.853* | 0.771+ | 0.809+ | 0.793* |
| | (0.43) | (0.41) | (0.42) | (0.40) |
| Dyadic distance (logged) | 0.513*** | 0.521*** | 0.474*** | 0.493*** |
| | (0.10) | (0.10) | (0.09) | (0.09) |
| Recipient EU member | −0.757*** | −0.746*** | −0.448* | −0.451* |
| | (0.19) | (0.19) | (0.18) | (0.18) |
| Origin EU member | −0.765*** | −0.733*** | −0.519*** | −0.477*** |
| | (0.10) | (0.10) | (0.09) | (0.09) |
| Constant | −0.569 | −0.487 | 2.455** | 2.300** |
| | (0.59) | (0.58) | (0.86) | (0.84) |
| Chi statistic | 251.701 | 255.071 | 328.187 | 320.017 |
| Wald test | 0.000 | 0.000 | 0.000 | 0.000 |
| Number of cases | 18,940 | 18,940 | 16,284 | 16,284 |

*Notes*: Cells present logistic regression coefficients. Standard errors (clustered by recipient country) in parentheses underneath. Main effects in **bold**.
+$p < .10$
*$p < .05$
**$p < .01$
***$p < .001$

the modifying impact of terrorism is nonlinear when we consider global terrorism. For autocracies, the coefficient picks back up to 0.03 and is significant at the 0.05 level. At the risk of speculation, autocracies are in general stricter in their migration policies, and their leaders may find it easier to use security fears as a justification to impose visa restrictions. These results speak volumes about the conditional effects of terrorism. Here we observe that democratic leaders are more likely to leverage the symbolic value afforded by tighter controls but also that these leaders are more sensitive to public fears about terrorist violence. Unsurprisingly, these fears become elevated when violence endangers the citizens and territory of democratic states. Lastly, the negative effects of economic ties on the likelihood of visa restrictions hold

Table 7. Impact of Terrorism on Visa Policies by Regime Type

| | Targeted Terrorism | | | Global Terrorism | | |
|---|---|---|---|---|---|---|
| Variable | Model 16 Democracies | Model 17 Anocracies | Model 18 Autocracies | Model 19 Democracies | Model 20 Anocracies | Model 21 Autocracies |
| Global terrorism | | | | 0.034*** (0.01) | 0.011* (0.00) | 0.031* (0.01) |
| Targeted terrorism (by victims) | 0.435* (0.18) | −0.001 (0.18) | 0.217 (0.89) | | | |
| Bilateral trade salience | −0.036** (0.01) | −0.037** (0.01) | −0.041 (0.04) | −0.039** (0.01) | −0.038** (0.01) | −0.038 (0.04) |
| Recipient to Origin GDP per capita ratio | 3.408*** (0.74) | −0.354 (0.79) | 3.936** (1.30) | 3.446*** (0.74) | −0.335 (0.79) | 3.953** (1.27) |
| Origin's democracy | −0.152*** (0.02) | −0.020+ (0.01) | −0.020 (0.03) | −0.148*** (0.02) | −0.019+ (0.01) | −0.019 (0.02) |
| Civil conflict in origin | 0.842*** (0.11) | 0.337* (0.13) | 0.746*** (0.20) | 0.565*** (0.09) | 0.233* (0.11) | 0.390** (0.13) |
| Recipient liberal state | −1.378*** (0.41) | −1.315** (0.47) | | −1.380*** (0.41) | −1.318** (0.47) | |
| Recipient's tourism revenue | 0.012 (0.01) | −0.039* (0.02) | −0.057** (0.02) | 0.011 (0.01) | −0.039* (0.02) | −0.056** (0.02) |
| Recipient migrant stock | −0.090** (0.03) | −0.028 (0.07) | −0.133 (0.13) | −0.088* (0.03) | −0.032 (0.07) | −0.141 (0.14) |
| Colonial link | 1.425* (0.59) | 1.582** (0.53) | 0.969 (0.62) | 1.437* (0.58) | 1.577** (0.54) | 0.782 (0.69) |

(continued)

Table 7 (continued)

| | Targeted Terrorism | | | Global Terrorism | | |
|---|---|---|---|---|---|---|
| Variable | Model 16 Democracies | Model 17 Anocracies | Model 18 Autocracies | Model 19 Democracies | Model 20 Anocracies | Model 21 Autocracies |
| Common language | -1.012*** | -1.433*** | -1.435* | -1.021*** | -1.436*** | -1.584* |
| | (0.24) | (0.25) | (0.70) | (0.24) | (0.25) | (0.74) |
| Dyadic alliance | -0.926* | -1.719*** | -2.954*** | -0.920* | -1.741*** | -3.055*** |
| | (0.39) | (0.29) | (0.85) | (0.40) | (0.29) | (0.82) |
| Militarized interstate dispute | 1.166* | 0.433 | 2.055** | 1.206* | 0.392 | 2.309*** |
| | (0.58) | (0.61) | (0.67) | (0.60) | (0.62) | (0.67) |
| Dyadic distance (logged) | 0.385** | 0.429* | 0.637*** | 0.379** | 0.418* | 0.651*** |
| | (0.12) | (0.18) | (0.12) | (0.12) | (0.18) | (0.13) |
| Recipient EU member | -0.910*** | | | -0.918*** | | |
| | (0.19) | | | (0.19) | | |
| Origin EU member | -1.035*** | -0.608** | 0.397 | -1.080*** | -0.622** | 0.335 |
| | (0.14) | (0.20) | (0.51) | (0.14) | (0.20) | (0.50) |
| Constant | -1.402+ | 1.987+ | -2.277 | -1.497* | 2.002+ | -2.351 |
| | (0.75) | (1.07) | (1.57) | (0.76) | (1.07) | (1.56) |
| Chi statistic | 366.048 | 165.178 | 166.599 | 348.992 | 227.739 | 502.935 |
| Wald test | 0.000 | 0.000 | 0.000 | 0.000 | 0.000 | 0.000 |
| Number of cases | 10,109 | 6,594 | 2,237 | 10,109 | 6,594 | 2,237 |

+$p$ < .10
*$p$ < .05
**$p$ < .01
***$p$ < .001

up for anocracies. Autocratic regimes have somewhat lower levels interdependence, which might partially account for the negative albeit insignificant coefficient for these regimes.[18]


## Substantive Importance and Robustness

The results provided heretofore boost confidence in the chapter's hypotheses. Unfortunately, however, logistic coefficients are difficult to interpret because the effects depend on the values of covariates. Interaction effects are cumbersome to interpret, particularly in logistic regression (Ai and Norton 2003). Beyond simply evaluating coefficients' significance, it is important to assess the range of values of the independent variables where the effects on the dependent variable are significant (Brambor, Clark, and Golder 2006). Following the advice of Brambor, Clark, and Golder (2006), I illustrate the interaction effects via marginal effects graphs. Figures 1 and 2 portray the marginal effect of global and targeted incidents, respectively, as trade salience is increased over its range of values from the minimum of 0 to approximately 80, as the maximum. More precisely, I raise the incident counts across their

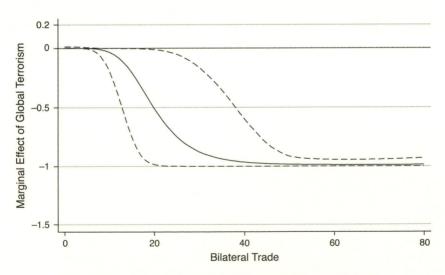

Figure 1. Global terrorism, trade salience, and visa restrictions.
This graph shows the marginal effect of maximal increase in terror
on visa restrictions as trade changes.

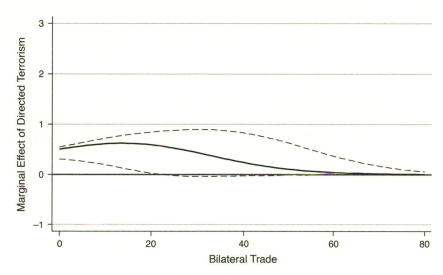

Figure 2. Targeted terrorism, trade salience, and visa restrictions.
This graph shows the marginal effect of maximal increase in terrorism
on visa restrictions as trade changes.

full range, 0 to 92 and 0 to 44, respectively, for global and targeted incident counts. The solid line sketches the marginal effect, while the dashed lines around the solid line show 95 percent confidence intervals.

The noticeably contrasting effects of global and targeted terrorist threats come to light when we compare the two figures. In Figure 1, the marginal effect of global terrorism hovers slightly above zero for low-trade interdependence dyads. As trade salience reaches about 17 percent of total trade value for the destination state, the positive marginal effect becomes insignificant and thereafter falls below the x-axis. In other words, economic ties overturn the positive marginal effect of global attacks on the probability of visa requirements. Figure 2 tells a different story. Here, the marginal effect of attacks against host citizens remains positive for the entire range of trade salience. It even rises slightly at first until the dyad attains 16 percent of the destination state's trade totals before starting to fall. Nonetheless, when trade salience attains 21 percent of total trade value, the effect becomes insignificant, as indicated by the fact that the lower bound of the confidence interval converges with and then crosses the x-axis.

Close to a quarter of dyads in the data set enjoy robust levels of interdependence that exceed sufficient levels of trade salience to render the impact of global terrorism insignificant. The patterns buoy support for the effects of economic ties. We should also bear in mind that the marginal effects shown here are for increasing the terrorism measures to their maxima. When we look at unit change (increase by a single incident), for example, we note that the marginal effect of global terrorism is insignificant for almost the entire range of trade values. The marginal effect of a unit increase in targeted terrorism hovers above zero for low-interdependent dyads and becomes insignificant when trade salience hits just 6 percent of total trade value. The marginal effect becomes negative (but insignificant) once trade salience nears 40 percent.

The main results utilize ITERATE as a source of terrorism data. As a secondary check of my hypotheses, I use a separate data set of terrorism, the Global Terrorism Database (GTD). The GTD records all terrorist attacks from 1970 onward. The original database includes transnational and domestic incidents. The GTD defines terrorism as "an intentional act of violence or threat of violence by a non-state actor" in which the violence is aimed at obtaining a social, political, or economic goal; there is evidence of intention to coerce, intimidate, or convey a message to a larger audience than the immediate victims; and the violent act falls outside of the precepts of international humanitarian law (GTD 2016).

Enders, Sandler, and Gaibulloev (2011) disaggregated the GTD into transnational and domestic components.[19] Enders, Hoover, and Sandler (2016) subsequently extended the disaggregated data to 2012.[20] Enders, Sandler, and Gaibulloev (2011) define transnational attacks as those where the nationalities of victims and the country where the attack transpires are not the same. One drawback of the GTD is that it does not include information on the nationality of perpetrators. This prevents me from creating a directed measure of transnational incidents and is the reason why my main analyses rely on ITERATE instead. Nonetheless, the GTD does afford a number of advantages. It includes an indicator titled "doubt terrorism proper," which refers to cases where the incident does not meet the definitional criteria for terrorism. For instance, incidents that have the qualities of insurgencies may report a "1" for doubt terrorism proper. The disaggregated Enders, Sandler, and Gaibulloev (2011) and Enders, Hoover, and Sandler (2016) data prune incidents that report "1" for doubt terrorism proper. Moreover, as Enders, Sandler, and Gaibulloev (2011) meticulously discuss, the GTD and ITERATE transnational counts differ for a number of reasons, which increases the utility of the robustness models.[21] I reevaluate my hypothesis using the GTD transnational terrorism measures.

Employing the GTD measures also lends a different empirical angle. The preceding analyses probed the effects of global and directed attacks. What remains unknown is whether transnational attacks on the country's own soil, regardless of the nationality of perpetrators, produces stiffer visa policies. On the one hand, we may expect countries that experience a high volume of transnational incidents to respond with a far-reaching crackdown. On the other hand, mobility rights are disproportionately shared among countries. We would thus anticipate that nondirected transnational attacks will also result in targeted visa restrictions. That is, regardless of which nationalities conducted previous attacks, terrorism will correspond to higher probabilities of visa controls imposed against a subset of states. This still does not mean that countries will overhaul their entire visa system. But it does mean that policy tightening is not necessarily calibrated to the source countries of terrorism. In order to test this assertion, I display models that include two counts of transnational attacks on destination states' territories; the first aggregates incidents from 1990 until 2009 and the second aggregates incidents from 2000 until 2009. These measures correspond to the post-1990 and post-2000 sums of global and directed terrorism I incorporated in the chief analyses in this chapter.

Table 8 presents six additional models. Models 22 and 23 include the post-1990 and post-2000 sums of all transnational incidents recorded by the GTD; models 24 and 25 focus on only fatal transnational incidents. The last two models, models 26 and 27, test the interactive dynamic between trade and terrorism by including an interaction term for bilateral trade and post-2000 incidents, and bilateral trade and post-2000 fatal transnational incidents. We immediately note that transnational incidents do not exercise significant influence over visa policies. Only fatal incidents reach the 0.10 level of significance. The coefficients on bilateral trade are on par with the coefficients given in Table 4. In model 27 we see that the interaction term and fatal incidents carry positive coefficients. However, the combined effect of bilateral trade and fatal incidents is negative, indicating that trade ties effectively overturn the substantively small positive effects of transnational ties. For the sake of brevity, all other controls mirror the effects observed before.

Overall, there is fairly weak evidence that the volume of transnational terrorism corresponds to higher visa-restriction probabilities. However, this

Table 8. Sensitivity Checks with Global Terrorism Database Transnational Terrorism Measures

| | All Incidents | | Fatal Incidents | | Interactive Effects | |
|---|---|---|---|---|---|---|
| Variable | Model 22 | Model 23 | Model 24 | Model 25 | Model 26 | Model 27 |
| GTD transnational terrorism post-1990 sum | −0.002 (0.00) | | | | | |
| GTD transnational terrorism post-2000 sum | | 0.009 (0.01) | | | 0.008 (0.01) | |
| Fatal transnational terror post-1990 | | | 0.004 (0.01) | | | |
| Fatal transnational terror post-2000 | | | | 0.037+ (0.02) | | 0.034+ (0.02) |
| Bilateral trade × GTD transnational post-2000 | | | | | 0.001+ (0.00) | |
| Bilateral trade × GTD fatal post-2000 | | | | | | 0.003 (0.00) |
| Bilateral trade salience | −0.035*** (0.01) | −0.032*** (0.01) | −0.033*** (0.01) | −0.031*** (0.01) | −0.036*** (0.01) | −0.035*** (0.01) |
| Recipient to origin GDP per capita ratio | 2.175*** (0.48) | 2.177*** (0.48) | 2.158*** (0.48) | 2.214*** (0.49) | 2.182*** (0.48) | 2.219*** (0.49) |
| Recipient's democracy | −0.038 (0.03) | −0.049 (0.03) | −0.047 (0.03) | −0.050 (0.03) | −0.049 (0.03) | −0.050 (0.03) |
| Origin's democracy | −0.090*** (0.01) | −0.088*** (0.01) | −0.089*** (0.01) | −0.088*** (0.01) | −0.088*** (0.01) | −0.088*** (0.01) |
| Civil conflict in origin | 0.631*** (0.09) | 0.662*** (0.09) | 0.653*** (0.09) | 0.672*** (0.09) | 0.660*** (0.09) | 0.670*** (0.09) |
| Recipient liberal state | −1.236** (0.39) | −1.152** (0.39) | −1.168** (0.39) | −1.128** (0.38) | −1.152** (0.39) | −1.128** (0.38) |

(continued)

Table 8 (continued)

| Variable | All Incidents | | Fatal Incidents | | Interactive Effects | |
|---|---|---|---|---|---|---|
| | Model 22 | Model 23 | Model 24 | Model 25 | Model 26 | Model 27 |
| Recipient's tourism revenue | -0.012 (0.01) | -0.011 (0.01) | -0.011 (0.01) | -0.009 (0.01) | -0.010 (0.01) | -0.009 (0.01) |
| Recipient migrant stock | -0.054+ (0.03) | -0.079* (0.03) | -0.071* (0.03) | -0.084** (0.03) | -0.079* (0.03) | -0.085** (0.03) |
| Colonial link | 1.710*** (0.41) | 1.729*** (0.42) | 1.713*** (0.41) | 1.748*** (0.43) | 1.733*** (0.42) | 1.752*** (0.44) |
| Common language | -1.295*** (0.18) | -1.266*** (0.17) | -1.268*** (0.17) | -1.274*** (0.17) | -1.267*** (0.17) | -1.276*** (0.17) |
| Dyadic alliance | -1.651*** (0.29) | -1.559*** (0.30) | -1.594*** (0.30) | -1.535*** (0.30) | -1.561*** (0.30) | -1.538*** (0.30) |
| Militarized interstate dispute | 0.955* (0.44) | 0.824+ (0.43) | 0.845* (0.43) | 0.722+ (0.43) | 0.825+ (0.43) | 0.718+ (0.43) |
| Dyadic distance (logged) | 0.539*** (0.10) | 0.511*** (0.10) | 0.517*** (0.10) | 0.510*** (0.10) | 0.510*** (0.10) | 0.508*** (0.10) |
| Recipient EU member | -0.807*** (0.19) | -0.718*** (0.19) | -0.709*** (0.20) | -0.653*** (0.19) | -0.718*** (0.19) | -0.655*** (0.19) |
| Origin EU member | -0.730*** (0.10) | -0.714*** (0.10) | -0.722*** (0.10) | -0.712*** (0.10) | -0.715*** (0.10) | -0.713*** (0.10) |
| Constant | -0.565 (0.58) | -0.555 (0.60) | -0.556 (0.60) | -0.626 (0.62) | -0.549 (0.60) | -0.618 (0.62) |
| Chi statistic | 250.768 | 250.442 | 252.348 | 250.643 | 257.524 | 256.095 |
| Wald test | 0.000 | 0.000 | 0.000 | 0.000 | 0.000 | 0.000 |
| Number of cases | 18,940 | 18,940 | 18,940 | 18,940 | 18,940 | 18,940 |

+$p < .10$
*$p < .05$
**$p < .01$
***$p < .001$

effect is limited to fatal incidents. The post-2000 sum produces a higher-magnitude effect. At the risk of speculation, this might be due to the war on terror and the consequent framing of transnational violence as a growing menace that has altered the global security landscape. After all, the new security paradigm rests on the individual as the transmitter of threats, and as such, high-profile events where perpetrators are foreigners stir governments into action. Fatal attacks set off alarm in policy circles, which translates into anxiety over transnational terrorism. Governments may underscore the vulnerability of borders and migration systems in general. They may call for indiscriminate migration restrictions, regardless of country of origin. For example, after the New York City truck attack that killed eight people on October 31, 2017, President Trump reiterated the need to discontinue the diversity visa. While the perpetrator was an Uzbek national, the diversity visa program encompasses a broad range of states from where the United States sought to encourage migration. However, discourse does not necessarily translate into policy. That said, the effects of overall transnational terrorism pale in comparison to those of directed terrorism where attacks can be pinned on specific nationalities. There is a closer correspondence between directed incidents and the likelihood of visa restrictions against specific countries.

In additional checks I do not display here, I also conducted a battery of supplementary tests.[22] First, I examine models 1–5 by utilizing logged aggregate counts of terrorism. This guards against sensitivity to outliers. Second, I confine the analysis to economically developed states, namely members of the OECD. This modeling choice aims to interrogate whether the impact of economic interdependence applies to a subset of states. The results depict substantively higher negative coefficients, providing modest support for this intuition. However, all terrorism terms yield significant and positive coefficients. Third, I utilize terrorism indicators that sum up incidents from 1990 until 2009. The results are virtually unaltered, showing that states' policies respond to the longer history of terrorism rather than simply to incidents in the previous decade. All terrorism terms emerge as statistically significant and positive. Importantly, the same pattern holds where targeted attacks exert a more acute impact on policy than do global attacks. Fourth, I cluster standard errors by dyad, which treats observations as independent across but not within dyads. This specification also allows me to control for unobservable factors that might be unique to the dyad. I also incorporate a number of alternative control variables to tap into dyadic ties: contiguity dummy in lieu of the logged distance measure and, to account for dyadic migration flows, bilateral migration stock instead of the total stock in the host state. The results survive robustness checks, enhancing confidence in the chapter's hypotheses.

What do the empirical patterns say in terms of the theoretical framework? These findings end on a buoyant note for scholars who endorse the pacifying effects of trade ties (Oneal and Russett 1999; Russett and Oneal 2001). That said, economic interests do not eradicate security concerns. Instead, a more subtle mechanism is at play whereby their relative influence will hinge on how close to home transnational violence strikes. Hence, we observe an interaction effect between economic ties and transnational terrorism whereby security concerns predominate given targeted attacks and economic incentives have a more pronounced impact given global and diffuse threats.

### CHAPTER 3

# Terrorism, Trade, and Visa Policies
# in the European Union

This chapter evaluates the book's hypotheses by studying bilateral visa restrictions. To reiterate, ideally we would track changes in visa policies over time. Visa requirements capture one component of how restrictive a state's policies are. For example, the same destination country can demand a visa from the nationals of origin states B and C, but citizens of B might find it easier to obtain a visa for travel. In this scenario, the destination state's policy toward state B may be viewed as more lenient. For example, Schengen countries are far more liberal in granting visas to Russian citizens than to citizens of Algeria. The dyadic visa-restrictions variable would not tap into this distinction because it records a visa requirement in force for citizens of Algeria and Russia seeking entry into the Schengen zone. To reiterate a broader point, borders vary in degree of permeability. Documentation requirements render the border less permeable (Boehmer and Peña 2012), but even given the same documentation requirements, we might find that nationals of specific origin countries have an easier time crossing the border. To be sure, the visa is a fundamental cornerstone of the global mobility regime (Guild 2009; Zureik and Salter 2005). The visa requirement is an important barrier to human mobility. However, the international mobility regime is multifaceted and must encompass not just whether visa requirements are in place but how strictly they are enforced. Furthermore, a visa is costly because of the logistical expenses imposed on travel (Hobolth 2012). The documentation requirements, waiting period, and travel to an application center are all costs travelers incur.

This chapter overcomes the limitations of the binary visa-requirements measure by utilizing a different indicator for visa policies: the visa rejection rate. As the data section elaborates, I draw on two sources of relatively new information: data reported by EU and Schengen member states to the Council of the European Union and data from the European Visa Database (EVD) (Hobolth 2013). From the former, I compiled a data set on EU and Schengen states' visa issuance practices from 2002 until 2015. From the EVD, I harnessed a measure for documentation requirements. I reevaluate the set of hypotheses analyzed in the previous chapter by introducing a longitudinal component into the analysis. This allows me to track whether changes in the main explanatory variables—terrorism and trade—influence shifts in visa-issuance practices.

The analysis is limited to EU and Schengen member states. As such, the policies of states in the sample are not independent from one another. In other words, EU member states devise and enact policies in the context of institutional cooperation. The Schengen as a border regime comprises both supranational and intergovernmental elements, with varying degrees of restrictiveness toward third-party states (Mau 2010). Uniform rules and procedures that regulate entry have allowed internal border controls to be dismantled (Lavenex 2010). In effect, a visa granted by one member state allows third-party nationals access to the entire Schengen zone. The European Union also shares a common visa list and extends visa liberalization to the same list of countries.

Despite these caveats, the narrower focus also has advantages. Confining the analysis to the subset of Schengen member states by default introduces a fair degree of similarity to the cases. It is not easy to identify the full set of push-and-pull factors on which destination states differ. Sampling European states allows me to hold these factors constant. With a narrower sample, we can be more confident in inferences and worry less about omitted variables from the analysis (Brady and Collier 2004). Additionally, despite the common visa list, as we will see, there is considerable variation in the restrictiveness of visa systems, as reflected in visa refusal rates. Put differently, European states share a visa regime but their implementation of visa practices offers rich variation. From a conceptual standpoint, the visa policies of countries in the sample are nested in a common regime. Hence, it is also important to understand how the harmonization of policies among full and partial members of the European Union's common visa policy (the Schengen Area) has affected member states' visa regimes.

## Harmonization of Visa Policies

EU-wide cooperation on migration gained steam in the 1980s (Geddes 2003). In the late 1980s and early 1990s, the process further accelerated with the collapse of communist governments. A significant spike in asylum applications to Europe followed, creating anxieties over undocumented migration and increasing the incentives to coordinate visa policies (Joppke 1998). Additionally, the Treaty of Rome in 1957 established the Single Market, removing barriers to the movement of people, goods, services, and capital within the EU bloc. This provided an important impetus for establishing cooperation, particularly in the area of border control (Monar 2001). In order to establish an area with unrestricted labor mobility, member states needed to establish a common border area. Coordination spurred deeper integration of border and migration control. The Schengen Agreement was signed in 1985, and the Schengen Implementation Agreement went into effect in 1990. As a result of these agreements, harmonization of immigration and border control topped the agenda for European states. The Schengen Agreement created the Schengen Area in 1995, which included Austria, Belgium, France, Germany, Greece, Italy, Luxembourg, and the Netherlands. New states have since joined, as the European Union has progressively expanded. As of 2017, the Schengen Area consists of the territories of twenty-six European states, with the United Kingdom poised to officially exit the union by 2019.

Harmonization was a gradual process, with member states initially maintaining a modicum of flexibility in how they implemented policies. For instance, at the advent of the Schengen regime, participating states retained discretion when extending visa waivers to sending states. An important stepping-stone came in 1992 when the Maastricht Treaty mandated that Schengen states adopt a common list of origin countries for visa requirements. In 1995, the Council of the European Union (the Council) passed a regulation that reiterated the requirement of the common list for all member states. Regardless, intergovernmentalism dominated policymaking in the late 1990s. It was not until the 1999 Amsterdam Treaty, which set up the European Union, that the Schengen acquis became institutionalized. The process culminated in the adoption of a "negative list" of 129 countries in 2001 (Annex I).[1] Annex I spelled out this shared list of sending states whose nationals would require a visa to travel to any of the participating states. At the same time, participating states adopted a "white list" of countries (Annex II) that enjoy visa-free travel to the Schengen zone. In addition, the Schengen acquis incorporated carrier sanctions, making transit companies liable for aiding unlawful entry into the Schengen zone (Article 27[1]). Both the negative and white lists were amended several times (Karanja 2008). The negative list was subsequently expanded to include 136 states by 2009, corresponding to 4.7 billion of the world's population (Hobolth 2013). In 2009, the Council passed resolution No. 810, approving the Visa Code, which systematizes the application procedure for the Schengen visa. In 2010, several Balkan states were moved to the white list, which now includes 58 states.

Both the initial adoption and eventual revision of the lists were done on a case-by-case basis. In the post-9/11 context, security concerns came to dominate migration policies (Guild 2009). However, securitization of migration is a nebulous process and not solely focused on terrorism. Rather, concerns over irregular migration played an important role, resulting in an effort to transfer prominent countries of irregular migration to the negative list; Ecuador and Bolivia are cases in point. Conversely, Macedonia, Montenegro, and Serbia were moved to the white list because of low migratory risks from these countries. However, not only source-country traits but also member countries' geopolitical concerns and historical ties with origin states shaped the common lists. Spain, for example, objected to requiring visas from citizens of former colonies. Even in the case of Ecuador and Bolivia, intra-EU dynamics among states played a role. The relatively latecomer states, Hungary, Poland, and Slovakia, backed Spain and Belgium for expanding the negative list in a bid to demonstrate their commitment to securing the external frontiers of the Schengen zone (Kovacks 2002). Thus the evolution of the Schengen visa regime shows that traditionally, historical ties and geostrategic considerations have hindered the unfettered use of the common visa regime as a general tool of immigration control (Finotelli and Sciortino 2013).

Within the immigration-control regime, visa policy stands out as one of the earliest and most successful areas of coordination. There are a number of complementary coordination schemes that comprise the heart of the visa regime. First, the regime rests on common standards for the issuance and regulation of visas, which all Schengen member states adhere to when granting short-term visas. Specifically, the European Community Visa Code regulates states' visa-granting practices through a highly structured procedure. Second, through carrier sanctions, member states shift the burden of control to third parties (Lahav 2004). Carrier sanctions also allow Schengen member states to extend surveillance and monitoring beyond the external border of the European Union (Mau et al. 2008). Third, members share identification databases as part of a coordinated effort at surveillance. In addition, states have designed common standards for border patrol and formed a specialized border-control agency, Frontex, to monitor the European Union's external borders (Brochmann and Hammar 1999). These endeavors form the cornerstone of the common visa system as well as the broader European immigration control regime. The Schengen visa regime establishes cooperation on short-term human mobility. The visa regime does not directly tackle longer-term labor migration, asylum determination, or the entry of refugees. Nevertheless, the visa system has important implications for regulating irregular migrants, as well as for asylum and refugee policies. Destination states capitalize on the preselection and screening function of visa requirements to ensure that foreigners do not intend to work or set up permanent residence. Visa policies theoretically run the risk that travelers from specific states will violate the terms of the visa, for example, by overstaying (Finotelli and Sciortino 2013).

With this common regime, we might expect considerable convergence among member states in visa policies. Empirical realities do not completely support this expectation, for a number of reasons. To reiterate, harmonization has featured concessions to member countries' historical, economic, and geopolitical concerns. Related to this, despite common lists, Schengen states allow some flexibility to accommodate the strategic interests of member states. This aspect allows for variation in visa granting rates. While EU harmonization has ignited debate about "Fortress Europe" (Bigo 2000; Huysmans 2006), the embedded liberal regime keeps restrictionism in check. Embedded liberalism, however, is not as influential on visa policies as it is on other aspects of migration control (Joppke 1998). Hence, whereas liberal tenets are an important influence on asylum and refugee determination, when it comes to short-term visas, states still enjoy considerable discretion.

Additionally, unilateral dynamics come into play in response to changes in migratory pressures. For instance, in 2011 France sought to reinstate internal checks along its border with Italy, and Denmark moved to introduce customs controls across its borders. More recently, European cooperation has experienced fissures in response to the outpouring of refugees from Syria and other conflict-ridden countries to Europe. Thus some states moved to fortify their external borders and, perhaps more stunningly, others announced intentions to fence their borders with other EU member states. These developments undercut cooperation, but from a deeper theoretical standpoint they also exhibit the trade-offs destination countries confront between security and economic incentives.

## Data Description

The empirical analysis in this chapter makes use of a new data set on EU and Schengen member states' visa policies. Countries provide annual reports to the Council of the European Union on the number of visa applications they receive and process, as well as on the number of visas granted or denied. Members of the Schengen Area report statistics on visas under the December 22, 1994, Decision of the Executive Committee on the issuance and exchange of information on the European Union's uniform visa policy (Council of the European Union 2009). The decision aims to foster transparency in reporting among Schengen states. The reports include information on short-state and transit visas that allow travel for up to three months for the purpose of business, family visits, or tourism.

The sample encompasses data for members of the Schengen Area, which are also EU member states, as well as Norway, Iceland, and Switzerland, which are Schengen states that are not members of the European Union. The data set also encompasses statistics for Schengen partial members, Bulgaria, Romania, and Cyprus; these states are not yet full-fledged members but are nevertheless bound by the Schengen acquis.[2] In addition, the European Visa Database encompasses data for the United Kingdom, an EU member state that is not part of the Schengen.[3] Data for the United Kingdom are available from 2005 until 2010. The data set is dyad-year in format and covers the years from 2002 until 2015. The visa-practice indicators gauge policies by destination toward origin state, given a specific year. The data set is panel: it contains information on member states across time. The number of years for which data are available varies across countries for two reasons. First, destination states file reports to the Council after they come under the purview of the Schengen acquis. Hence the coverage of the data grows with each successive expansion of the European Union and, by extension, the Schengen zone. The years 2002–2003 comprise data for the original EU members (EU-15).[4] The years 2004–2007 cover the EU-25, adding Cyprus, the Czech Republic, Estonia, Hungary, Latvia, Lithuania, Malta, Poland, Slovakia, and Slovenia to the list. The years 2007 onward integrate Romania and

Bulgaria. The coverage consists of 28 states comprising 27 Schengen states plus the United Kingdom. Second, there is cross-national and temporal variation in the sets of sending (origin) countries that produce visa applications. To illustrate, Estonia received applications from only 20 countries in 2015 compared to 47 countries in 2010. The full data comprise up to 198 origin states.[5] This yields 21,896 dyad-years.

The dependent variable in this chapter is the visa refusal rate, which is the total number of A, B, and C visas denied out of the total number applied for. A and B visas are for airport and land transit whereas the C type is the more common short-term Schengen visa, which allows the holder to reside in any Schengen country for up to three months (COM 2013a). The UK data list the number of visa denials out of the total requested for general tourism, allowing visits up to six months. The total numbers include both single-entry and multiple-entry visas granted. They also include limited territorial validity (LTV) visas, which permit travel to only a specific Schengen state. The data exclude national visas (D visas) designed for long-term stay, for example, for longer-term study or work or for permanent residence.[6]

The data on the number of visa applications submitted, issued, and denied were culled from portable digital files (pdfs) reported by member states to the Council of the European Union. From 2002 until 2009, the raw statistics were contained in scanned pdf files. From 2010 onward, the Council began converting reports to Excel files available for public use. Using the commercial software Cogniview, I converted the data contained in the pdf files into digital format in Excel (Høyland, Sircar, and Hix 2009). As an accuracy check, I then selected subsets of the data from each of the years 2003–2009 and compared against the original pdf files. Finally, I extended the data to cover 2015 after the release of the Excel files on the Council of the European Union website (COM 2015). Subsequently, Hobolth (2013) released the European Visa Database (EVD), which contains visa refusal rates assembled independently via a parallel method.[7] As a final safeguard, I checked for discrepancies in my data against the data provided by EVD.

The Council reports contain information by consulate or embassy. I calculate the dyad-year rejection (refusal) rate as the number of applications denied (not issued) out of the total number submitted per year, summed across consulates and embassies. To give a brief example, citizens of Turkey can file a visa application for France, a Schengen member, at the embassy in the capital, Ankara, or at a consulate, in Istanbul. The visa rejection rate in this case is computed by summing the application and denial numbers reported by the embassy and the consulate. The rejection rate is expressed as a percentage and varies (theoretically and empirically) from 0 to 100. Cases where no applications were submitted are taken out of the analysis. This means that a visa rejection rate of 0 percent is a true zero: none of the applications filed were rejected. For instance, in 2015, Austria received 14 visa applications from Argentina and granted all 14; accordingly, the data register 0 for the Austria-Argentina dyad for 2015. Conversely, 100 percent means all applications filed in that year were rejected.[8]

It is worth mentioning a number of limitations that pertain to the visa rejection measure. The EVD's visa-issuance data include Schengen and EU states in the list of origin states. To create a dyad-year data set, I similarly followed EVD's template and included all countries in the system from which destination states receive visa applications. This list does include Schengen and EU states whose citizens enjoy visa-free short-term travel to EU destination states. This is because the raw data contained in the Council reports are collected by consulate or embassy. Consequently, the data can theoretically encompass applications by both citizens and residents of the origin state. For a dyad with joint Schengen membership, this means that (most) applicants from sending states are not citizens of the latter.[9] Factoring this into account, I eliminated from the analysis origin states that are members of the Schengen or European Union.

A second and related issue is that the visa refusal rate may not directly reflect destination policy vis-à-vis citizens of the origin state. Instead, it can be treated as visa practices by the destination country oriented toward applications stemming from the origin country. The analysis redresses this issue by controlling for diplomatic representation in the region. For example, Austria does not have diplomatic representation in Iraq. Iraqi nationals therefore travel to nearby states, for example, submitting applications for a Schengen visa in the embassy or consulates in Turkey. Accordingly, the data on visa issuance for the Austria-Turkey dyad might capture applications by nationals of states, such as Iraq, without diplomatic representation in the destination state (Austria). I thus leverage the diplomatic representation data developed by Hobolth (2013). We may also imagine that noncitizen migrants who reside in the origin state may also submit their applications in the origin state. Using the same example, the Austria-Turkey dyad may also reflect applications by Iranian residents of Turkey, even though Austria does have diplomatic representation in Iran. As a second check, I also control for the ratio of total migrant stock to origin population. Regardless, the global pool of migrants is low, and in most countries, the total migrant stock represents a small portion of the population, which should allay concerns over remaining bias in the visa rejection measure (Czaika and Haas 2015).

A related concern is the representativeness gap between the applicant pool and the population writ large. Insofar as there is a gap, then visa rejection rates reflect how strict visa practices are toward the applicants from the origin country, as opposed to the country's larger population. However, this would only be a concern for inferences based on cross-national comparison if there were systematic differences across countries in representativeness of the applicant pool. We might surmise, for example, that the gap is wider for lower-income countries where the costs of travel impose an undue burden, making for an applicant pool that is more affluent than the larger population. Statistical analysis includes controls for origin-country economic development, which partially accounts for this possibility.

## Independent Variables

### Transnational Terrorism

Data sources, with a few exceptions that are disclosed subsequently, are identical to those that Chapter 2's analyses draw upon. Data for transnational terrorism stem from ITERATE (Mickolus et al. 2012). To capitalize on temporal variation, I include a cumulative sum of terrorist incidents. I develop two specifications: the first is a moving sum of incidents over the previous five years and the second is a running sum that cumulates incidents from 1990 until the current year. Mirroring specifications in Chapter 2, I distinguish between global and targeted incidents. For the *global* sum, the previous five years' sum captures total incidents perpetrated by origin-country nationals anywhere in the world in the previous five years not including the current year. Similarly, the *targeted* measures cumulate incidents by origin nationals executed against the destination state's citizens and staged on destination soil; I refer to these as victim nationality- and venue-based indicators, respectively. These sums do not include the current year and hence encode the lagged effects of transnational terrorism. This modeling choice (partially) controls for endogeneity bias.[10] Supplementary models reevaluate the hypotheses using the post-2000 sums utilized in the previous chapter. To

Table 9. Transnational Terrorism Measures

| Terrorism Sums | Obs. | Mean | Std. Dev. | Min. | Max. |
|---|---|---|---|---|---|
| Global previous five years' sum | 21,896 | 0.42 | 3.95 | 0 | 120 |
| Global post-2000 running sum | 21,896 | 1.36 | 8.12 | 0 | 288 |
| Targeted, sum of previous five years (by nationality) | 21,896 | 0.08 | 0.79 | 0 | 35 |
| Targeted, post-2000 running sum | 21,896 | 0.05 | 1.04 | 0 | 51 |
| Targeted, sum of previous five years (by venue) | 21,896 | 0.01 | 0.23 | 0 | 12 |
| Targeted, post-2000 running sum (by venue) | 21,896 | 0.04 | 1.07 | 0 | 48 |
| GTD domestic sum of previous five years' incidents | 21,896 | 10.63 | 26.48 | 0 | 180 |
| GTD domestic sum of previous five years' fatal incidents | 21,896 | 11.05 | 24.65 | 0 | 108 |

refresh readers, these indicators compute total incidents from 2000 until 2009. Table 9 contains descriptive information on the transnational terrorism measures.

In terms of the global cumulative sum, Pakistan generates the greatest volume of worldwide terrorist attacks. The UK-Iraq dyad tops the cumulative sum by nationality, followed by the Netherlands-Nigeria dyad. In other words, the United Kingdom has experienced the greatest volume of terrorism, and these attacks were staged by Iraqi nationals. The venue-based coding produces fewer attacks, which is in line with the claim that transnational terrorism is short-gun violence. If we consider targeted incidents by venue, Spain emerges as the country that has witnessed the highest volume of terrorism carried out by Moroccan nationals on its territory.

*Economic Interdependence*

The COW Bilateral Trade Data (version 3) provide information on trade between destination and origin countries. I calculate trade interdependence as follows:

Dyadic trade to total trade ratio:

$$\frac{imports\ from\ state\ B\ (the\ sending\ state)\ to\ state\ A\ (the\ recipient)}{total\ trade\ value\ of\ state\ A}$$
$$+ exports\ from\ A\ to\ B$$

The measure is lagged by one year as a check against endogeneity. The most recent version of the COW trade data covers 2009 (Barbieri, Keshk, and Pollins 2009; Barbieri and Keshk 2012). In order to leverage the full range of availability for the dependent variable, I extend the 2009 values for trade until 2015. Capital interdependence is measured using data on bilateral foreign direct investment (FDI). The measure is drawn from the work of Neumayer (2011). This measure is the average bilateral FDI stock from 2005 until 2008.

In the interest of space, I briefly document the control variables. Similar to before, these variables assess push-and-pull dynamics between destination and sending states. The Polity IV regime score assesses the level of democracy in origin states (Marshall and Jaggers 2013); we expect Schengen countries to be more welcoming of visitors from democratic states. While the destination states studied here are all democracies, there may be different pull factors among them.[11] Specifically, we may anticipate that states that host longer-term migration may have more relaxed migration practices in general. To account for this, I bring in the total migrant stock to population ratio from the World Bank's data (WDI 2015). In addition, we expect travelers to favor countries with touristic assets, and destination states that exhibit greater dependence on tourism as a source of revenue may on average be more permissive in visa-issuance practices. To capture both dynamics, I utilize tourism expenditures as a proportion of export revenue, again leveraged from WDI (2015). Physical distance between countries should also impact states' visa policies. I thus include the logged distance between the capitals of destination and sending states. Affluent destination states may be reticent to grant visas to nationals of significantly poorer states. As such, I computed the dyadic disparity in GDP per capita; data for GDP per capita came from the World Bank (WDI 2015). This variable is expressed as a ratio of the origin state's GDP per capita to the dyadic total so that higher values correspond to greater disparity between recipient and sending countries. States also routinely express concerns over visa transgressions and are hesitant to relax policies toward poor states in case their nationals use legal means of entry to gain a foothold in developed countries (Czaika and Hobolth 2016). Therefore, this variable also indirectly accounts for concerns over undocumented migration. Similarly, destination states fear that migrants from turbulent origin countries may exploit the short-term visa as a means for longer-term territorial access. Hence they may be reluctant to grant visas to citizens of countries plagued by domestic conflict. To tap into this, I include a dummy for civil war, coded 1 if the origin state suffered civil war in the previous year and 0 otherwise. This measure derives from the UCDP/PRIO Armed Conflict data set version 4 and records 1 if the origin experienced civil conflict exceeding 1,000 battle deaths in the prior year and 0 otherwise (Gleditsch et al. 2002).

Beyond physical proximity, cultural and linguistic similarities may function as a draw for origin-country nationals. With this in mind, I include a dummy measure taking the value of 1 and 0 otherwise for common language. European countries' visa practices have traditionally factored in colonial ties; on the other hand, host states may face higher demand for short-term travel from former colonies and hence develop stricter visa practices. These dynamics necessitate the inclusion of a dummy for former colonial ties. The data for these dummies are sourced from the replication data in Avdan (2014a). Next, to factor in the possibility that European destination states are less lenient toward travelers from Muslim states, I include a dummy variable, coded 1 if the origin state is majority Muslim. I created this variable from the COW World Religion Database, which charts information on worldwide religious adherence since 1945 (COW 2013; Maoz and Henderson 2013). Specifically, I treated countries with at least 80 percent of the population that adheres to Islam (regardless of sect) as majority Muslim.

The final set of controls aims to remedy the limitations of the data discussed above. To refresh, the visa rejection rate is calculated from applications originating from embassies and consulates in origin states. The rejection rate would exhibit bias to the extent that the measure also includes applications from non-nationals of origin states. To mitigate this caveat, I eliminated from the sample sending states that are members of the European Union and/ or Schengen. As an additional safeguard, I generated a measure from the EVD's consular representation component.[12] The EVD provides a dummy indicator if the recipient has full diplomatic representation in the origin state. To refer to an earlier example, Turkey's visa applications for Schengen states without diplomatic representation in Iraq (for example, Austria, Belgium, Bulgaria, and Cyprus) may also reflect demand by Iraqi nationals. Or putting it more generally, Iraqi citizens may travel to nearby states to submit

Table 10. Descriptive Statistics of Model Covariates

| Variable | Obs. | Mean | Std. Dev. | Min. | Max. | Data Source |
|---|---|---|---|---|---|---|
| ECONOMIC INTERDEPENDENCE | | | | | | |
| Trade salience | 17,092 | 0.00 | 0.01 | 0.00 | 25.42 | COW Trade Data (Barbieri and Keshk 2012; Barbieri, Keshk, and Pollins 2009) |
| GDP per capita difference (logged) | 17,701 | 9.53 | 1.00 | 0.00 | 10.84 | WDI 2015 |
| FDI to GDP | 20,341 | 8.64 | 24.41 | −58.98 | 255.42 | WDI 2015 |
| DESTINATION TRAITS | | | | | | |
| Tourism to GDP | 21,896 | 8.21 | 5.95 | 1.80 | 32.86 | WDI 2015 |
| Civil liberties | 15,863 | 6.87 | 0.33 | 6.00 | 7.00 | Freedom House (Annual Surveys of Freedom Country Ratings 2014) |
| Migrant to population | 21,896 | 2.66 | 5.79 | 0.00 | 43.96 | WDI 2015 |
| Regime type | 19,507 | 9.75 | 0.54 | 8.00 | 10.00 | Polity IV (Marshall and Jaggers 2014) |
| ORIGIN TRAITS | | | | | | |
| Regional restrictions | 18,711 | 5.61 | 8.00 | 0.00 | 47.00 | EVD (Hobolth 2013) |
| Migrant to population | 5,174 | 8.07 | 14.62 | 0.05 | 88.40 | WDI 2015 |
| Regime type | 18,644 | 1.86 | 6.50 | −10.00 | 10.00 | Polity IV (Marshall and Jaggers 2014) |
| Civil war | 21,896 | 0.18 | 0.38 | 0.00 | 1.00 | UCDP/PRIO Armed Conflict Data (Gleditsch et al. 2002) |
| Majority Muslim | 21,885 | 0.05 | 0.22 | 0.00 | 1.00 | COW WRD 2013 (Maoz and Henderson 2013) |
| DYADIC TRAITS | | | | | | |
| Common language | 18,524 | 0.04 | 0.19 | 0.00 | 1.00 | Avdan 2014a |
| Logged distance | 18,525 | 8.41 | 0.75 | 2.13 | 9.88 | Avdan 2014a |
| Colonial link | 21,896 | 0.03 | 0.18 | 0.00 | 1.00 | Avdan 2014a |

applications for the Schengen visa. The variable I employ to account for this is total count of regional countries lacking diplomatic representation.[13] It is possible that greater restrictions in the region result in more demand being funneled through countries where the destination state has diplomatic representation.

Potential bias is more likely in the case of visa applications submitted from countries with a higher ratio of migrant stock to population. Accordingly, following Hobolth's (2013) recommendations, models control for migrant stock in origin states; this measure comprises the total migrant stock divided by the population of the country.

Table 10 provides an overview of summary statistics for this chapter's variables.

## Statistical Analysis

Before proceeding to the multivariate analysis, let's take a look at Figure 3, which offers a snapshot of visa rejection rates for the destination countries in the sample. The graphs illustrate the visa rejection rate from 2002 until 2015 (depending on temporal availability of the data, as the preceding section discussed). The graphs showcase rich variability in visa rejection rates, which further reassures us that harmonization does not necessarily rule out significant differences among Schengen members. Considering longitudinal variation in the refusal rates, we cannot definitively ascertain a trend toward restrictiveness. To be sure, this snapshot is limited because it does not parse apart variance by origin states; neither does it confer insights into the determinants of the visa rejection rate. Toward that end, I now turn to the multivariate analysis.

## Analysis

Because of the panel structure of the data, ordinary least squares (OLS) would yield inconsistent estimates (Greene 1997). As an alternative, panel-corrected standard errors (PCSEs) are a suitable technique to account for panel-level heteroscedasticity and serial correlation (Beck 2001; Beck and Katz 1995). Beck and Katz (1995) recommend that scholars utilize PCSEs when dealing with wide data sets where, for example, the number of countries exceeds the

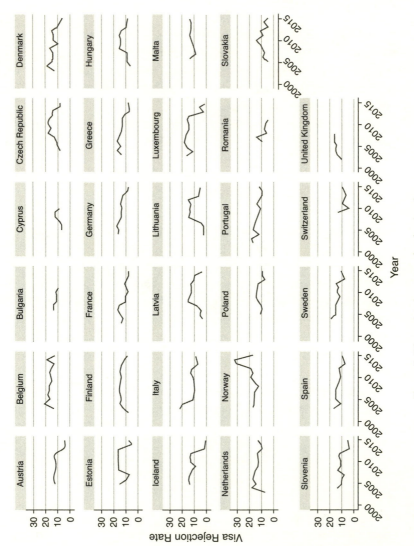

Figure 3. Visa rejection rates by destination state.

number of years. As such, this technique is particularly well suited for the data at hand. As previously explained, the panel is unbalanced in that the number of dyads—destination and origin pairs—is not constant across time. Econometricians have shown that PCSEs accommodate unbalanced panels well and are advantageous in small samples (Franzese 1996).[14] This technique also permits a stricter test of theoretical assumptions in that we can be more confident in statistically significant findings. As a final methodological note, the inclusion of a battery of controls for host- and origin-country traits may introduce multicollinearity to the models. The bivariate correlation coefficients for the variables, however, are reassuring. The migrant stock values for host and sending states give the highest Pearson's r of 0.41. This simply tells us that there is a positive association between short-term emigration and immigration stocks. As another shield against multicollinearity, I evaluated variance inflation factors (VIFs). All values remained below 1.46, well below the threshold of 5, reassuring us that multicollinearity does not present a problem.

Table 11 displays the first four models that compare the effects of global and targeted terrorism on European visa rejection rates. Models 1 and 2 employ the previous five years' sum and cumulative sums for global terrorism; models 3 and 4 use the counterparts for targeted terrorism. Across all four models, the coefficients on the terrorism indicators are positive and significant. These results bolster confidence in hypotheses 1 and 2, which postulate that global and targeted effects of terrorist attacks will be toward policy stringency. Substantively, global attacks executed by origin nationals produce an increase of about 0.3 percentage points in the visa rejection rate of applications emanating from the origin state. If we consider the cumulative sum, the increase is slightly less: over 0.2 percentage points. At the risk of speculating, the accumulation of global incidents does not necessarily compound the impact on visa-issuance practices. Turning to the coefficients on directed terrorism measures, in models 3 and 4, we note a discernibly stronger impact. The results portray an increase in the visa rejection rate of close to 2 percentage points (1.8) for terrorist incidents in which nationals of the destination state have been harmed. Again, if we consider the aggregate number of attacks post-2000, the effect is fairly similar but not larger: 1.4 percentage points. These patterns resonate with Chapter 2's findings with respect to visa requirements: targeted incidents result in stricter policies toward origin states compared to terrorist events worldwide.

Turning to hypothesis 3 on economic interdependence, we note the negative coefficient on trade and capital interdependence across all models.

Table 11. European Visa Rejection Rates, Terrorism, and Economic Interdependence, 2002–2015

| | *Global Terrorism* | | *Targeted Terrorism* | |
|---|---|---|---|---|
| *Variable* | *Model 1* | *Model 2* | *Model 3* | *Model 4* |
| Global terrorism, past 5 previous years | 0.309*** (0.05) | | | |
| Global terrorism, 2000s cumulative sum | | 0.211*** (0.02) | | |
| Targeted terrorism, past 5 previous five years' sum | | | 1.884*** (0.39) | |
| Targeted terrorism, 2000s cumulative sum | | | | 1.450*** (0.38) |
| Dyadic trade salience | −0.385** (0.13) | −0.364** (0.13) | −0.397** (0.13) | −0.405** (0.13) |
| Dyadic FDI stock (logged) | −0.952*** (0.05) | −0.981*** (0.05) | −0.935*** (0.05) | −0.922*** (0.05) |
| Destination migrant stock as ratio of population | −0.044+ (0.02) | −0.037 (0.02) | −0.050* (0.02) | −0.052* (0.02) |
| Destination tourism revenue as ratio of GDP | −0.063** (0.02) | −0.067*** (0.02) | −0.059** (0.02) | −0.061** (0.02) |
| Origin migrant stock as ratio of population | −0.145*** (0.01) | −0.144*** (0.01) | −0.146*** (0.01) | −0.146*** (0.01) |
| GDP per capita difference (logged) | 1.762*** (0.13) | 1.757*** (0.13) | 1.785*** (0.13) | 1.806*** (0.13) |
| Distance between capitals (logged) | −2.604*** (0.20) | −2.577*** (0.20) | −2.584*** (0.20) | −2.630*** (0.20) |
| Origin's democracy | −0.302*** (0.02) | −0.309*** (0.02) | −0.303*** (0.02) | −0.303*** (0.02) |
| Civil war in origin (lagged) | 2.000*** (0.25) | 2.045*** (0.25) | 2.004*** (0.26) | 1.990*** (0.26) |
| Origin majority Muslim | 4.964*** (0.55) | 4.789*** (0.54) | 5.123*** (0.55) | 5.176*** (0.55) |
| Total regional diplomatic restrictions | 0.239*** (0.02) | 0.243*** (0.02) | 0.237*** (0.02) | 0.237*** (0.02) |
| Constant | 17.635*** (1.73) | 17.316*** (1.73) | 17.279*** (1.74) | 17.518*** (1.74) |

(*continued*)

Table 11 (continued)

| Variable | Global Terrorism | | Targeted Terrorism | |
| --- | --- | --- | --- | --- |
| | Model 1 | Model 2 | Model 3 | Model 4 |
| Chi statistic | 1742.229 | 1771.753 | 1742.567 | 1739.151 |
| Wald test | 0.000 | 0.000 | 0.000 | 0.000 |
| Number of cases | 11,624 | 11,624 | 11,624 | 11,624 |

*Note*: Panel-corrected standard errors are in parentheses under coefficients.
$+p < .10$
$*p < .05$
$**p < .01$
$***p < .001$

Across the board, trade salience has a modest negative impact where by increasing the dyadic trade to total trade ratio by one standard deviation (1.20 percent of total trade), we witness a 0.48 drop in the visa rejection rate. Similarly, the dyadic FDI stock expressed as total capital investments between the receiving and sending states has a sizably negative impact. For a standard deviation increase in the logged dyadic FDI value, there is a 2.47 reduction in the visa rejection rate. These patterns enhance confidence in the proposition that trade and capital ties between destination and origin countries result in more generous visa-issuance practices. The results in Table 11 also complement the previous chapter's findings and provide a somewhat different angle on policy. The previous chapter demonstrated that robust trade and capital ties pave the way toward visa liberalization. The results here show that, in addition, even absent visa waivers, host states are generous in approving visas to citizens of commercial partners.

Turning to the control variables, we note that across the board, all regressors are significant and in line with what we would expect. In short, countries are more liberal in their visa-issuance practices toward physically distant and democratic states. Hence the visa is used as a barrier where distance is not a major hindrance. Applicants from majority Muslim states and countries bedeviled by civil war in the previous year confront tighter visa granting rates. As expected, tourism dependence dampens visa refusal rates while significant wealth differentials in the dyad—indicating poorer source states—result in tighter visa-issuance practices. Next, the models incorporate an array of measures to factor in the possibility that visa applications emanating from origin states include submissions from noncitizens. Among these, we note that regional diplomatic restrictions correspond to higher visa rejection rates, ceteris paribus. This is not surprising considering regional clustering on travel restrictions. Thus states that border or are proximate to countries with diplomatic restrictions are likely to encounter tighter controls. The migrant stock of origin states, somewhat surprisingly, shows a fairly weak negative impact on the visa refusal rate. To reiterate, the impetus behind this variable's inclusion is to factor in the visa refusal rate's responsiveness to applications from noncitizens of origin countries. We may surmise that the migrant stock surrogates for general openness of the origin state to international flows, which in turn could result in more permissive policies on the part of destination countries.

These findings harness the targeted terrorism measure by nationality, which sums attacks by origin nationals in which destination citizens are victimized. Table 12 presents the alternative indicator by venue, aggregating attacks staged by origin nationals that have taken place on destination countries' territories. All other covariates are identical and once again, the models estimate the PCSEs. Models 5 and 6 deploy indicators of targeted terrorism as the previous five years' sum of attacks and cumulative sum of attacks; these specifications mirror their counterparts in Table 11. I also consider attacks by origin citizens on the European continent. The attacks in Paris and Brussels reverberated across the European continent and compounded the impetus toward policy stringency across the European Union. Even countries that had not witnessed attacks on their soil expressed alarm. For instance, the United Kingdom feared its liberal border policies could leave it open to transnational militants (Hope, Barrett, and Turner 2016). If these recent examples point to broader patterns, we would expect states to respond to attacks in geographically proximate and similar countries. These events are more visible and salient and at the same time engender fears about the spread of transnational violence. Given this logic, the final two models in Table 12 utilize measures of terrorism that sum incidents conducted by origin citizens in Western Europe.[15] Both models count total attacks carried out within the previous five years; model 8 looks exclusively at fatal attacks on European soil. The terrorism variable in model 7 varies between 0 and 35 where the maximum number of incidents were staged by Iraqi nationals; the maximum corresponds to the number for 2003, which represents the sum of incidents in the previous five years (1998–2002). Fatal attacks are fewer, with a maximum of 10, in line with established patterns (Sandler, Arce, and Enders 2009): the deadliest years are 2011 and 2012, again due to violence in the region at the hands of Iraqis.

Across the board, the coefficients on the terrorism counts bear positive signs, but they attain statistical significance only in models 6 and 7. Because distance impedes flows of violence, targeted counts defined by the venue of attack are fewer in number. As Table 9 displays, the previous five years' sum by venue varies between 0 and 12; equally important, its mean is markedly lower than that of the targeted sum by nationality. Put differently, incidents orchestrated by foreign perpetrators on destination countries' territories are rarer. Hence, we cannot definitively conclude from the lack of significance that these terrorist events have no policy impact. In fact, model 6 considers the cumulative sum of attacks by venue and shows a significant modest impact. A single event increases the visa refusal rate by approximately 0.2 percentage points, an effect comparable to that of global terrorism. Considering attacks on European soil, the coefficient in model 7 emerges as substantively stronger and statistically significant. In fact, the impact is commensurate with that of targeted attacks whereby the visa rejection rate increases by 1.8 percentage points in response to a unit-level change in the terrorism count. These findings inform us that destination states treat terrorist events in other Western European countries as a threat to their own security. In other words, the empirical evidence conforms to expectations generated by anecdotal pronouncements. Nonetheless, as featured in model 8, fatal attacks do not exert a significant positive effect. Again, however, fatal attacks are fewer in number. Given the substantive magnitude of the coefficient, we can speculate that over time, deadly incidents may produce a significant increase in visa denials.

The coefficients on other covariates behave as expected. Trade and capital interdependence exercise a downward and significant effect on the visa rejection rate, reassuring us on the veracity of hypothesis 3. The controls similarly portray patterns in congruence with those observed in Table 11. Thus autocratic origin states, origin states that have undergone civil war, and poorer states encounter a significantly higher visa refusal rate. As before, origin countries situated in regions with poor diplomatic representation by European destination states face tighter visa-issuance practices.

So far, models 1–8 have examined the direct effect of economic interdependence. Table 13 shifts to evaluating the modulating effect put forward in

## Table 12. Visa Rejection Rates and Targeted Terrorism by Venue

| Variable | Incidents by Venue | | Incidents in Europe | |
|---|---|---|---|---|
| | Model 5 | Model 6 | Model 7 | Model 8 |
| Targeted incidents, past five years' sum (by venue) | 0.515 (0.32) | | | |
| Incidents by venue, cumulative sum | | 0.207** (0.06) | | |
| Incidents in Europe, previous five years' sum | | | 1.484*** (0.20) | |
| Fatal incidents in Europe, previous five years' sum | | | | 2.412 (2.94) |
| Dyadic trade salience | −0.402** (0.13) | −0.401** (0.13) | −0.372** (0.13) | −0.402** (0.13) |
| Dyadic FDI stock (logged) | −0.926*** (0.05) | −0.931*** (0.05) | −0.938*** (0.05) | −0.925*** (0.05) |
| Destination migrant stock as ratio of population | −0.052* (0.02) | −0.052* (0.02) | −0.050* (0.02) | −0.053* (0.02) |
| Destination tourism revenue as ratio of GDP | −0.062** (0.02) | −0.063** (0.02) | −0.059** (0.02) | −0.061** (0.02) |
| Origin migrant stock as ratio of population | −0.146*** (0.01) | −0.146*** (0.01) | −0.142*** (0.01) | −0.146*** (0.01) |
| GDP per capita difference (logged) | 1.809*** (0.13) | 1.803*** (0.13) | 1.834*** (0.13) | 1.812*** (0.13) |
| Distance between capitals (logged) | −2.624*** (0.20) | −2.606*** (0.20) | −2.500*** (0.20) | −2.629*** (0.20) |
| Origin's democracy | −0.303*** (0.02) | −0.304*** (0.02) | −0.307*** (0.02) | −0.303*** (0.02) |
| Civil war in origin (lagged) | 1.965*** (0.26) | 1.966*** (0.26) | 1.886*** (0.25) | 1.972*** (0.26) |
| Origin majority Muslim | 5.163*** (0.55) | 5.162*** (0.55) | 5.183*** (0.55) | 5.152*** (0.55) |
| Regional diplomatic restrictions | 0.236*** (0.02) | 0.236*** (0.02) | 0.236*** (0.02) | 0.237*** (0.02) |
| Constant | 17.482*** (1.74) | 17.384*** (1.74) | 16.061*** (1.75) | 17.480*** (1.74) |

(continued)

Table 12 (continued)

| Variable | Incidents by Venue | | Incidents in Europe | |
|---|---|---|---|---|
| | Model 5 | Model 6 | Model 7 | Model 8 |
| Chi statistic | 1715.868 | 1723.806 | 1759.847 | 1713.006 |
| Wald test | 0.000 | 0.000 | 0.000 | 0.000 |
| Number of cases | 11,624 | 11,624 | 11,624 | 11,624 |

*Note*: Panel-corrected standard errors are in parentheses under coefficients.
+$p < .10$
*$p < .05$
**$p < .01$
***$p < .001$

hypothesis 4. The models add interaction terms: models 9 and 11 interact global and targeted terrorism with trade interdependence; models 10 and 12 add interaction terms with bilateral FDI. The results provide robust support for the contention that economic ties mitigate the impact of concerns over terrorism. First, we note that the coefficients on the terrorism counts retain their positive and significant effects. Second, as it did before, targeted terrorism yields more powerful substantive effects: whereas the visa rejection rate increases from 0.33 to 0.47 percentage points in response to attacks worldwide by origin-state citizens, it jumps from 0.87 to 2.5 percentage points given targeted terrorist events, ceteris paribus. In the presence of interaction terms, the coefficients on terrorism terms convey the impact on the dependent variable when trade and capital interdependence equal zero. Third, the strongly negative coefficients on trade and capital ties capture the reductive effect, in the absence of terrorism. In a perfectly benign context, a percentage-point increase in the bilateral trade to total trade ratio, for example, leads to a 1.11 percentage-point decrease in the visa refusal rate. Again, setting terrorism to zero, a unit increase in bilateral FDI yields close to a percentage-point drop in the refusal rate.

Fourth, we turn to the tempering effect of trade and capital ties. Except in the final model, the coefficients on the interaction terms are negative and show that as levels of economic interdependence increase, the positive impact of terrorism weakens. Trade interdependence is expressed as a percentage of the destination state's total trade value. Therefore, in model 9, setting trade interdependence to zero produces a modest positive impact on global

Table 13. Economic Interdependence and Transnational Terrorism, Interaction Effects

| Variable | Global Terrorism | | Targeted Terrorism | |
|---|---|---|---|---|
| | Model 9 | Model 10 | Model 11 | Model 12 |
| Global terrorism, previous five years' sum | 0.333*** (0.05) | 0.471*** (0.07) | | |
| Targeted terrorism, previous five years' sum | | | 2.529*** (0.44) | 0.872** (0.31) |
| Dyadic trade salience | −1.114*** (0.14) | | −1.122*** (0.14) | |
| Dyadic FDI stock (logged) | | −0.930*** (0.04) | | −1.002*** (0.04) |
| Global terrorism × dyadic trade salience | −0.211+ (0.13) | | | |
| Global terrorism × dyadic FDI | | −0.059*** (0.01) | | |
| Targeted terrorism × dyadic trade salience | | | −1.757*** (0.48) | |
| Targeted terrorism × dyadic FDI | | | | 0.705*** (0.11) |
| Destination migrant stock/ population | −0.033 (0.02) | −0.019 (0.02) | −0.038+ (0.02) | −0.025 (0.02) |
| Destination tourism revenue/ GDP | −0.004 (0.02) | −0.062*** (0.02) | −0.003 (0.02) | −0.062*** (0.02) |
| Origin migrant stock/ population | −0.151*** (0.01) | −0.150*** (0.01) | −0.150*** (0.01) | −0.147*** (0.01) |
| GDP per capita difference (logged) | 1.740*** (0.13) | 1.745*** (0.12) | 1.758*** (0.13) | 1.725*** (0.12) |
| Distance between capitals (logged) | −2.112*** (0.20) | −1.813*** (0.18) | −2.129*** (0.20) | −1.763*** (0.18) |
| Origin's democracy | −0.241*** (0.02) | −0.247*** (0.02) | −0.246*** (0.02) | −0.254*** (0.02) |
| Civil war in origin (lagged) | 2.136*** (0.26) | 1.376*** (0.24) | 2.129*** (0.26) | 1.288*** (0.24) |
| Origin majority Muslim | 5.104*** (0.55) | 4.963*** (0.54) | 5.233*** (0.56) | 5.039*** (0.54) |

(continued)

Table 13 (continued)

| Variable | Global Terrorism | | Targeted Terrorism | |
|---|---|---|---|---|
| | Model 9 | Model 10 | Model 11 | Model 12 |
| Regional diplomatic | 0.296*** | 0.210*** | 0.293*** | 0.206*** |
| restrictions | (0.02) | (0.02) | (0.02) | (0.02) |
| Constant | 11.662*** | 11.126*** | 11.687*** | 11.056*** |
| | (1.78) | (1.61) | (1.78) | (1.61) |
| Chi statistic | 1236.084 | 1665.384 | 1238.244 | 1732.363 |
| Wald test | 0.000 | 0.000 | 0.000 | 0.000 |
| Number of cases | 11,624 | 13,757 | 11,624 | 13,757 |

*Note*: Panel-corrected standard errors are in parentheses underneath model coefficients.
$+p < .10$
$*p < .05$
$**p < .01$
$***p < .001$

terrorism, where each additional attack raises the visa rejection rate by 0.33 percentage points. However, the combined effects of the interaction term and trade interdependence are significant ($p < .001$); in other words, trade ties lower the visa refusal rate both directly and indirectly by conditioning the effect of global terrorism. Turning to model 11 and setting trade interdependence to zero shows directed terror's impact on the visa rejection rate to be significantly positive, where each attack raises the rate by 2.53 percentage points. Compared to global terrorism's impact of 0.33 percentage points, directed attacks have greater policy impact. A unit increase in targeted terrorism gives a positive coefficient, albeit with a significance level just below conventional levels of statistical significance ($p < .059$). The Wald test of joint significance demonstrates that across the first three models in Table 13, the negative effect of commercial ties maintains its statistical significance. In the final model, we note that in the absence of directed attacks, the effect of bilateral FDI is negative and significant. In contrast, as terrorism increases, the combined effect becomes positive and significant. This tells us that targeted events overwhelm the liberalizing effect of capital ties in the dyad.

An intuitive way to substantively interpret interaction effects is by considering the linear combination of coefficients, which also permits analysts to consider the range of values over which the interactive effects are significant

(Brambor, Clark, and Golder 2006). Toward that end, Figures 4a and 4b illustrate the marginal effects of transnational terrorism across levels of trade interdependence. Specifically, I vary trade salience across its full spectrum of values and juxtapose the marginal effects of global and targeted terrorism. The solid line in each panel captures the marginal effect while the 95 percent confidence intervals are represented by the dashed lines. Figure 4a shows that at low levels of trade, a unit increase in global attacks obtains a positive, albeit statistically insignificant, coefficient. Trade quickly overwhelms the marginal effect of global terrorism and the effect loses significance, as indicated by the dashed lines that cross the x-axis. For the range of trade values, the marginal effect is negative but insignificant. This pattern shows that trade ties do overturn the positive effect of security incentives, but the effects are indistinguishable from zero.

These figures show the marginal effect of *terrorism* and treat trade interdependence as the modifying variable. Using the linear combination of coefficients, I also evaluated the marginal effect of economic interdependence. The conclusion is rather positive for advocates of interdependence, as can also be seen from the negative signs on both the interaction and trade salience variables in Table 13. In short, the negative effect of trade salience on the visa refusal rate survives even as global attacks mount up. The reductive effect of trade falls below the 0.05 level of significance only when global attacks reach about forty-three.

Figure 4b engages in the same endeavor, charting the marginal effect of targeted terrorism, as we vary trade salience across its range of values. Again on a sanguine note for interdependence advocates, the graph demonstrates that the marginal effect of terrorism dips below zero. That said, for low levels of interdependence, the marginal effect is positive and significant. More concretely, the marginal effect of targeted terrorism remains positive and significant until the dyadic trade value reaches just under 1 percent of the total trade value of the recipient state. This aligns with the analysis in Table 13: targeted terror has a positive but marginally insignificant coefficient ($p < .059$) when we set trade salience to 1 percent. Because the graph charts the marginal effect across the full range of trade salience, this value may seem trivial. Nevertheless, close to 90 percent of the destination-origin dyads in the sample fall below this level of trade interdependence. Hence for these destination states, terrorism would dominate policy decisions when attacks harm their own citizens, and origin nationals would see tougher policies enacted against them if their compatriots perpetrated these attacks. A range of

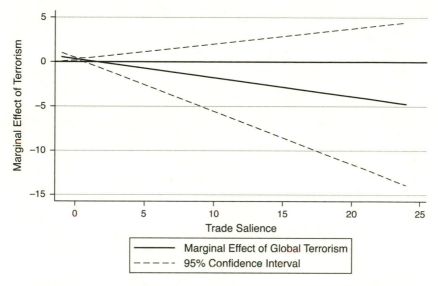

Figure 4a. Marginal effect of global transnational terrorism and trade ties. This graph shows the marginal effect of global terrorism on visa rejection rate as trade salience changes.

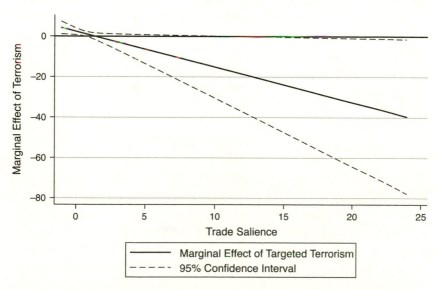

Figure 4b. Marginal effect of targeted transnational terrorism and trade ties. This graph shows the marginal effect of targeted terrorism on visa rejection rate as trade salience changes.

dyads in the sample benefit from modest levels of trade interdependence and fall between the 70th and 90th percentiles on trade salience. For these states, the marginal effect is positive but statistically insignificant, as evidenced by the lower bound of the confidence interval traversing the horizontal axis.

Figures 5a and 5b display the marginal effects of global and targeted terrorism across the range of bilateral FDI stock values. Bilateral FDI is logged and has a maximum of 12.7. The two graphs sharply illustrate the contrast between the two measures of terrorism. The marginal effect of global terrorism plotted across dyadic FDI runs fairly parallel to the marginal effect across dyadic trade. However, it remains significant and positive until the log of FDI attains 5.5, at which point the lower bound of the confidence interval passes zero. Until the log of FDI reaches 7, the marginal effect of global terror is positive but insignificant; after this point, it is negative and insignificant. If we consider the distribution of bilateral FDI, we note that 70 percent of the dyads in our sample feature capital interdependence below 5.5. This pattern illustrates that in practice, the moderating effect of capital ties is similar in spirit to that of trade ties. However, this is only true when global terrorism is concerned. Figure 5b, illustrating targeted terrorism, paints a starkly different picture: here, capital interdependence fails to override the effect of security concerns. Instead, the marginal effect's positive value survives across the full range of values for bilateral FDI. The 95 percent confidence intervals fan out slightly, showing decreasing certainty around the estimate, but the effect remains statistically significant throughout.

### Sensitivity Analysis

A series of supplementary analyses serve to address the deficiencies inherent in the visa rejection rate. Precisely because visa restrictions grant governments prescreening and selection mechanisms, visa controls may deter citizens of countries that confront a high visa rejection rate from applying. This would limit the cross-national comparability of visa rejection rates. As a panacea, I triangulate the results using an alternative indicator of barriers to mobility, derived from the European Visa Database (Hobolth 2012). The mobility index provides an ordinal score that also incorporates whether visa restrictions are in force. As such, I use the full sample of origin states, rather than restricting it to countries without visa waivers. This indicator reports 0

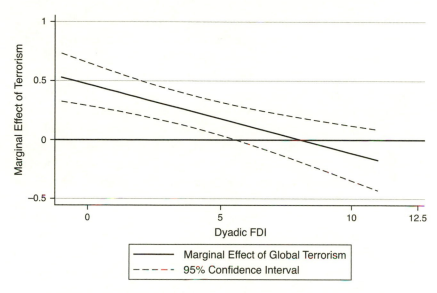

Figure 5a. Marginal effect of global transnational terrorism and capital ties. This graph shows the marginal effect of global terrorism on visa rejection rate as dyadic FDI changes.

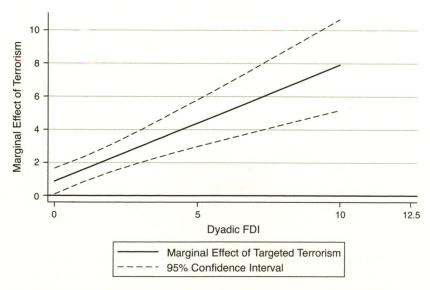

Figure 5b. Marginal effect of targeted transnational terrorism and capital ties. This graph shows the marginal effect of targeted terrorism on visa rejection rate as dyadic FDI changes.

for the absence of visa requirements. It varies between 0 and 3, denoting increasing barriers encountered by source-state citizens. A 1 signifies low barriers, 2 medium, and 3 high barriers to mobility. Hobolth (2012) canvassed government records to ascertain the ease of access for citizens of the origin state to visa application centers and the ease of application procedures, including documentation requirements, whether applications had to be submitted in person, whether interviews were conducted, and whether fingerprints were collected from applicants. Thus the mobility index allows us to ascertain whether concerns over terrorism amount to stricter mobility restrictions in terms of a lengthier and more cumbersome application process.

The further advantage of utilizing the mobility index is that it captures barriers on mobility that are conceptually dyadic. That is, it assesses policies that destination countries tailor toward origin countries. That is, unlike the visa refusal rate, the index is not affected by the volume of applications filed by non-nationals of origin countries. It also offers a more granular look into mobility restrictions by tapping into the transaction and procedural costs of filing visa applications. For example, citizens of Afghanistan and India may both require a visa to travel to France, but the former may encounter steeper restrictions. The rejection rate measures the stringency of visa admittance practices, but it is not informative on procedural requirements and consular restrictions. The mobility index redresses this limitation. The main drawback of the index is that its coverage is temporally limited to the period from 2005 until 2012 and that it is missing data within that period.

The mobility index lends an ordinal dependent variable. In order to take into account the panel structure of the data, I fit a series of random effects ordinal logits. We would expect variation in targeted transnational terrorist events to affect cross-national variation. We would also expect temporal variation that responds to changes in security threats. Random effects accommodate both temporal and cross-sectional changes in the index by decomposing the error term into within and between variance (Allison 2009). Errors are clustered by dyad to account for panel heteroscedasticity. Table 14 contains seven additional models. The baseline model remains the same with the exception that I omit the controls designed to factor in applications from non-nationals of the origin state.[16] Models 13 and 14 evaluate the impact of global terrorism and include the previous five years' sum and cumulative sum from 2000 until 2009. Models 15 and 16 utilize the counterparts for directed terrorism; models 17 and 18 shift focus to the venue-based targeted terrorism term. Finally, model 19 probes the impact of terrorist events in Western Europe.

For the sake of brevity, I reserve the discussion of Table 14's findings to the main independent variables. Across the board, the terrorism terms carry positive coefficients; however, the effects are significant in only three of seven models. Consistent with the patterns outlined in the chapter, global terrorist events exert a less powerful impact on policy. The first two models depict a negligible impact on the mobility barriers index. Two findings are noteworthy: attacks within Western Europe show a significant and positive impact on mobility barriers. Specifically, each attack in the region raises the logged odds of observing a higher category of mobility restrictions by a factor of 3. Stated differently, if we hold all independent variables at their respective mean values, using model 19 coefficients, a maximal change in the number of attacks in Europe (from 0 to 35) reduces the probability of visa exemptions by 17 percent. It also dampens the probability that the mobility index takes the value of 1 for low barriers by 20 percent and 2 for moderate barriers by 47 percent, but heightens the probability of 3, the highest level of barriers recorded by the index, by 85 percent. Second, in line with the results presented so far, targeted terrorism's policy impact is more potent; however, this comes to light only when we consider the cumulative count of attacks (model 18). Again considering the changes in predicted probabilities and using model 18's coefficients, with all covariates held at their means, reveals a similar pattern: maximal change in targeted attacks in destination states lowers the probability of mobility without visa restrictions by 17 percent, and low and moderate barriers by 18 percent and 19 percent. It increases the probability of high mobility barriers by 57 percent. These results provide further confirmation that attacks at home and in similar countries matter, as do attacks against compatriots. We also note that the impacts of trade and capital ties maintain their negative effect. Specifically, a highly interdependent dyad (defined as at the 90th percentile level of trade interdependence) has an 85 percent higher probability of enjoying visa-free travel, compared to a dyad with negligible levels of interdependence. I also conduct supplementary analyses by looking at standard deviation changes in independent variables. According to these analyses, even a standard deviation increase in trade salience increases the probability of visa liberalization by 15 percent while also reducing each level of restriction on the mobility index by 8–10 percent. The impact of capital ties remains more modest and increases the probability of visa-free travel by 2.5 percent and low-barrier travel by 1.9 percent and lowers

Table 14. Mobility Barriers, Terrorism, and Economic Interdependence

| Variable | Global Terror | | | Targeted Terror | | | |
|---|---|---|---|---|---|---|---|
| | Model 13 | Model 14 | Model 15 | Model 16 | Model 17 | Model 18 | Model 19 |
| Global terrorism, previous five years' sum | 0.002 (0.01) | | | | | | |
| Global terrorism, 2000s cumulative sum | | 0.001 (0.01) | | | | | |
| Targeted terrorism, previous five years' sum (by victims) | | | 0.356* (0.17) | | | | |
| Targeted terrorism, 2000s cumulative sum (by victims) | | | | 0.144 (0.11) | | | |
| Targeted terrorism, previous five years' sum (by venue) | | | | | 0.002 (0.46) | | |
| Targeted terrorism, 2000s cumulative sum (by venue) | | | | | | 2.947*** (0.61) | |
| European attacks, previous five years' sum | | | | | | | 0.178*** (0.04) |
| Dyadic trade salience | -1.057*** (0.19) | -1.057*** (0.19) | -1.065*** (0.19) | -1.058*** (0.19) | -1.057*** (0.19) | -1.071*** (0.20) | -1.06*** (0.19) |
| FDI (normalized) | -0.671* (0.31) | -0.671* (0.31) | -0.664* (0.31) | -0.666* (0.31) | -0.671* (0.31) | -0.664* (0.31) | -0.662* (0.31) |
| Destination migrant stock/population | -0.005 (0.00) | -0.005 (0.00) | -0.005 (0.00) | -0.005 (0.00) | -0.005 (0.00) | -0.005 (0.00) | -0.005 (0.00) |
| Destination tourism revenue/GDP | 0.018 (0.01) | 0.018 (0.01) | 0.018 (0.01) | 0.018 (0.01) | 0.018 (0.01) | 0.018 (0.01) | 0.017 (0.01) |
| GDP per capita difference (logged) | 0.331** (0.11) | 0.331** (0.11) | 0.327** (0.11) | 0.330** (0.11) | 0.331** (0.11) | 0.312** (0.11) | 0.331** (0.11) |

(continued)

Table 14 (continued)

| Variable | Global Terror | | | Targeted Terror | | | |
|---|---|---|---|---|---|---|---|
| | Model 13 | Model 14 | Model 15 | Model 16 | Model 17 | Model 18 | Model 19 |
| Distance between capitals (logged) | 2.229*** (0.24) | 2.230*** (0.24) | 2.232*** (0.24) | 2.229*** (0.24) | 2.230*** (0.24) | 2.263*** (0.24) | 2.236*** (0.24) |
| Origin's democracy | -0.110*** (0.01) | -0.110*** (0.01) | -0.109*** (0.01) | -0.110*** (0.01) | -0.110*** (0.01) | -0.109*** (0.01) | -0.11*** (0.01) |
| Civil war in origin (lagged) | 1.389*** (0.20) | 1.389*** (0.20) | 1.390*** (0.20) | 1.391*** (0.20) | 1.390*** (0.20) | 1.387*** (0.20) | 1.402*** (0.19) |
| Origin majority Muslim | -0.094 (0.08) | -0.094 (0.08) | -0.093 (0.08) | -0.093 (0.08) | -0.094 (0.08) | -0.097 (0.08) | -0.070 (0.08) |
| $\tau_1$ | 16.418*** (2.15) | 16.419*** (2.15) | 16.405*** (2.14) | 16.407*** (2.15) | 16.420*** (2.15) | 16.546*** (2.12) | 16.479*** (2.13) |
| $\tau_2$ | 20.705*** (2.18) | 20.705*** (2.18) | 20.691*** (2.17) | 20.693*** (2.18) | 20.707*** (2.18) | 20.831*** (2.16) | 20.76*** (2.17) |
| $\tau_3$ | 27.589*** (2.22) | 27.589*** (2.22) | 27.576*** (2.22) | 27.577*** (2.22) | 27.591*** (2.23) | 27.718*** (2.20) | 27.65*** (2.21) |
| Constant | 27.392*** (2.01) | 27.390*** (2.01) | 27.329*** (2.00) | 27.376*** (2.00) | 27.402*** (2.01) | 27.206*** (1.98) | 27.28*** (1.99) |
| Chi squared | 401.890 | 401.946 | 403.637 | 401.652 | 400.954 | 409.466 | 421.991 |
| $p >$ chi$^2$ | 0.000 | 0.000 | 0.000 | 0.000 | 0.000 | 0.000 | 0.000 |
| Number of cases | 20,154 | 20,154 | 20,154 | 20,154 | 20,154 | 20,154 | 20,154 |

*Note:* Standard errors are clustered by dyad and presented in parentheses under model coefficients.

+$p < .10$
*$p < .05$
**$p < .01$
***$p < .001$

the probability of medium- and high-barrier travel by 3 and 1.7 percent, respectively.

The previous analyses examine the connection between transnational terrorism and migration policies. Yet some of the most sensationalized attacks were homegrown in the sense that the assailants were citizens of the state in which the attack transpired. For example, the Manchester attack on May 22, 2017, was homegrown (Burke 2017). It was carried out by a second-generation British national, Salman Abedi, whose family had migrated from Libya. Nonetheless, the foreign connection entered the discourse in the wake of these attacks. Pundits stress that second-generation migrants in Western democracies are particularly vulnerable to radicalization (Roy 2017). They argue that the experience with migration is a risk factor to the degree that geographic dislocation exposes individuals to radical views, cultural alienation, and disillusionment with the host society. The public and media response tended to disregard the nationalities of perpetrators and again cast the threat as external, or at least made references to the migration-terrorism nexus. We may imagine that states that suffer fatal homegrown attacks overhaul their border and migration policies. Or they may tighten up controls against certain states, even if the past attacks did not originate from these countries. Do homegrown attacks inspire the same type of policy response? Looking at domestic terrorism helps answer this question.

In order to shed light on the connection between homegrown terrorism and migration control, I separately analyze the impact of domestic terrorism on visa rejection rates in Europe. For this, I computed various sums of domestic terrorism from the Global Terrorism Database (GTD). As in the previous chapter I made use of the Enders, Sandler, and Gaibulloev (2011) and Enders, Hoover, and Sandler (2016) disaggregated data. Using the domestic attacks data file, I generated moving sums of total domestic and total domestic fatal GTD incidents. These sums total the number of incidents within the previous five years, not accounting for the current year. Therefore, the domestic counts parallel the transnational sums I used in Tables 11 and 12. As we can see in Table 9, domestic counts have considerably larger means and maxima compared to the transnational sums. This is consistent with what we know about terrorism patterns: domestic attacks outstrip transnational attacks (Sanchez-Cuenca and Calle 2009). Table 15 is concerned with domestic terrorism. The table presents panel-corrected standard errors, mirroring the previous models.

Table 15. Domestic Terrorism and Visa Rejection Rates

| Variable | Additive Models | | Interactive Models | |
|---|---|---|---|---|
| | Model 20 | Model 21 | Model 22 | Model 23 |
| GTD domestic terrorism, previous five years' sum | 0.020*** (0.00) | | 0.022*** (0.00) | |
| GTD fatal domestic terrorism, previous five years' sum | | 0.114** (0.04) | | 0.123** (0.04) |
| Domestic terrorism × dyadic trade | | | −0.011** (0.00) | |
| Fatal domestic terrorism × dyadic trade | | | | −0.050 (0.07) |
| Dyadic trade salience | −0.396** (0.13) | −0.401** (0.13) | −0.369** (0.13) | −0.397** (0.13) |
| Dyadic FDI stock (logged) | −0.917*** (0.05) | −0.922*** (0.05) | −0.911*** (0.05) | −0.920*** (0.05) |
| Destination migrant stock/ population | −0.057* (0.02) | −0.056* (0.02) | −0.057* (0.02) | −0.056* (0.02) |
| Destination tourism revenue/ GDP | −0.101*** (0.02) | −0.072*** (0.02) | −0.100*** (0.02) | −0.072*** (0.02) |
| Origin migrant stock/ population | −0.146*** (0.01) | −0.147*** (0.01) | −0.147*** (0.01) | −0.147*** (0.01) |
| GDP per capita difference (logged) | 1.785*** (0.13) | 1.807*** (0.13) | 1.790*** (0.13) | 1.808*** (0.13) |
| Distance between capitals (logged) | −2.661*** (0.20) | −2.653*** (0.20) | −2.660*** (0.20) | −2.653*** (0.20) |
| Origin's democracy | −0.303*** (0.02) | −0.303*** (0.02) | −0.302*** (0.02) | −0.302*** (0.02) |
| Civil war in origin (lagged) | 1.984*** (0.26) | 1.981*** (0.26) | 2.006*** (0.26) | 1.987*** (0.26) |
| Origin majority Muslim | 5.139*** (0.55) | 5.145*** (0.55) | 5.146*** (0.55) | 5.149*** (0.55) |
| Regional diplomatic restrictions | 0.242*** (0.02) | 0.239*** (0.02) | 0.243*** (0.02) | 0.239*** (0.02) |
| Constant | 18.115*** (1.75) | 17.755*** (1.74) | 18.034*** (1.75) | 17.738*** (1.74) |
| Chi statistic | 1734.804 | 1721.534 | 1785.455 | 1733.565 |
| Wald test | 0.000 | 0.000 | 0.000 | 0.000 |
| Number of cases | 11,624 | 11,624 | 11,624 | 11,624 |

+$p < .10$
*$p < .05$
**$p < .01$
***$p < .001$

Models 20 and 21 focus on direct effects, using the GTD domestic and fatal domestic sums, respectively. Models 22 and 23 examine conditional effects, interacting domestic and fatal domestic sums with dyadic trade salience. Otherwise, the models replicate the same sets of regressors I included in Tables 11–14. Two patterns stand out. First, across all models, the GTD domestic sums impose significant positive effects on the visa refusal rate. Second, fatal domestic attacks exercise a more potent impact on the refusal rate. Bilateral trade salience assumes a coefficient commensurate with its effects in the main models in Tables 11 and 12 with the ITERATE transnational terrorism sums. The difference between fatal and total attacks is apparent when we consider the interactive dynamic. Across all models, the combined effects of bilateral trade salience and the interactive terms are negative and significant. However, the coefficient on the interaction term in model 23 does not reach significance. The combined effect falls below the .05 threshold of significance once the total number of fatal domestic attacks passes 5 incidents. The takeaway is that domestic terrorism matters, but trade ties can offset its policy effects. Fatal domestic terrorism, however, drives up the visa refusal rate, despite trade ties. These effects resonate with the patterns we observed with directed transnational attacks.

In separate models that I do not present here, I also analyzed the impact of domestic terrorism on visa restrictions, using Chapter 2's data. These analyses showed positive but insignificant effects on visa probabilities. At the risk of speculation, for European host countries, domestic terrorism may perceptually be similar to transnational attacks within the states' borders. That is, what is powering the results is not just that attacks are perpetrated by foreign nationals but that they occur on the countries' own soil. In addition, public debate and polemic may accentuate the migration-terrorism nexus, even if the perpetrators are not foreigners. It may be that only targeted terrorism significantly influences which countries' citizens are required to obtain visas but that homegrown terrorism also influences how easy it is for those countries' citizens to procure a legal visa for travel.

Finally, I also consider whether the ideological disposition of the incumbent conditions the effects of transnational terrorism on visa rejection rates. Right-wing populist leaders draw strength from anti-immigration sentiments and exclusionary zeal (Müller 2016). When in power, such leaders may also energize opposition to immigration and sell hard-line policies. Hence, right-wing leaders directly influence migration policies. Right-wing leadership can also compound the effects of terrorism insofar as public anxieties play into the hands of leaders' draconian agendas (Davis and Silver 2004). Thus right-wing leaders may frame terrorism as an existential threat and play up the migration-security nexus by emphasizing the dangers of lax migration policies. To assess these insights, I coded a dummy for whether the destination state in the European sample had a right-wing executive party. Data for this were sourced from the Database of Political Institutions (DPI) (Beck et al. 2001). I created the dummy from the DPI's execrlc indicator, which measures the executive party's orientation as right, left, centrist, or other. My indicator takes the value of 1 if execrlc reports 1 for right wing.[17] Other researchers note that recurrent terrorist attacks can bring right-wing leaders to power as the electorate favors hard-line and authoritarian leaders as one important coping mechanism (Merolla and Zechmeister 2009). I lag the right-wing incumbent indicator and look at whether a right-wing party was in power in the previous electoral cycle of that country. To account for modifying effects, I also created interaction terms with previous five years' sums of global, targeted, and European transnational terrorist events.

Table 16 presents four models, adding in the global, targeted, targeted by venue, and European attack sums. All of these models include the interaction terms with right-wing executive.

Several patterns are noteworthy. First, parallel to the previous results, global terrorism has a temperate positive impact on the visa rejection rate compared to the targeted terrorism indicators. Targeted terrorism measured by venue—that is, attacks on the host country's soil—has by far the largest coefficient. Second, as expected, a right-wing executive heightens the rejection rate. That is, when we set terrorism to zero, the coefficient on the right-wing executive indicator is positive. Even absent terrorism, when right-wing parties are in power stricter visa policies result. This effect is significant at the 0.05 level across all four models. Model 24 demonstrates that global terrorism increases the visa rejection rate by 0.28 percentage points. Although global terrorism has a modest impact on visa rejection rates, right-wing leadership can compound this effect. Model 24 shows that a right-wing executive increases the effect of global terrorism. The coefficient on the interaction term is positive (0.05) but does not gain statistical significance. However, the combined effect is significant and positive; given a right-wing executive, an incident of global terrorism produces an increase in the visa rejection rate of 0.33 percentage points. This can be seen by adding the coefficient on the interaction term (0.05) and the coefficient on right-wing executive (0.28). The effects of targeted terrorism in model 25 stand out. Absent a right-wing party

## Table 16. Terrorism, Right-Wing Leadership, and Visa-Rejection Rates

| Variable | Model 24 Global | Model 25 Targeted | Model 26 Venue | Model 27 European |
|---|---|---|---|---|
| Global terrorism, previous five years' sum | 0.283*** (0.06) | | | |
| Targeted terrorism, previous five years' sum | | 4.012*** (0.85) | | |
| Targeted incidents, by venue, previous five years' sum | | | 0.124 (0.33) | |
| Incidents in Europe, previous five years' sum | | | | 1.459*** (0.28) |
| Right-wing executive (lagged) | 0.469* (0.24) | 0.597* (0.24) | 0.508* (0.24) | 0.502* (0.24) |
| Global terrorism × right-wing executive | 0.050 (0.09) | | | |
| Targeted terrorism × right-wing executive | | −2.842** (0.94) | | |
| Targeted by location × right-wing executive | | | 1.360+ (0.73) | |
| European terrorism × right-wing executive | | | | 0.061 (0.39) |
| Dyadic trade salience | −0.380** (0.13) | −0.387** (0.13) | −0.396** (0.13) | −0.366** (0.13) |
| Dyadic FDI stock (logged) | −0.952*** (0.05) | −0.944*** (0.05) | −0.925*** (0.05) | −0.937*** (0.05) |
| Destination migrant stock/ population | −0.039+ (0.02) | −0.044+ (0.02) | −0.047* (0.02) | −0.045* (0.02) |
| Destination tourism revenue/ GDP | −0.067*** (0.02) | −0.064** (0.02) | −0.066** (0.02) | −0.064** (0.02) |
| Origin migrant stock/ population | −0.146*** (0.01) | −0.146*** (0.01) | −0.147*** (0.01) | −0.143*** (0.01) |
| GDP per capita difference (logged) | 1.719*** (0.14) | 1.735*** (0.14) | 1.764*** (0.14) | 1.792*** (0.14) |
| Distance between capitals (logged) | −2.619*** (0.20) | −2.580*** (0.20) | −2.637*** (0.20) | −2.514*** (0.20) |
| Origin's democracy | −0.301*** (0.02) | −0.301*** (0.02) | −0.302*** (0.02) | −0.306*** (0.02) |

(continued)

Table 16 (continued)

| Variable | Model 24<br>Global | Model 25<br>Targeted | Model 26<br>Venue | Model 27<br>European |
|---|---|---|---|---|
| Civil war in origin (lagged) | 2.008*** | 2.011*** | 1.975*** | 1.894*** |
|  | (0.26) | (0.26) | (0.26) | (0.26) |
| Origin majority Muslim | 4.954*** | 5.108*** | 5.150*** | 5.180*** |
|  | (0.55) | (0.55) | (0.56) | (0.55) |
| Regional diplomatic | 0.242*** | 0.240*** | 0.239*** | 0.239*** |
| restrictions | (0.02) | (0.02) | (0.02) | (0.02) |
| Constant | 17.979*** | 17.466*** | 17.800*** | 16.372*** |
|  | (1.75) | (1.76) | (1.76) | (1.77) |
| Chi statistic | 1723.381 | 1730.899 | 1700.874 | 1744.143 |
| Wald test | 0.000 | 0.000 | 0.000 | 0.000 |
| Number of cases | 11,453 | 11,453 | 11,453 | 11,453 |

*Note*: Panel-corrected standard errors are presented in parentheses beneath model coefficients.
$+p < .10$
$*p < .05$
$**p < .01$
$***p < .001$

in power, attacks within destination states raise the visa rejection rate by over 4 percentage points.

Perhaps the more puzzling finding is the negative coefficient on the interaction term. While the effect remains positive and significant ($p < .001$) regardless of the executive's ideological disposition, it decreases when the country has a right-wing party in power. At the risk of post hoc explanations, it may be that targeted attacks affect policy regardless of who is in power. The targeted terrorism sum here measures attacks against nationals, and not attacks within territory per se, and hence capture attacks elsewhere as well. That is, right-wing parties may not be able to use attacks against the nationals of a country to their advantage to push for stiffer migration policies. In contrast, attacks on the country's own soil may be politicized to a greater extent. Hence, model 26 shows us that targeted attacks (by venue) do not yield a significant positive impact, absent right-wing leadership, but when a right-wing party is in power, the effect is positive and significant. The combined effect produces an increase of 1.48 percentage points on the visa rejection rate and is significant with $p < .02$. Model 27 illustrates the effects of European terrorism, bringing in the sum of all attacks on the European continent within the previous five years. In congruence with Table 14's findings, European terrorism lends a statistically significant coefficient of decent magnitude, increasing the visa rejection rate by almost 1.5 points. The coefficient on the interactive term is insignificant and the combined effect of European terrorism given a right-wing executive in the destination state is slightly over 1.5 points. In other words, attacks in Europe are significant in their own right, but a right-wing party in power does not necessarily magnify their policy impacts. The emerging conclusion from this discussion is that the political climate generally or the ideological orientation of incumbents more specifically can shape the policy salience of terrorism. Nonetheless, Table 16 also shows that the main effects are not perturbed by these domestic factors.

## Conclusion

This chapter bolsters Chapter 2's findings by providing substantial evidence that security concerns and economic incentives have opposing effects on states' visa policies. The effects carry over to several dimensions of visa policy: visa-waiver programs, visa-issuance practices, and overall barriers to human mobility. Also, the results demonstrate that trade and capital ties function as a counterweight to security concerns. Destination countries that enjoy strong commercial links with sending countries are more likely to liberalize their visa programs vis-à-vis nationals of their economic partners. In addition, targeted attacks had a discernibly different impact when compared to global terrorism. These results underscore that the balance shifts in favor of security concerns when the destination state's own citizens have been victimized; however, we observe the difference between directed and diffuse threats most acutely at low levels of trade salience.

Theoretically, the patterns outlined in both chapters offer two initial conclusions. First, they highlight that economic ties have implications beyond international war. Maintaining secure borders and monitoring short-term human mobility are part and parcel of tackling transnational security threats. From that perspective, economic interdependence shapes how states seek security, given transnational threats. Second, and equally important, the results ask us to unpack the effects of international terrorism. Harm to the state's own citizens and territory most starkly involve national interests. That said, national interests may be more broadly defined and include threats that imperil the citizens and territory of geographically and culturally proximate states. EU and Schengen countries adjust policies in response to attacks that affect citizens of or unfold on the territory of Western European states, which testifies to the broader nature of the national interest.

CHAPTER 4

# Terrorism, Trade, and Border Fences

## Border Fences

In stark contrast to globalist expectations of a borderless world, the practice of building fences has gained steam. Since the end of World War II, the world has seen sixty-two new border barriers between neighboring states. Strikingly, states built forty-eight of these barriers after the end of the Cold War. Regional turmoil in the wake of the Arab Spring motivated several states in the Middle East to encircle their borders with fences. The war in Syria animated EU member states to begin constructing fences along their borders. From a globalist perspective, these trends are puzzling insofar as we expect the material benefits of transnational exchange to guide states to prefer open borders.

The previous two chapters demonstrated that transnational terrorism tightens visa policies. While the reasons for building fences are varied, terrorism is frequently cited as a justification for building border barriers (Jones 2012a). Israel extols the Gaza fence as a successful antiterrorism initiative that inspired the construction of the West Bank barrier. Following the Reyhanli terrorist attacks of May 2013, Turkey began wall construction on its southeastern border with Syria (Afanasieva 2014). Saudi Arabia has pointed to Yemen's inability to monitor its borders and touted the new 9,000-foot fence as an impediment to Al-Qaeda operations (Nuseibeh 2009). Neither have European states been immune from the rising popularity of fenced borders. While managing the refugee influx is a prominent driving force in Europe, some right-wing leaders have been quick to point to the attacks in Paris and Brussels as the impetus for harder borders. Hungary's right-wing government rushed to link terrorism to migration, with the foreign minister declaring: "We are talking about a stretch of border 175-kilometres-long, whose physical closure can happen with a four-meter-high fence" (Nordstrom 2015). In

the face of the migration crisis, hawkish politicians blend together nationalist fervor and fears over terrorist infiltration to propel border closure. Recently
many other states have voiced their intentions to seal their borders by building walls. For example, Iran is installing a 435-foot-long fence against Pakistan, and Tehran explicitly names militancy and terrorism among the reasons
for the barrier (Ghasmalee 2011). More recently, Israel has cited the prominence of the Muslim Brotherhood in Egypt as the impetus for raising a
150-mile-long fence along its border with Egypt (Weiken 2013). Israel also
announced in June 2014 that it would institute fences along its borders with
Jordan and Syria to thwart flows of radical militants ("Israel" 2014).

Avdan and Gelpi (2017) show that border fences are effective in undercutting the probability of transnational terrorist events. Notwithstanding the
objective effectiveness of fences, their perceived utility against clandestine entry can justify their construction (Hassner and Wittenberg 2015). To illustrate, the Israeli public firmly believes that the Gaza fence is effective against
Palestinian terrorism, a conviction that created consensus that physical barriers could derail cross-border terrorist events. More generally, states sometimes implement harder policies to subdue public fears (Andreas 2000). In
this fashion, policy stringency serves to symbolically assert the state's commitment and ability to protect its citizenry and maintain territorial integrity.
This symbolic aspect is less apparent when it comes to visa controls insofar
as they are not readily observable by the public. In contrast, border barriers
are easily observable by domestic and external audiences.

To be sure, border fences are an attractive policy tool against transnational
threats. They are, however, a pricey policy initiative. The 670 miles of fence
along the U.S. border with Mexico, for example, came with a $2.4 billion price
tag and is forecasted to require another $6.1 billion to operate over twenty
years (Sais 2013). In early 2018, Trump asked lawmakers for $18 billion to ex-
tend the fence and bolster the existing barrier. The price tag is slated to exceed $33 billion overall for enforcement and construction of the new fence
(Miroff and Werner 2018). Beyond the costs of construction, harder borders
detract from economic exchange. Commenting on France's reintroduction
of border controls after the Paris attacks, Roger Weber, former mayor of
Schengen village in Luxembourg, noted: "The impact on the economy is huge.
It's suicidal, especially at a time like this when economic prospects are poor.
We can't live with closed borders" (Traynor 2016). In addition to direct monetary costs, fences have reputational costs in the sense that barriers may
strain relationships with neighboring states. Especially when viewed as a

hostile signal by neighbors, fences erode economic ties (Donaldson 2005). Hence, states do not undertake fence construction lightly.

The security theater perspective suggests that fences may represent policymakers' benign yet perhaps inflated response to public anxiety. Or, from a less edifying perspective, governments may deliberately point to the specter of terrorism and engage in fear mongering in order to advance more draconian agendas. In either instance, states build walls regardless of their actual efficacy. Yet we do not know whether actual terrorist events trigger the installation of barriers. Barricading borders pits perceived and actual security benefits against potential economic loss. The theoretical chapter stipulated that economic incentives will steer policy toward open borders. As such, states confront the trade-off between security and material interests when fortifying their borders.


## Border Fences in International Politics

Borders marked by physical barriers occupy a middle position between fully militarized border zones and delimited borders (Hassner and Wittenberg 2015). On one end of the continuum lie borders defined by treaties. Demarcated borders represent the next step in border institutionalization where markers such as signs or posts may be installed to demonstrate the boundary line between countries (Gavrilis 2011). As the boundary is reinforced via a physical marker, it moves away from a symbolic line and can function as a physical impediment to transborder movement. A border barrier takes demarcation one step further and refers to the imposition of a physical obstacle at the interstate boundary line. Border barriers are unilateral measures and imposed without the explicit support of the neighbor state. Thus barriers often elicit rebukes from the neighbor. Given disputed territory, neighbors may object that the barrier constitutes a fait accompli, such as Pakistan does with respect to India's Line of Control (LoC). Nevertheless, barriers more often arise on undisputed than on disputed borders (Donaldson 2005).

Border barriers run the gamut from tattered fences, to razor fences, to solid walls, to walls with sophisticated surveillance technology.[1] Several European states, for example, Bulgaria, Hungary, Macedonia, and Slovenia, are constructing razor-wire fences to stem the flow of migrants (Coelho 2017). A more sophisticated structure is Israel's Gaza fence, which is equipped with military technology, surveillance cameras, motion sensors, watchtowers, and guard posts. On the other end of the spectrum is Saudi Arabia's fence with Yemen, described by the Saudi government as resembling a screen rather than a wall (Whitaker 2004). States may reinforce an existing weak structure: for example, terrorist attacks along the Iranian border hinterland in 2007 motivated Iran to erect a solid wall in place of a tattered wire fence on its boundary with Pakistan. And the war in Syria animated Turkey to replace its wire fence with a concrete wall. Barriers may engulf the entire boundary line, or states may place partial barriers along segments of the border: Spain barricaded its border with Morocco at two separate segments, along the cities of Ceuta and Melilla. And fencing may occur in fits and starts, whereby states seal off segments of the border at different points in time. Spain fenced Ceuta and Melilla in 1993 and 1998, respectively. At the extreme end of the spectrum, states may pursue border security through electrified fences, the deployment of military forces, or minefields (Jellissen and Gottheil 2013). States may install minefields independently of fences, as is the case in Angola, Bosnia-Herzegovina, and Cambodia, or they may accompany border fences, as in the case of Egypt and Iran.

Border barriers are not new: construction of the Great Wall of China began in the fifth century BC; Hadrian's Wall in northern England was built in the first century; Offas Dyke between Wales and England was constructed in the eighth century; and Danevirke in Schleswig-Holstein was imposed in the ninth century. Twentieth-century fences and walls have served a strategic military purpose (Sterling 2009). The French erected the ill-fated Maginot Line in the interwar era in a failed bid to block German military expansion. Germany built Maginot's counterpart, the Siegfried Line, as a defensive effort against the French. In both cases, states built fortifications to repel conventional military forces. States have also installed fortifications as a protective barrier against unconventional forces—for example, insurgencies— during military conflict. The French installed the Morice Line in 1956 along its border with Tunisia to impede the FLN (Front Liberation Nationale) during the Algerian War of Independence (Keiger and Alexander 2002). Barriers also support states' solidification of authority over territorial conquests. The Bar-Lev Line established Israel's territorial control of the Sinai Peninsula in the 1967 war. Other examples include Eritrea's fence with Ethiopia pursuant to their border dispute and India's fence on its side of the LoC in Kashmir. States have also built walls against ideological rivals. Throughout the Cold War, the Berlin Wall was emblematic of the ideological divide between the capitalist West and the communist East. The longest-standing wall, the Korean demilitarized zone (DMZ), is a stark reminder of the enduring rivalry between North and South Korea.

Since the fall of the iron curtain, the world has witnessed new barriers being installed at a rapid pace. The defining feature of modern border barriers is that they aim to repel non-state threats: "Their primary function is border control, not military defense or territorial demarcation" (Hassner and Wittenberg 2015, 160). Alongside the shift in focus on non-state threats, states' border enforcement emphasizes policing rather than military defense (Bigo 2014). Fence construction aligns with this shift. Additionally, walls must be understood in the context of states' strategies to tackle the negative externalities of globalization (Naim 2005). Border scholar Elisabeth Vallet views fences as a backlash against globalization: "We assumed September 11 triggered the proliferation of walls in the world, but we backtracked and discovered that the walls were on the minds of [states] already" (quoted in John 2015). Globalization paves the way toward the "re-articulation and expansion of sovereign authority," which along with other developments such as the increasing number of border agents, new surveillance technologies, and deployment of military troops in border spaces redefines the significance of borders (Jones and Johnson 2016, 195). More concretely, states strive to stymie illicit flows, such that significant wealth differentials between neighboring countries increase the likelihood of border fences (Carter and Poast 2015). Unmonitored transborder flows undercut border stability, which is pivotal to states' security in the face of globalization (Gavrilis 2008a).

### The Terrorism and Trade Trade-off

Instead of impeding conventional armed forces, modern-day border barriers seek to derail unauthorized and clandestine human mobility (Andreas 2003a). In other words, border fences are built to monitor clandestine transnational actors (CTAs). While CTAs encompass a broad array of people, none has received more attention than transnational terrorists. This attention is not unwarranted and has rewritten the security paradigm (Salehyan 2008b). There is growing recognition that individuals can wreak devastation that was previously the preserve of state armed forces. Barrier construction has increased considerably since September 11, and scholars underscore that the global war on terror underpins the accelerated pace of border fencing (Jones 2012b; Jones and Johnson 2016).

Fences are undeniably also symbolic. Regardless of actual effectiveness, a physical barrier—even in the case of a flimsy fence—instills a psychological sense of safety (Jones 2012a). Physical barriers are part of a broader "imperative to at least project an impression of territorial control and to symbolically signal official commitment to maintaining such control" (Andreas 2000, 5). Demonstrating the actual success of the fence may prove difficult, but policymakers find it easier to portray the initiative as successful. Israel has time and again touted the West Bank and Gaza fences as an antiterrorism tool and lauded them for significantly reducing cross-border suicide terrorist attacks from Palestine (Steves 2013). Defending the West Bank separation against petitions to dismantle it, Netanyahu remarked: "I hear they are saying today that because it's quiet, it's possible to take down the fence. My friends, the opposite is true. . . . It's quiet because a fence exists" ("Netanyahu: Israel Won't Dismantle" 2009).

Moreover, even when terrorism is not directly tied to the construction of a border wall, by invoking terrorism, governments muster support for the initiative. Accordingly, Jones (2012a) notes that the "decision to build the barrier on the U.S.-Mexico border is a direct result of the discourse on terror" (50). Terrorist attacks can reanimate stagnant agendas in favor of border fortifications or, similarly, add renewed zeal to existing construction projects. For instance, the 2008 Mumbai attacks compelled India to reinforce the India-Pakistan fence and resume construction on the partially fenced border.

*Hypothesis 1: Global*

*States are more likely to construct a border barrier against neighbor states that generate transnational terrorist attacks.*

*Hypothesis 2: Targeted*

*States are more likely to construct a border barrier against neighbor states that generate transnational terrorist attacks if their own nationals and territory are harmed in these incidents.*

Although fences have symbolic value, there are concrete ways through which terrorism incentivizes fence construction. Fences are a relatively economical and less risky initiative compared to offensive antiterror initiatives such as cross-border incursion, aerial bombardment, or decapitation campaigns (Staniland 2006). Fences may complement or supplant offensive initiatives, especially when the latter prove unsuccessful, as in the case of Israel's West Bank fence (Jellissen and Gottheil 2013). Fences strive to deny access to transnational terrorists by sealing leaky borders. If Hassner and Wittenberg (2015) are correct, territorial denial will be particularly effective against transnational threats given limited alternative routes of access and robust cooperation with neighboring countries. States also erect barriers to impose additional logistical impediments on groups, for example, by impeding the flow of funding, supplies, and militants. For instance, spearheaded by the United States, the international community encouraged Turkey to repair its fence with Syria in order to hinder the flow of foreign recruits and funds to the ISIS (Banco 2014).

The foregoing discussion links transnational terrorism to a higher probability of border fences. In parallel to the separate effects of global and targeted terrorism, we may imagine two scenarios. Terrorist groups seek havens of high-volume terrorist activity—terrorist hot spots (Braithwaite and Li 2007). Hot spots create and accentuate the impression that neighboring space is lawless and ungovernable; these perceptions in turn motivate states to close their borders (Jones 2012a). Hence we expect countries to wall off borders against neighbors that generate a significant volume of terrorism. Alternatively, given the pecuniary and reputational costs of fences, countries may be more selective in that they build walls against terrorism-exporting neighbors only when their own interests are harmed in these attacks. The preceding discussion leads to the following hypotheses.


*Hypothesis 3: Interdependence*


*Economic interdependence will reduce the probability that states build border barriers against neighbors.*

Fences may be an attractive option, but they are costly. Beyond the expense of construction and maintenance, walls may damage commercial ties. They may do so both directly by hampering cross-border exchange and indirectly through deleterious effects on the dyadic relationship. Jellissen and Gottheil note that "states are often forced to weigh the opportunity costs of allowing such border intrusions to go unchecked against the costs of imposing barriers to prevent or at least curb such intrusions" (2013, 10). Kazakhstan's decision to institute a fence along its border with Kyrgyzstan, a trade partner and friendly state, provides an empirical illustration of the opportunity costs of walls. Construction came on the heels of Kazakhstan's accession to the Eurasian Economic Community Customs Union and drew criticism for undermining the spirit of the Customs Union (Smith 2012). Nonetheless, Kazakhstan defended the fence on the grounds that it aims to stop rampant smuggling and human trafficking. Even in the absence of prior territorial disputes, a fence can anger a neighbor. This is especially true because fences are asymmetrical policy tools. While neighbors may agree upon the need to bolster border security, states unilaterally initiate fences (Hassner and Wittenberg 2015). To the degree that fences constitute "barriers to movement rather than bridges enabling contact," they undermine cultural integration at the local level (Newman 2006, 150). This is also true because while states may subsequently dismantle barriers (Avdan and Gelpi 2017), they conjure a formidable sense of permanence (Donaldson 2005). Neighbors may regard them as violation of sovereignty and contest their location, as was the case when Mexico denounced the U.S.-Mexico fence ("Mexican Anger over US 'Trespass'" 2007). Border populations that are economically integrated by virtue of simple proximity are particularly vulnerable to the ill effects of artificial barriers (Vallet 2016); Mexico decried the U.S. fence on the grounds that it would diminish bilateral trade. Lastly, barriers exact direct costs on economic exchange. Interstate borders inhibit trade; this reductive effect trumps the inhibitory effects of physical distance (Disdier and Head 2008; McCallum 1995; Rodrik 1998). McCallum (1995) shows for example that trade between Canadian provinces was almost 22 times that of Canada-U.S. trade in 1990, ceteris paribus. Fences are likely to compound border effects. In addition to personnel and infrastructure costs, increased waiting and document-processing times result in trade losses. Thus, anticipating negative effects on cross-border exchange, economically interdependent states will be less likely to build fences.

## Data and Measurement

This chapter utilizes an original data set of border fences, originally inspired by the paucity of quantitative measures on border closure (Gavrilis 2008a). The sample is restricted to dyads that share land or river boundaries, that is, states with a contiguity score of 1 according to the COW Direct Contiguity guidelines (COW 2007; Stinnett et al. 2002).[2] The main resource for data construction was the online archives of the International Boundaries Research Unit (IBRU), a searchable database on border-related news maintained by the University of Durham. I conducted a keyword search for "barriers," "fences," "fortifications," and "walls" using IBRU's *Boundary & Security Bulletin*.[3] While the bulletin extends only to 2001, IBRU also captures current news on borders. I supplemented IBRU's archives with several other online resources, including the list of contemporary separation barriers provided by Borderbase and Wikipedia.[4] Additionally, I undertook general Google searches to check the accuracy of the list of barriers.[5] Finally, I referred to several publications on border walls in order to cross-check my work, including Carter and Poast 2015, Hassner and Wittenberg 2015, Jellissen and Gottheil 2013, and Jones 2012a. The final data cover border fences from 1968 until 2012.

The data set records three key pieces of information: whether the border is fenced, the date the fence was instituted, and the builder and target states. The data set also contains additional variables that register whether the dyad had a prior fence in place that was subsequently dismantled and the date the fence was taken down. The unit of analysis is the dyad-year. The data set thus records variation in fenced borders across time. To demonstrate how the data are coded, here is an example: Saudi Arabia began fencing its border with Oman in 2009. The data identify Saudi Arabia as the builder, Oman as the neighboring target state, and the date of construction as 2009. The dependent variable "border fence" is coded 0 for the Saudi Arabia-Oman dyad for years until 2009 and records 1 for the dyad thereafter. Oman-Saudi Arabia, however, reports 0 because Oman does not have a fence along its border with Saudi Arabia. The date of fencing refers to the date construction began. It is difficult to ascertain the exact date of completion of a fence because construction can often stagnate for years while stretches of the border remain unfenced. As an example, the Israel-Egypt fence was begun in 2010 but not completed until 2013. It was therefore easier to obtain information on the date construction began. Table 17 displays the list of fences recorded by the data.

The data set identifies 77 fences; the 1968–2012 period comprises 48 fenced interstate borders. Two of these, Ceuta and Melilla fences, belong to the same dyad: Spain-Morocco. The data exclude the most recent fences that are underway and states' intentions to build fences.[6] First, the list shows that border fences are directional: we can distinguish between building and target states. The list also affirms that fences are asymmetrical policy tools; there are no cases where the target state reciprocates by building a wall against the builder. Second, although some states—such as Israel and Saudi Arabia—encircle their borders with multiple neighbors with a barrier, this is not the norm. Third, the fences that arose in the time period under investigation have not been dismantled, with the lone exception of the Israel-Egypt fence, which Israel took down in 1973. This observation aligns with Jones's (2012a) insight that fences are often permanent. Fourth, it is rare for a dismantled fence to be replaced with a newer one; the exception is the Bulgaria-Turkey fence. While Bulgaria had a fence in place during the Cold War to prevent flight from the country, the contemporary construction aims to screen out migrants (Lyman 2015). Finally, because of data unavailability, by default, the statistical analysis omits three fences across territorial boundaries in which one of the parties is not a sovereign state: Israel-Gaza, Israel-West Bank, and Spain-Western Sahara.[7]

## Independent Variables

In line with the previous empirical chapters, data for transnational terrorism are acquired from ITERATE, which records terrorist attacks based on sources such as Reuters, the Associated Press, United Press International, Foreign Broadcast Information Services (FBIS), and major U.S. newspapers (Mickolus et al. 2012). As with the prior analyses, I differentiate between global and targeted counts; each variable aggregates terrorist events in the previous five years. As before, targeted attacks leverage two separate computations, one cumulating attacks by neighbor nationals against the builder's citizens, and the second one by nationals unfolding on the builder's territory. I refer to these variables as victim-based and venue-based measures, respectively. Trade salience expresses the total bilateral imports from and exports to the neighbor state divided by the builder's total trade value. Trade data derive from the COW Bilateral Trade Data version 3.0 (Barbieri and Keshk 2012). To account for reverse causality—the possibility that an existing barrier affects flows of trade in the dyad—I lag the trade-salience variable.[8]

## Control Variables

The models incorporate a battery of control variables grounded in emerging empirical scholarship on border barriers. Carter and Poast (2015) argue that

Table 17. Border Fences

| Builder | Neighbor | Year Built | Year Dismantled |
|---------|----------|------------|-----------------|
| 1901–2000 | | | |
| Norway | Sweden | 1901 | 1920 |
| Finland | Russia (Soviet Union) | 1920 | 1939 |
| Russian Federation | Estonia | 1922 | 1939 |
| Russia (Soviet Union) | Latvia | 1922 | 1939 |
| Russia (Soviet Union) | Lithuania | 1922 | 1939 |
| Russia (Soviet Union) | Poland | 1922 | 1939 |
| France | Germany | 1930 | 1940 |
| Greece | Bulgaria | 1936 | 1941 |
| Vietnam | China | 1946 | 1989 |
| German Democratic Rep. | Rep. of Germany | 1947 | 1989 |
| Czechoslovakia | Austria | 1947 | 1989 |
| Czechoslovakia | Rep. of Germany | 1947 | 1989 |
| Bulgaria | Turkey | 1947 | 1989 |
| Russia (Soviet Union) | Finland | 1947 | 1989 |
| Korea, Rep. | Korea, Dem. Rep. | 1953 | |
| Algeria (French) | Morocco | 1957 | 1962 |
| Algeria (French) | Tunisia | 1957 | 1962 |
| Zimbabwe | Zambia | 1966 | |
| **Israel** | **Egypt** | **1968** | 1973 |
| **Israel** | **Syria** | **1973** | |
| **South Africa** | **Mozambique** | **1975** | |
| **Nigeria** | **Cameroon** | **1981** | |
| **India** | **Bangladesh** | **1986** | |
| **South Africa** | **Swaziland** | **1986** | |
| **Kuwait** | **Iraq** | **1991** | |
| **Russian Federation** | **China** | **1991** | |
| **Russian Federation** | **Korea, Dem. Rep.** | **1991** | |
| **Russia** | **Mongolia** | **1991** | |
| **Russia** | **Norway** | **1991** | |
| **India** | **Pakistan** | **1992** | |
| **Spain** | **Morocco** | **1993** | |
| **Botswana** | **Namibia** | **1997** | |
| **Uzbekistan** | **Kyrgyz Republic** | **1999** | |
| **Iran** | **Afghanistan** | **2000** | |
| **Israel** | **Lebanon** | **2000** | |
| 2001–2012 | | | |
| **Thailand** | **Malaysia** | **2001** | |
| **Turkmenistan** | **Kazakhstan** | **2001** | |
| **Turkmenistan** | **Uzbekistan** | **2001** | |
| **Uzbekistan** | **Afghanistan** | **2001** | |
| **India** | **Myanmar** | **2003** | |

(continued)

Table 17 (continued)

| Builder | Neighbor | Year Built | Year Dismantled |
|---|---|---|---|
| **1901–2000** | | | |
| **Botswana** | **Zimbabwe** | **2003** | |
| **Lithuania** | **Belarus** | **2005** | |
| **Pakistan** | **Afghanistan** | **2005** | |
| **United States** | **Mexico** | **2005** | |
| **China** | **Korea, Dem. Rep.** | **2006** | |
| **Jordan** | **Iraq** | **2006** | |
| **Kazakhstan** | **Uzbekistan** | **2006** | |
| **Saudi Arabia** | **Iraq** | **2006** | |
| **Iran** | **Pakistan** | **2007** | |
| **Saudi Arabia** | **Jordan** | **2007** | |
| **Saudi Arabia** | **Kuwait** | **2007** | |
| **United Arab Emirates** | **Oman** | **2007** | |
| **United Arab Emirates** | **Saudi Arabia** | **2007** | |
| **Egypt** | **Gaza** | **2009** | |
| **Myanmar** | **Bangladesh** | **2009** | |
| **Saudi Arabia** | **Oman** | **2009** | |
| **Saudi Arabia** | **Qatar** | **2009** | |
| **Saudi Arabia** | **UAE** | **2009** | |
| **Kazakhstan** | **Kyrgyz Republic** | **2010** | |
| **Azerbaijan** | **Armenia** | **2011** | |
| **Greece** | **Turkey** | **2011** | |
| **Israel** | **Jordan** | **2011** | |
| **South Africa** | **Lesotho** | **2012** | |
| **Turkey** | **Syria** | **2012** | |
| **Uzbekistan** | **Tajikistan** | **2012** | |
| **Turkey** | **Syria** | **2012** | |
| 2013–PRESENT | | | |
| Bulgaria | Turkey | 2015 | |
| Hungary | Croatia | 2015 | |
| Slovenia | Croatia | 2015 | |
| Austria | Slovenia | 2015 | |
| Macedonia | Greece | 2015 | |
| Slovakia | Hungary | 2015 | |
| Hungary | Serbia | 2015 | |
| INTENDED FENCES | | | |
| Estonia | Russia | | |
| Ukraine | Russia | | |
| Russia | Ukraine | | |
| Iran | Pakistan | | |

*Note*: The statistical analysis includes the cases in **bold.**

economic disparity in the dyad is a positive determinant of border barriers. Taking their insights into account, I construct the *dyadic GDP per capita ratio*: this variable is constructed as the builder's GDP per capita weighted by the total dyadic GDP per capita. Higher values on this variable represent a wealthier builder state compared to its neighbor. Given the economic burden of fence construction, I also control for the *builder's GDP*; given the right-skewed distribution of GDP, I take its natural log. GDP and GDP per capita stem from the World Bank's WDI (WDI 2015). Jones (2012a, 2012b) underlines that three of the most controversial barriers belong to democracies: Israel, India, and the United States. Nonetheless, democratic states may be hesitant to erect barriers against fellow democracies. Following this intuition, I create a *joint democracy* variable that is coded 1 when both building and neighbor states enjoy Polity IV scores of 6 or higher (Marshall and Jaggers 2013). Next, although countries may build fences mostly to mollify domestic audiences, they may be interpreted by the neighbor as a violation of sovereignty or a bid to alter the location of the border (Donaldson 2005; Hassner and Wittenberg 2015). This may even be an issue in the absence of a territorial dispute. By way of illustration, Botswana professes that the three-hundred-mile fence on its border with Zimbabwe is intended to block cattle from straying across the border. Zimbabwe believes the wall aims to forestall refugee outflows and views it as a diplomatic insult (Donaldson 2005). Accordingly, I inject a dummy, coded 1 for a *prior territorial dispute* or 0 otherwise. The source data for this measure is Simmons's (2005) update of Huth's (1996) measure. Huth codes a territorial dispute as present when the state: (1) expresses disagreement over the location of the border, (2) challenges the sovereignty of another state over some portion of territory within the border, (3) seizes control over a part of the border and refuses to withdraw, or (4) does not recognize the independence of another country (for example, a colonial territory). The dispute is considered resolved upon the formal recognition of the boundary as legitimate.

A slew of neighbor characteristics are likely to influence the propensity of states to erect fences. Hassner and Wittenberg (2015) note that border walls are more prevalent in the Muslim world, especially in the post–Cold War context. Therefore, I create a dummy that gives 1 if the *neighbor is a majority Muslim state* and 0 otherwise. I construct this indicator from the Correlates of War Project's World Religion Database version 1.1 (COW 2013). I deem countries with at least 85 percent of the population subscribing to Islam (regardless of sect) as majority Muslim. Bearing in mind that populous neighbors may cultivate migratory pressures, I also control for *neighbor-country population*; I employ the natural log of raw data incorporated from WDI. Carter and Poast (2015) postulate that the threat of violence spillover from civil war in neighboring states will spur on wall construction. The civil war in Syria, for example, led to a string of bombings in the border cities in Turkey, in addition to reigniting the conflict between Kurdish militants and the government (Pitel 2016). Therefore, I include a dummy for *civil war in the neighboring state*. I follow the UCDP/PRIO guidelines and register 1 for intrastate conflict with at least 1,000 battle deaths and 0 otherwise (Gleditsch et al. 2002). I use the UCDP/PRIO Armed Conflict Dataset version 4; intrastate conflict corresponds to the data set's type 2 (internal) and type 3 (internationalized internal) conflict (Pettersson and Wallensteen 2015). Some scholars have noted that refugee flows from neighbors may transmit militancy and terrorism (Milton, Spencer, and Findley 2013; Salehyan 2008a). Correspondingly, a large influx of refugees may motivate states to install barriers. This insight prompts me to control for *refugee outflows* from the neighbor. The variable stems from the United Nations High Commissioner for Refugees (UNHCR) Global Trends 2013 (UNHCR 2014); the models included the natural log of refugee flows. Finally, while the sample is restricted to contiguous dyads, distance should still hinder undesirable flows between countries. Given this logic, I expect distance to negatively affect the propensity to build walls. Models also add the *logged distance between capitals,* originating from Gleditsch and Ward's (2001) distance between capitals data.

## Analysis

Before proceeding to the multivariate analysis, let's look at Tables 18, 19a, and 19b, which present a thumbnail illustration of the association between global and directed terrorism, respectively, and fenced borders. Tables 19a and 19b employ the nationality- and venue-based operationalizations of terrorism. To create the bivariate cross-tabulations, I created dummies for global and directed terrorism that take the value of 1 if the volume of terrorism was at least at the 95th percentile of the past five years' event sums. For global terrorism, the threshold corresponds to a total of 31 attacks and for directed terrorism (by nationality) to at least 1 attack.

The tables demonstrate that fenced borders are rare. The period from 1968 to 2012 yields 19,483 fenced dyad-years; less than 3 percent of such dyads are

Table 18. Global Terrorism and Fenced Borders

|  | Border Policy | | |
|  | Not Fenced | Fenced | Total |
|---|---|---|---|
| No terror | 17,944 | 549 | 18,493 |
| Row % | 97.03% | 2.97% | 100% |
| Terror | 958 | 32 | 990 |
| Row % | 96.77% | 3.23% | 100% |
| Total | 18,902 | 581 | 19,483 |
| Row % | 97.02% | 2.98% | 100% |

*Notes*: Pearson chi-square (1 d.f.) = 0.23; $p < .635$.

fenced. Table 18 reports a small but statistically insignificant difference in the frequency with which fences are constructed, comparing a benign context (absent terrorism) with one marked by a high volume of terrorism. We observe that tranquil borders result in fences being constructed 2.97 percent of the time, which is only 0.01 percent less than the percentage of fenced borders. A high global count of terrorism culminates in an increase in the frequency with which border barriers are built: 3.23 percent. The chi-squared statistic is well below the threshold for statistical significance, however, indicating no discernible difference in the frequency of barriers between these two contexts.

Table 19a shows a statistically significant ($p < .000$) difference between peaceful dyads and dyads afflicted with terrorism. Terror-plagued interstate borders witness barriers being built at a rate more than double that experienced by peaceful dyads (6.18 versus 2.86 percent). This pattern is all the more important given the rarity of border fences. Table 19b paints a fairly similar picture for directed terrorism in which neighbor nationals commit acts of terror on the state's territory. Dyads vexed by terrorism encounter a noticeably higher frequency of border fences. While dyads free of terrorism witness fences at a frequency slightly lower than the total percentage of fenced borders—2.92 percent—close to 6 percent of interstate borders that have experienced directed terrorism are fenced. The chi-square is significant at 0.001. In sum, at first glance, the bivariate analyses cast doubt on whether fences are installed in response to terror-prone neighbors. Contrarily, they support the contention that directed terrorism from the neighbor prompts fence construction. The bivariate correlations are illustrative but preliminary;

Table 19a. Directed Terrorism (by Victims' Nationality)
and Fenced Borders

|  | Border Policy | | |
|---|---|---|---|
|  | Not Fenced | Fenced | Total |
| No terror | 18,204 | 535 | 18,739 |
| Row % | 97.14% | 2.86% | 100% |
| Terror | 698 | 46 | 744 |
| Row % | 93.82% | 6.18% | 100% |
| Total | 18,902 | 581 | 19,483 |
| Row % | 97.02% | 2.98% | 100% |

*Notes*: Pearson chi-square (1 d.f.) = 27.39; $p < .000$.

Table 19b. Directed Terrorism (by Venue of Attack)
and Fenced Borders

|  | Border Policy | | |
|---|---|---|---|
|  | Not Fenced | Fenced | Total |
| No terror | 18,534 | 558 | 19,092 |
| Row % | 97.08% | 2.92% | 100% |
| Terror | 368 | 23 | 391 |
| Row % | 94.12% | 5.88% | 100% |
| Total | 18,902 | 581 | 19,483 |
| Row % | 97.02% | 2.98% | 100% |

*Notes*: Pearson chi-square (1 d.f.) = 11.06; $p < .001$.

they cannot account for confounding factors. With this in mind, I now turn
to multivariate analysis.

## Multivariate Analysis

Fenced interstate borders are relatively rare, comprising less than 3 percent
of the sample. As a consequence, standard logit might overestimate treatment
effects, downward biasing the standard errors on estimated effects King and

Zeng (2001). I use rare events logit to assess the impact of terrorism and trade on the probability of whether states build border fences. Table 20 reports the results, presenting six models. Model 1 investigates the impact of global attacks while models 2 and 3 focus on directed attacks, using the counts by victims' nationality and venue of incident, respectively. Models 4 and 5 probe the impact of fatal attacks, again, by victims' nationality and venue of attack. Finally, model 6 sharpens the focus on high-magnitude attacks. I constructed this variable by restricting the count of attacks to incidents for which ITERATE assigns a damage score of at least 2; this translates to incidents with at least $10,000 in material damage. To recap, all terrorism measures aggregate attacks over the previous five years. Another modeling concern is temporal dependence, which necessitates a conceptual distinction between the dynamics of barrier construction and maintenance. Taking a cue from Carter and Signorino (2010), I created a cubic polynomial of years elapsed since fence construction began. All models in Table 20 include the cubic polynomial, but the coefficients are not of substantive importance and hence are suppressed.

Hypotheses 1 and 2 propose that global and directed attacks will heighten the probability of fence construction. The former hypothesis finds dubious support in model 1; the coefficient is positive but insignificant. Paralleling the previous two chapters' findings, directed terror casts a substantively stronger effect, significantly elevating the likelihood that states will build walls. Hypothesis 2, however, receives clear support, as the strongly positive and significant coefficients on all the directed terrorism terms testify. A second noteworthy observation is that where border barriers are concerned, attacks on territory are a more powerful motive for fence construction than are attacks carried out against the state's citizens. Turning to the final three models, it bears mentioning that fatal and high-magnitude attacks elicit a discernibly greater impact on the propensity to build fences. Interestingly, there are no substantive differences in coefficients on fatal attacks that victimize the state's nationals (model 4) and deadly attacks on the state's territory (model 5). In fact, all three types of attacks yield a commensurate impact.

Table 20 sketches a hierarchy of impact where fatal attacks within the state's borders have the greatest coefficient magnitude, followed by high-magnitude attacks, and global attacks by neighbor citizens produce an impact indistinguishable from zero. We observe that the effect of global terrorism pales in comparison to that of directed terrorism. Again illustrating the clear hierarchy, we note that ceteris paribus, directed terrorism aimed at nationals of the builder has more than ten times the magnitude on the propensity to build barriers. The coefficient on directed terrorism on the builder's soil is more than forty times larger than global terrorism's coefficient. Corroborating hypothesis 3, trade salience bears a negative and significant coefficient across all models.

In line with emerging scholarship on border barriers (Carter and Poast 2015; Hassner and Wittenberg 2015), the positive and significant coefficient on the GDP per capita ratio indicates that affluent states are more likely to build barriers and that income differentials positively impact the likelihood that fences will be constructed. Several other control covariates are significant: more populous neighbors face a higher likelihood that fences will be built along their border. As we might expect, joint democracy dampens the probability that border barriers will be built. In line with Donaldson's (2005) argument, we have also found that extant territorial disputes cause fences to be built. Contrary to expectations, the Muslim population proportion, the incidence of civil war, and refugee outflows do not emerge as significant determinants of fence construction.

Next, in order to accommodate unobserved heterogeneity across panels, I reanalyze the same set of models with random and fixed effects logistic regression. It is possible that the models omit some factors on which the dyads differ. In other words, dyads are heterogeneous because of these unobserved factors. Random effects and fixed effects take stock of heterogeneity in different ways. Random effects regression accounts for heterogeneity by including a dyad-specific and overall error term (Beck 2001; Kennedy 2003). Rather than including a dyad-specific intercept, the panel structure of the data is treated through the error term that is allowed to vary across units (Kennedy 2003). Fixed effects capture differences among countries that the models may not account for by including an intercept for each country. This is akin to running separate regressions for each country. This also means, however, that we only focus on over-time variation within each dyad (King and Zeng 2001). Dyads that were never fenced—where the DV does not change from 0—are removed from the analysis. Lastly, the first three models incorporate the time since fence cubic polynomial.[9]

The first three models boost confidence in the chapter's hypothesis. Parallel with Table 20's findings, Table 21 shows us that targeted attacks exercise a more powerful impact on the propensity to build walls compared to global attacks. Model 7 shows global incidents to be statistically significant ($p < .01$). Hypothesis 3 on economic interdependence, however, is not strongly

Table 20. Border Fences, Terrorism, and Trade

| Rare Logit Results | Global Terrorism | Directed Terrorism | | Fatal Attacks | | High-Magnitude Attacks |
| --- | --- | --- | --- | --- | --- | --- |
| VARIABLE | Model 1 | Model 2 | Model 3 | Model 4 | Model 5 | Model 6 |
| Global terrorism | 0.004 (0.00) | | | | | |
| Directed terrorism, by victims | | 0.058** (0.02) | | | | |
| Directed terrorism, by venue | | | 0.165*** (0.03) | | | |
| Fatal terrorism, by victims | | | | 0.559** (0.22) | | |
| Fatal terrorism, by venue | | | | | 0.548** (0.17) | |
| High-magnitude attacks, by venue | | | | | | 0.590* (0.30) |
| Trade salience | −3.521+ (1.97) | −3.483+ (1.98) | −3.276+ (1.95) | −3.383+ (1.96) | −3.422+ (1.96) | −3.471+ (1.97) |
| Builder GDP (logged) | 0.437*** (0.04) | 0.433*** (0.04) | 0.434*** (0.04) | 0.433*** (0.04) | 0.436*** (0.04) | 0.436*** (0.04) |
| Dyadic GDP/pc per capita ratio | 0.569*** (0.12) | 0.571*** (0.12) | 0.586*** (0.12) | 0.572*** (0.12) | 0.573*** (0.12) | 0.569*** (0.12) |
| Territorial dispute | 0.460** (0.16) | 0.449** (0.15) | 0.434** (0.15) | 0.440** (0.15) | 0.439** (0.15) | 0.439** (0.15) |

(continued)

Table 20 (continued)

| Rare Logit Results | Global Terrorism | Directed Terrorism | | Fatal Attacks | | High-Magnitude Attacks |
|---|---|---|---|---|---|---|
| | Model 1 | Model 2 | Model 3 | Model 4 | Model 5 | Model 6 |
| VARIABLE | | | | | | |
| Distance between capitals | 0.089 | 0.096 | 0.119 | 0.100 | 0.098 | 0.092 |
| | (0.11) | (0.11) | (0.12) | (0.11) | (0.11) | (0.11) |
| Neighbor population (logged) | 0.184*** | 0.188*** | 0.183*** | 0.186*** | 0.188*** | 0.189*** |
| | (0.04) | (0.04) | (0.04) | (0.04) | (0.04) | (0.04) |
| Civil war in neighbor | 0.129 | 0.131 | 0.108 | 0.139 | 0.145 | 0.144 |
| | (0.21) | (0.21) | (0.21) | (0.21) | (0.21) | (0.21) |
| Neighbor Muslim | 0.306 | 0.311 | 0.292 | 0.313 | 0.314 | 0.313 |
| | (0.26) | (0.26) | (0.26) | (0.26) | (0.26) | (0.26) |
| Joint democracy | -1.147*** | -1.148*** | -1.155*** | -1.127*** | -1.138*** | -1.141*** |
| | (0.26) | (0.26) | (0.26) | (0.26) | (0.26) | (0.26) |
| Refugee outflows (logged) | -0.021 | -0.021 | -0.021 | -0.019 | -0.020 | -0.019 |
| | (0.04) | (0.04) | (0.04) | (0.04) | (0.04) | (0.04) |
| Constant | -18.370*** | -18.367*** | -18.502*** | -18.377*** | -18.452*** | -18.420*** |
| | (1.04) | (1.04) | (1.05) | (1.04) | (1.04) | (1.04) |
| Number of cases | 8,029 | 8,029 | 8,029 | 8,029 | 8,029 | 8,029 |

*Note:* All models also include the cubic time polynomial of years since fence was installed.
+*p* <.10
\**p* < .05
\*\**p* < .01
\*\*\**p* < .001

Table 21. Random Effects and Fixed Effects Logistic Regression of Border Fences

| | Random Effects | | | Fixed Effects | | |
| --- | --- | --- | --- | --- | --- | --- |
| Variable | Model 7 | Model 8 | Model 9 | Model 10 | Model 11 | Model 12 |
| Global terrorism | 0.045** (0.02) | | | 0.003 (0.13) | | |
| Directed terrorism, by victims | | 0.351*** (0.10) | | | 0.823 (2.78) | |
| Directed terrorism, by venue | | | 0.616** (0.21) | | | 5.940 (67.25) |
| Trade salience | | | | -32.418+ (19.37) | -32.136+ (18.58) | -32.719+ (18.62) |
| Trade salience | -8.283 (9.75) | 0.333 (7.86) | -6.788 (11.74) | | | |
| Builder GDP (logged) | 3.475*** (0.28) | 4.304*** (0.24) | 4.769*** (0.39) | 7.978*** (1.77) | 7.924*** (1.74) | 7.916*** (1.75) |
| Dyadic GDP per capita ratio | 3.471*** (0.59) | 4.817*** (0.52) | 4.514*** (0.82) | 2.667 (1.67) | 2.723 (1.66) | 2.659 (1.66) |
| Territorial dispute | -0.295 (1.69) | 1.570 (1.23) | -2.552 (2.86) | | | |
| Distance between capitals | -1.436** (0.48) | -1.293** (0.50) | -1.741* (0.68) | | | |
| Neighbor population (logged) | 1.225* (0.51) | 1.567*** (0.30) | 1.895*** (0.55) | 111.389*** (25.11) | 110.733*** (24.62) | 110.645*** (24.74) |

(continued)

Table 21 (continued)

| Variable | Random Effects | | | Fixed Effects | | |
|---|---|---|---|---|---|---|
| | Model 7 | Model 8 | Model 9 | Model 10 | Model 11 | Model 12 |
| Civil war in neighbor | 0.948 | 1.266* | 0.984 | 2.086 | 3.147 | 3.064 |
| | (0.60) | (0.61) | (0.70) | (5.73) | (8.34) | (8.58) |
| Neighbor Muslim | −0.824 | −0.938 | −0.944 | | | |
| | (0.56) | (0.60) | (0.61) | | | |
| Joint democracy | −0.908 | −1.345+ | −0.868 | 0.849 | 0.850 | 0.832 |
| | (0.80) | (0.74) | (0.94) | (2.51) | (2.50) | (2.47) |
| Refugee outflows (logged) | −0.527* | −0.497** | −0.549* | −1.049 | −1.048 | −1.041 |
| | (0.22) | (0.19) | (0.24) | (1.75) | (1.73) | (1.74) |
| Constant | −122.580*** | −150.478*** | −171.498*** | | | |
| | (6.84) | (7.06) | (9.31) | | | |
| Chi-square | 699.244 | 752.842 | 726.206 | 371.853 | 371.986 | 371.917 |
| p > chi-square | 0.000 | 0.000 | 0.000 | 0.000 | 0.000 | 0.000 |
| Number of cases | 9,459 | 9,459 | 9,459 | 627 | 627 | 627 |

*Notes:* Models 7, 8, and 9 included the cubic time polynomial. Standard errors are in parentheses under model coefficients.

+$p < .10$
*$p < .05$
**$p < .01$
***$p < .001$

supported. While trade salience bears a negative coefficient in models 7 and 9, the effect is indistinguishable from zero; the coefficient is positive in model 8. The fixed effects results tell a different story: while the terrorism measures carry positive coefficients, they are below the threshold for significance. Although trade salience is again marginally significant, it assumes a markedly larger negative coefficient. The takeaway from the final three models is that when within-dyad variation is considered, neither global nor directed terrorism proves to be an important determinant of barrier construction. Put differently, terrorism's influence is driven mostly by variation among dyads. In short, states plagued with targeted terrorism from neighbors are statistically more likely to erect barriers against neighbors than are states that share borders with peaceful neighbors. The lack of significance in models 10–12, however, tells us that increases in transnational terrorism over time do not drive fence construction. The temporal insignificance of terrorism lends confidence in the assertion that barrier construction is in part driven by symbolic motivations. The largely negative substantive effect of trade offers good news for advocates of interdependence theory. Over time, trade salience lowers the probability of border barrier construction, ceteris paribus.

Very briefly, most of the controls perform as expected and in congruence with the rare events logistical results. As before, income differentials are positively associated with the construction of fences although this effect disappears when dyad fixed effects are included. A few exceptions are notable. Joint democracy fails to retain its negative significant effect. As expected, civil war returns a positive and significant coefficient. The log of refugee outflows, however, depicts a negative and significant effect. Hence the results fail to corroborate the argument that higher volumes of refugees manifest in a greater propensity to install barriers. Neither are Muslim neighbors associated with the propensity to build barriers. States are, however, more likely to build walls against populous countries. The coefficient's magnitude on logged population of the neighbor is remarkably large, especially when compared to fixed effects. Over-time shifts in population emerge as powerful determinants of barrier construction. At the risk of speculation, this might also indicate that countries erect barriers in response to mounting migratory pressure rather than to increases in terrorism outflows from neighbors. Territorial disputes appear to exert contradictory effects; this might be because ongoing disputes reduce rather than increase the likelihood of border wall construction (Carter and Poast 2015).

While the coefficients in Tables 20 and 21 convey the direction of each variable's impact and statistical significance, they are unable to illustrate the substantive impact of the explanatory variables on the probability that a state builds a wall against its neighbor. Accordingly, I provide a visual illustration of these substantive effects in Figure 6. In line with King and Zeng's (2001) advice, I evaluate substantive effects in terms of changes in relative risks of the dependent variable. Relative risk assessment is a useful tool for analyzing rare events: given a very small mean probability of border fences, significant t-values on individual coefficients are dependent on the scale of the explanatory variable. The change in the relative risk of a border fence being built is calculated as the ratio of the probability of a fence when the independent variable in question is held at one value to the probability of a fence when the independent variable is held at another value. Figure 6 depicts the relative risks as the main variables of interest are moved from 0 to the 99th percentile. All other explanatory variables are held at their respective median values. The relative risks are computed from the models presented in Table 20. The horizontal lines portray the relative risk while the black vertical lines capture the 95 percent confidence intervals around the risks.

Changes in relative risks are evaluated with respect to 1, with values exceeding 1 indicating an increase in the relative risk and values below 1 signifying a decrease in the relative risk. Values that are less than 1 denote a reduction in the relative risk of an attack. For example, a relative risk of 0.5

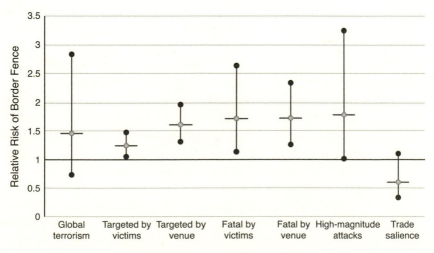

Figure 6. Relative risk of border fences.

would indicate a 50 percent reduction in the risk of an attack. Values that are greater than 1, on the other hand, indicate an increase in the incidence of terrorism. Thus a relative risk of 2.0 would indicate a 100 percent increase in the relative risk. Considering the impact of global terrorism first, the relative risk of observing a fence goes up by approximately 48 percent, when we move terrorism from 0 to its 99th percentile. However, the lower bound of the confidence interval crosses 1. Values below 1 stand for a reduction in the relative risk. Therefore, if the confidence interval crosses 1 here, it means that the effect of global terrorism is not significant. All other effects presented in Figure 6 are significant and the confidence intervals are above 1 for the terrorism variables and below 1 for trade salience. Raising targeted terrorism counts changes the relative risk of barriers being built by 25 percent for the nationality-based indicator and a substantial 62 percent for the venue-based indicator.

When moving the variables from 0 to the 99th percentile, we should keep in mind, however, that the distributions of global and targeted terrorism counts are markedly different. Thus, for example, the global count has a maximum of 208 and its 99th percentile corresponds to 87 attacks. To compare, the directed count by victims' nationality has a maximum of 57 with 5 attacks corresponding to the 95th percentile. I thus also analyzed the changes in relative risk for a unit change in each term. We note that the targeted count by nationality produces a 6 percent increase in relative risk whereas the increase is 18 percent for targeted attacks by venue. A unit change in global attacks, in contrast, results in an increase of only 0.4 percent in the relative risk. Also worth noting is that while statistical uncertainty is greater for the targeted sum by venue, as the wider confidence interval indicates, the impact on the relative risk is strikingly higher, denoting a 62 percent uptick as opposed to 19 percent for the targeted sum by victims. Mirroring Table 20's patterns, we find fatal and high-magnitude events to be potent predictors of fence construction. The effects on the relative risk of fence construction are fairly parallel, standing at a 72 percent increase for both counts of fatal incidents and a 79 percent increase for high-magnitude attacks. Lastly, consistent with Table 20's findings, trade salience, on average, yields a significant 40 percent drop in the relative risk of fence construction.

Next, in order to inspect the combined effects of trade salience and terrorism, I repeat the same exercise by moving the terrorism measures from 0 to the 99th percentile while also increasing trade values. I compare the relative risks for when trade salience is increased from the 5th percentile to the

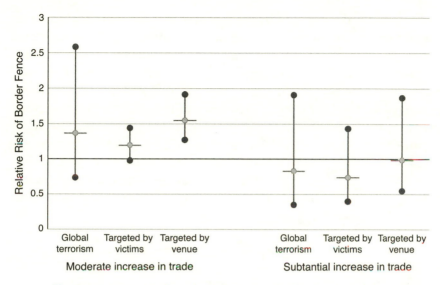

Figure 7. Relative risk of border fences across levels of trade salience.

50th percentile, which I refer to as a moderate increase, and for when trade salience is increased to the 99th percentile, which I label a substantial increase. Figure 7 depicts the relative risks, again with the horizontal lines denoting the impact and the arrows representing the lower and upper bounds of the 95 percent confidence interval.

Looking at the left side of Figure 6, moderate increase in trade reveals a pattern in tune with the average effects in Figure 7. When we increase trade moderately, increasing terrorism (by venue) to the 99th percentile results in a 54 percent as opposed to a 62 percent increase in the relative risk of fence construction, when we hold trade at its median value. Similarly, for targeted terrorism (by victims), the increase is 18 percent as opposed to 25 percent. Both effects are significant. Again, however, global terrorism has a large positive impact on the relative risk, but the lower bound of the interval dips below 1, which indicates a reduction in the relative risk. Hence, global terrorism is again insignificant in terms of its impact on the relative risk of barrier construction.

The effects depicted on the right side of Figure 7 plot relative risks resulting from moving the terrorism variables from 0 to their 99th percentiles, while at the same time raising trade salience from 0 to the 99th percentile. First and foremost, uncertainty over all three effect estimates increases, as illustrated by the larger confidence intervals. Two of the effects are negative but insignificant. Global terrorism's impact becomes negative, reducing the relative risk by 13 percent; however, the upper bound is above 1: in other words, the effect is not statistically significant. The same is true for the second effect depicted in the figure; targeted terrorism (by victims) shows reduction in the relative risk by 25 percent, but again the effect is insignificant. Finally, targeted terrorism by venue, which on average has the greatest impact on the relative risk, is indistinguishable from 0. In fact, the relative risk is near unity (0.99), signifying almost no change in the relative risk. Given a substantial increase in trade salience, then, all three counts of terrorism fail to significantly heighten the relative risk that the state erects a border fence.

### Supplementary Checks

In addition to the models presented, I also conduct a bevy of sensitivity checks.[10] As the opening paragraphs of the chapter discussed, fence construction has gained steam since the end of the Cold War. Its pace has further accelerated in the past decade and a half. Taking the accelerated pace into account, I evaluate the impact of terrorism, considering fences in the post–Cold War and post-2000 contexts. For the former, I restrict the analysis to 1990 until 2012 and for the latter to 2000 until 2012. I find the effect to be fairly similar for the former, with a clear hierarchy in impact magnitude for targeted attacks by venue, followed by targeted attacks by victims' nationality, and, finally, global effects. I observe the effect magnitudes to be noticeably stronger for fences post-2000. Specifically, global terrorism assumes a positive (0.02) and significant coefficient ($p < .01$). The substantive magnitudes of the coefficients on targeted terrorism are about 4 times their magnitudes in Table 20; both variables are significant at the 0.001 level. The coefficients on the fatal and high-magnitude attack variables, however, are commensurate in magnitude to their effects in the full-time analysis.

Second, I probe the impact of capital openness, utilizing a variable that gauges the capital openness of the building state. The World Bank's WDI lends a series that expresses net foreign direct investment (FDI) as a ratio of the country's GDP. The raw data contain negative values on FDI for countries that generate net outflows of capital. For ease of interpretation and to control for sensitivity to outliers, I normalize the variable to run from 0 to 1.[11] FDI returns a negative but insignificant coefficient. I should stress, however, that this does not speak to the association between bilateral capital ties and the propensity to build fences.

Third, terrorism may be endogenous to fence building whereby the presence of a border fence will influence terrorism flows within dyads. In order to accommodate this dynamic, I estimate a simultaneous equations model where the propensity to erect a fence is regressed on terrorism in one equation and terrorism is regressed on the presence of a border fence in another equation. I implement the two-stage estimation method recommended by Keshk et al. (2004) for simultaneous equations models in which one of the endogenous variables is continuous and the other endogenous variable is dichotomous.[12] To fulfill the exclusion criteria, I instrument terrorism by using the peace-years spline, capturing spells of zero terrorism within the dyad (Beck, Katz, and Tucker 1998). Following the democratic vulnerability argument (Eubank and Weinberg 1994; Li 2005), I also include the builder's Polity IV score as an instrumental variable. In line with Avdan and Gelpi (2017), I find that the presence of a border fence reduces terrorism, while terrorism retains its positive impact on the likelihood of observing a border fence.

Fourth, conflict and cooperation within the dyad can affect decisions to build walls (Avdan and Gelpi 2017; Carter and Poast 2015). To tap into animosity toward neighbors, I include a *dyadic rivalry* dummy, based on Goertz et al.'s (2006) revised data set on enduring rivals. Enduring rivalries represent militarized interstate disputes that are not isolated conflicts and exhibit spatial consistency. To capture dyadic cooperation, I include an indicator for *alliance ties*. I measure the impact of alliance ties based on the COW data set on alliances (Gibler 2009). Specifically, the indicator takes the value of 1 if the builder and neighbor states have a COW alliance of any kind (defense pact, entente, or neutrality pact). The dummy for alliance ties produces a negative but insignificant coefficient; the coefficient on dyadic rivalry, in contrast, is positive and insignificant. While states are significantly more likely to build walls against rival states, alliance ties are not systematically related to fence construction.

## Conclusion

This chapter offered a different vantage point on how transnational terrorism fuels policy stringency. Fences and walls are visible incarnations of the trend toward tighter border controls. Border barriers are by no means new to world politics (Sterling 2009). Notably, however, fence construction has continued apace since the end of the Cold War and is a trend at odds with globalist pronouncements that borders will wither away as economic flows traverse borders with increasing volume and speed (Ohmae 1990; Strange 1997). On the contrary, borders remain fundamental to world politics.

Yet others view fences as last-gasp attempts by states to salvage territorial sovereignty (Brown 2010). Others still take a tempered view that border fences represent rebordering, which permits states to forge a compromise between conflicting objectives (Jones and Johnson 2016). One such compromise is between maintaining trade ties with neighboring states and mitigating security concerns. Given the growing consensus that uncontrolled and clandestine transborder flows are destabilizing (Naim 2005), border management comes to occupy a pivotal role in states' pursuit of security.

Walls are ultimately about monitoring cross-border mobility of illicit goods and people. Both can prove dangerous and destabilizing; both involve threats transported on the backs of humans. In that respect, they complement and bolster other instruments of border control, particularly those aimed at controlling human mobility. Whereas visas screen and preselect people, border barriers obstruct entry. Man-made barriers call to mind archetypical fears over surreptitious and unauthorized entry. Nevertheless, scholars stress that apart from actual effectiveness in hindering illegal entry, walls may be likened to a public relations campaign designed to assuage public fears (Rosiere and Jones 2012; Vallet 2016). Walls represent security performance with the public as the audience (Andreas 2009). A more cynical version of this perspective suggests that walls merely represent an effort by politicians with a stake in stronger border control to push forward their agendas.

Both perspectives raise doubts about the empirical association between objective threats and walls. If border walls were solely about audience dynamics, we would observe a tenuous link between transnational terrorism and the likelihood of observing border barriers. This chapter sheds light on the empirical linkage, showing that border walls do in fact mirror visa policies by responding to targeted terrorism from neighboring states. Nevertheless, the statistical findings uncover patterns that are consonant with the security performance argument. There is a clear hierarchy in impact magnitude of types of terrorism flows. Fatal attacks on the state's own soil, followed by fatal attacks that involve the state's own nationals, surpass nonfatal and global terrorist events, in terms of effect size. Importantly, global terrorism has a minute impact on the predilection to build walls. States that border countries whose citizens are involved in attacks elsewhere are not significantly motivated to build walls. Thus we can imagine that targeted fatal and/or high-magnitude events are more salient, granting governments more leeway in justifying the border barrier. Salient terrorist events may compound the immediacy of the terrorism threat. In the event of such assaults, building a wall becomes a politically appealing and politically salable means of alleviating public anxiety while at the same time responding to actual threats.

CHAPTER 5

# Turkey's Migration Policy:
# An Illustrative Case Study

## Turkey as an Illustrative Case

How did Turkey's economic liberalization affect its visa and border-control policies? Did concerns over terrorism stymie policy liberalization? The previous chapters presented quantitative evidence that economic considerations function as a counterweight to security concerns when threats from terrorism are remote. They also showed, however, that terrorism does result in policy tightening when terrorism directly undermines the security of the state's citizens and territory. This chapter provides a qualitative assessment of the theoretical framework. It also unpacks the mechanisms that underpin the empirical results of Chapters 2, 3, and 4. Using archival data and secondary sources, this chapter outlines the causal processes driving changes in Turkey's migration policies. Turkey presents an ideal case for showing how security and material interests operate in tandem to shape migration policies. The primary variables of interest—economic liberalization and terrorism—exhibited variation in this time period. Turkey underwent trade and financial liberalization, after Özal took office, with the return to civilian rule after the 1980 military takeover. Concerns over terrorist violence gained prominence at the same time that the country undertook a vigorous program of economic liberalization. Ethnic terrorism was on the rise after the Kurdish militant group, the Parti Karkeran Kurdistan (PKK), launched its terrorist campaign in 1984. Anxiety over terrorism increased as other types of terrorist organizations proliferated in the following decades. These fears were widespread in policy circles as Turkey morphed into a trading state.

These patterns mirror and bolster the insights from the preceding chapters. They show that material and security imperatives exert the hypothesized opposing effects on migration policies. The theoretical framework posited that economic interdependence influences policy by generating opportunity costs and by creating vested domestic interests. This chapter illustrates how these mechanisms came to influence policy. In parliamentary debates, policymakers referenced the gains from commerce to make a case for policy relaxation. This framing served as a check against the effects of security parameters. As Turkey liberalized, policymakers began to recognize that changes in Turkey's migration policies had repercussions for commercial partners. Parliamentary debates showed concerns that tight policies might backfire by inciting reprisals from economic partners. Additionally, liberalization created domestic interests who espoused liberal migration policies. The prioritization of economic motivations cast doubt on the utility of tight border- and migration-control measures as a counterterrorism strategy.

The theoretical chapter stated that security imperatives are conditionally influential on policy. Qualitative assessment verifies this proposition by showing that perception of security threats matters. The record also shows that border policies serve a symbolic function. Threat perception conditions the effect of security concerns. It hinged on the frequency and visibility of attacks within Turkish territory or against its citizens and on the salience and lethality of such incidents. Beliefs about the prospective failure or success of governmental efforts to curb terrorism also affected perceptions of threat.

## Case Study Approach

The post-1980 time period captures over-time changes in the primary variables of interest as terrorism fears grew against the backdrop of economic liberalization. The 1980s marked the beginning of a comprehensive program of trade and financial liberalization under the Özal administration. At the same time, the intensification of the Kurdish insurgency, the proliferation of Armenian terrorist groups, and anxiety over terrorist infiltration from Turkey's borders in the Middle East augmented security concerns. This chapter utilizes process tracing, an analytical tool for drawing descriptive and causal inferences about the temporal sequence of events (Collier 2011). The historical narrative is structured according to the theoretical framework and links changes in trade and terrorism—the primary variables of interest—to changes in migration policies. The core focus of this book has been on upstream migration-control policies—instruments that states enact to control migration before anyone crosses a border. The case study adheres to the core focus, with special attention paid to Turkey's visa and border policies.

The qualitative data for this chapter come from both primary and secondary sources I collected during field research in Istanbul and Ankara during the summers of 2008 and 2009 at both sites. I trace more recent changes in the country's migration policies by leveraging secondary sources. Two types of primary documentation proved especially informative: (1) the proceedings of the Turkish Grand National Assembly (TBMM Tutanakları), and (2) primary legislation recorded in various government documents. These two sources were obtained from the Library of the Turkish Grand National Assembly (TBMM Kütüphanesi) in Ankara. The secondary sources covered scholarly articles on the topic of migration and border control, Turkish jurisprudence on asylum and refugee law, and relevant migration and newspaper pieces in both Turkish and English. Secondary qualitative material came from the Library of the Turkish Grand National Assembly and National Library (Milli Kütüphane) in Ankara, the Center for Migration Research at Bilgi University (Bilgi Üniversitesi Göç Çalışmaları Araştırma ve Uygulama Merkezi), the European Union Information Center (Avrupa Birliği Bilgi Merkezi), and the Helsinki Citizens' Assembly (Helsinki Yurttaşlar Derneği) in Istanbul. Additionally, statistical figures on asylum and visa applications were drawn from the Ministry of the Interior (İçişleri Bakanlığı), the General Directorate of Security (Emniyet Genel Müdürlüğü), and the Turkish branch of the United Nations High Commissioner for Refugees (UNHCR).

This chapter complements the large-n analyses in several ways. First, it offers a granular look into the causal processes that link economic and security incentives to policy change. It also provides a "plausibility probe" by showing the consistency of theoretical propositions (Eckstein 1975). While quantitative chapters demonstrated how trade and terrorism shape policies, the case study sheds light on the underlying dynamics. Second, the single case study design by default eliminates country-specific confounders in large-n analysis (Bennett 2010). Statistical techniques may account for country-specific effects but may still omit relevant confounders from the analysis. By providing a historical narrative, process tracing sharpens the focus on temporal variation (Buthe 2002). The chapter thus links changes in the primary variables of interest—trade and terrorism—to policy change.

## Explaining Change

Migration policies are historically embedded and grounded in legacies of state building and ideas about what constitutes the nation (Brubaker 1992). Policy change or lack thereof may be tied to historical context. In the Turkish case, the founding interpretation of the country's migration regime as a nationalist project delimited the pace and quality of policy change (İçduygu and Aksel 2013). Owing to lack of macrodata on earlier time periods, quantitative analysis may miss the embedded nature of policies. This chapter redresses this potential shortcoming. Although the focus of this chapter is on the post-1980 period, the discussion documents the broader historical context underpinning policies. Toward that end, the next section sketches the historical context that defined Turkey's migration regime.

Turkey switched from an emigration to an immigration state in the after 1980. The country's reliance on remittances dropped as foreign currency flooded in. It also experienced a marked shift in the types of immigration flows and encountered the first significant wave of non-Turks in its history. Globalization facilitated the movement of people just as Turkey began a program of trade and financial liberalization. On Turkey's western borders, political turmoil in the Balkans after the Soviet Union dissolved propelled non-Turkic migrant inflows to Turkey. On its eastern borders, the repressive practices of Iran, Iraq, and Afghanistan and the Iran-Iraq War unleashed refugee flows to Turkey.

Shared Turkic ethnicity and Sunni identity formed the cornerstones of Turkey's approach to migration. To the extent that foundational ideas predicated a homogeneous and exclusionary sense of national identity, we would expect further policies to be governed by these ideas (Brubaker 1992). Hence, we would expect little variation over time. In addition, security concerns should bolster the case for stringency. Nationalist agendas derive strength from the securitization of migration (Bigo 1997). When migrants are defined as an existential threat, leaders can push forward exclusionary sets of policies. Populist leaders exploit public fears to whip up support for tighter migration control. Growing concerns over terrorism should have appealed to leaders vested in adhering to cultural homogeneity. However, Turkey's visa regime experienced several waves of liberalization.

Beginning in 1980, economic opening facilitated the liberalization of Turkey's migration policies. However, identity questions remained at the core of the state's perspectives toward migration. The binary distinctions between Turk and non-Turk and Muslim and non-Muslim continued to undergird policymaking. These distinctions became more salient after the 1980 coup and were influential throughout the 1990s. The 2000s brought further relaxation of some of these criteria. Turkey slowly moved toward civic citizenship and pruned the ethnicity component from its asylum and refugee policies. For example, as part of EU pre-accession reforms, it committed to removing the exception to the 1951 Geneva Convention. While the state made a concerted effort to politicize the Turkish communities abroad, it also acknowledged the dual loyalties of its citizens (Ünver 2013). Toward that end, in 1981, Turkey revised its citizenship code to permit dual citizenship. The 1982 Turkish constitution explicitly charged the Turkish government with providing social services for and attending to the cultural needs of its citizens abroad.

In sum, Turkey's migration policies experienced varying degrees of relaxation. Why would we observe such change over time? In particular, how did economic liberalization shape migration control?

## Economic Liberalization and Rise of the Trading State

From the founding of the modern republic, Turkey's economy had been characterized as an import-substitution economy (ISI) (Ahmad 1993). ISI stipulated cheap credits, protectionism, and state intervention in infrastructure development. Turkey held to a tradition of state planning and a strong presence of state-run firms. Up until the 1980s, "the Turkish economy had a very 'Soviet' touch to it" (Kirişçi and Kaptanoğlu 2011, 706). The Turkish government routinely formulated five-year plans. This system tethered the country to an agricultural economy. It also restricted commercial flows and advocated for state intervention to stabilize the monetary market.

Turkey commenced a program of wholesale liberalization and restructuring in the post-1980 years. The interim military regime that took over on September 12, 1980, embraced economic readjustment and passed a wave of measures toward that end. While these measures came on the heels of the February 1980 reforms, full-scale liberalization was to await the return to civilian rule in 1983. Enacted by the administration of Süleyman Demirel, it was the brainchild of his economic advisor, Turgut Özal (Yalpat 1984). On July 1, 1980, Turkey liberalized interest rates, and Özal took office as prime minister and leader of the ruling party, Motherland Party (Anavatan Partisi), known by its Turkish acronym, ANAP. A staunch liberalization advocate, Özal took on the arduous task of opening Turkey's economy to international trade and finance. The Özal administration reformed the economy in order to break with state-planned growth and encourage privatization. During this decade, the country made great strides in trade liberalization. In contrast, capital controls were relaxed gradually and capital liberalization proceeded a step behind.

The result of ANAP's reforms was nothing short of miraculous. Inflation dropped from over 100 percent to under 40 percent. Turkey's agricultural economy transformed with the emergence and growth of the manufacturing and services sectors. The sectors of banking, communication, tourism, and health took off. Exports rose by a spectacular 62 percent in spite of a worsening world recession. International trade expanded substantially and consistently. In terms of raw figures, imports grew from $4.8 billion in 1975 to $11.3 billion by 1985. Exports grew even more impressively, burgeoning from around $1.4 billion in 1975 to $8 billion by 1985. In subsequent decades, total trade value enlarged by over sixfold. In 1975, foreign trade constituted a relatively small proportion of Turkey's GDP, less than 14 percent. This figure grew steadily in the next decades, more than doubling by 1985 and eventually reaching almost 50 percent by 2015. Table 22 provides macroeconomic statistics for Turkey's trade from 1975 to 2015.

Financial deregulation accompanied the growth of international trade. In previous decades, the Turkish government had significantly curtailed

Table 22. Turkey's Foreign Trade, 1975–2015 (in millions of USD)

|  | 1975 | 1985 | 1995 | 2005 | 2015 |
|---|---|---|---|---|---|
| Exports | 1,401 | 7,958 | 21,637 | 73,476 | 143,839 |
| Imports | 4,789 | 11,343 | 35,709 | 116,774 | 207,234 |
| Total trade | 6,190 | 19,301 | 57,346 | 190,251 | 351,073 |
| GDP | 44,633.71 | 66,404.14 | 169,485.94 | 482,979.84 | 717,879.79 |
| Trade as % of GDP | 13.76 | 28.71 | 33.84 | 39.39 | 48.91 |

*Sources*: GDP figures are drawn from the World Bank's World Development Indicators (WDI). Trade figures come from the Turkish Statistical Institute (TUIK), www.turkstat.gov.tr.

financial flows into and out of the country. The military regime had lifted restrictions on interest rates in 1981, but in 1984 this was followed by full liberalization of exchange trade. The Özal administration relaxed restrictions—tariffs, quotas, and red tape—on imports and promoted exports, encouraging Turkish industrialists to import raw products and intermediate materials. Ankara opened the country's doors to foreign investors. As a result, foreign direct investment (FDI) increased over tenfold in a decade, from an annual average of $65.4 million for the 1980–1984 period to $716.4 million for the 1990–1994 period.[1] The government eased capital restrictions through a range of other developments. It established the Istanbul Stock Exchange in 1986 and opened the Central Bank to market operations the following year. The year 1989 was a landmark one for full-scale liberalization as the remaining barriers to capital flows were dismantled and the Turkish Lira (TL) became fully convertible (Arin 1998).

Liberalization also spelled a normative shift that deemphasized protectionism and state regulation (Aktan 1991 [1993]). A firm belief in the virtues of liberalism guided Turkey's reforms.[2] Özal was committed to underwriting a revolutionary transformation. This commitment was seen in televised speeches where he opted for the term "transformation" (devrim) instead of "simple change" (değişim) (Özal 1983). Turkey's accession to NATO in 1952 had constituted a preliminary and important step into integration into the capitalist global economy (Yalpat 1984). Nonetheless, liberal ideas resulted in policy manifestations three decades later. Cold War dynamics also assisted the growth of liberal norms. Turkey's role as an ally of the Western bloc and within NATO reinforced the commitment to liberalism.

My theoretical framework expects economic liberalization to exert several complementary effects. First, we anticipate liberalization to foster an ideational change that deemphasizes geopolitical security in state grand strategy and emphasizes material incentives (Rudolph 2005). In the spirit of classical liberalism, Özal believed that increased economic contact could mitigate belligerence between states (Aktan 1996). "The Özalist vision and reprioritizing of the principles of Turkey's national security led to an outward-looking policy. Overcoming the rigidity of physical and political borders, Turkey tried to extend its influence, primarily economically, to all surrounding areas, to act as a broker between the West and the expanded Middle East, and to benefit economically and politically from Turkey's increasing importance as a gateway" (Özel 1995, 176). The transformation of the Turkish economy paved the way for the rise of the Turkish trading state.

Turkey moved from regarding its neighbors through the lens of national security to seeing them through the lens of commerce. Economic integration also entails a reconfiguration of power within the state, whereby a wider range of actors come to participate in foreign policymaking. Prior to the 1980s, the military and the Ministry of Foreign Affairs had been influential and attached greater weight to preserving territorial integrity and social cohesion. As the power of these domestic players diminished, Turkey went from a territorial state to a trading state (Kirişçi 2009).

The theoretical chapter posited that the trading state favors liberalization of flows across borders. New actors gain voice in politics and advocate liberal border and migration policies. Turkey's migration policies conformed to these expectations, with varying degrees of liberalization across dimensions of migration control. The liberalization of trade and finance enabled the growth of a new business elite, and the liberal market policies put into place in the 1980s eventually led to the emergence of strong business interest groups with growing political leverage: the Independent Industrialists and Businessmen's Association (MÜSİAD) and, later on, the Turkish Industrialists and Businessmen's Association (TÜSİAD) and the Turkish Union of Chambers and Commodity Exchanges (TOBB). These new actors were influential in pushing Turkey to lift visa restrictions for citizens of commercial partners.

We also expect economic incentives to offset security concerns. The 1980s put this insight to a tough test as the threat of terrorism gained ground in policy circles just when the economic liberalization project was getting underway. Terrorist violence originated from homegrown leftist movements that proliferated in the Cold War context. Although unrest can be traced back to the 1950s, rapid industrialization and urbanization brought class struggles to the fore (Zehni 2008). At the same time, Kurdish secessionism was on the rise in the 1970s, resulting in the formation of the National Liberation Army (NLA) in 1973 (Button 1995). The NLA, motivated by the establishment of an independent Kurdish state, was the precursor to the Parti Karkeran Kurdistan (Kurdish Workers' Party [PKK]). The PKK was founded in 1978 by Abdullah Öcalan, who had also led the NLA. The military regime's repressive tactics in the 1980s also fed ethnically charged violence (Ciftci and Kula 2015). In an effort to stanch ethnic separatism, the regime had severely cut into Kurdish minority rights, for example by prohibiting the use of Kurdish and forcibly changing Kurdish names to Turkish. These tensions fueled the PKK. Blending Kurdish nationalism with Marxist-Leninist tenets, the PKK rose to notoriety as the leading terrorist threat to national security for the Turkish state in the following decades. In 1984 the group accelerated its campaign against the Turkish regime. In subsequent decades, the terrorist campaign inflicted over 30,000 fatalities and cost the government $125 billion (Cakar, Cengiz, and Tombul 2011).

Initially embracing a leftist ideology, the PKK capitalized on class struggles and exploited ideological disunity (Wyne 2005). Socioeconomic grievances stemming from the rapid modernization and transformation of Turkish society empowered the organization. In response, the Turkish state adopted heavy-handed tactics, precluding compromise and relying on a military approach to crush the organization. Figures 8 and 9 capture patterns of terrorism from 1980 until 2000. In both figures, the lines depict the total number of incidents that transpired on Turkish soil. Figure 8 displays total terrorist incidents recorded in the Global Terrorism Database (GTD). Figure 9 traces incidents carried out by the PKK. Figure 9 shows a discernible uptick in violence by the PKK in the 1980s, as the group took the fight to urban centers and embraced indiscriminate tactics.

Although concerns over terrorism focused on the PKK and its offshoots in these two decades, other groups also contributed to fears over security. Foremost among these were groups that aimed to avenge the mass killings of Armenians during World War I: the Armenian Secret Army for Liberation Armenia (ASALA) and Justice Commandos of the Armenian Genocide (Mango 2005). Parliamentary proceedings from the 1980s express concerns among the Turkish policy establishment of cooperation between Kurdish and Armenian terrorist groups (TBMM 1984). The proceedings also underscore fears over Armenian groups' attacks triggering PKK activity and creating an escalation in terrorist activity.

The scale and extent of violence affect how threats are perceived and interpreted. Empirical results in previous chapters demonstrated that the volume and magnitude of violence influenced border and migration policies. However, perception is not simply a direct function of the raw number of incidents. There were other factors that influenced threat perceptions. Foremost among them was the quality of the violence. The PKK adapted its tactics in response to state repression and its violence went through several phases. While the violence initially targeted the police and symbols of state authority, by the late 1980s it had branched out to targeting civilians. Violence shifted from the countryside to urban centers. The PKK's violence also became more indiscriminate and the group began resorting to suicide terrorism.

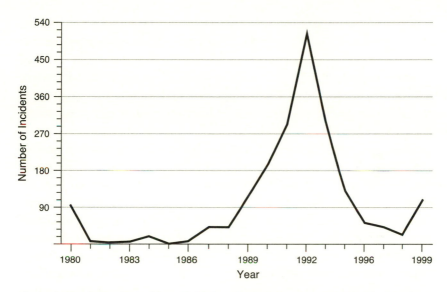

Figure 8. Total terrorist incidents in Turkey, 1980–1999. Source: GTD. The data here skip 1993 because the GTD lost the data for that year. See Enders, Sandler, and Gaibulloev 2011.

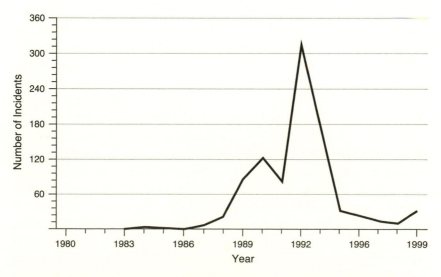

Figure 9. Terrorist incidents by the PKK in Turkey, 1980–1999. Source: GTD. The data here skip 1993 because the GTD lost the data for that year. See Enders, Sandler, and Gaibulloev 2011.

While unsuccessful in wrangling concessions from the Turkish government (Pape 2003), the tactic was an indication that the group had upped the ante in its war against the government.

The foreign connections of the PKK also motivated the Turkish government to take action. The PKK was a domestic terrorist group, and most of its attacks conformed to the definition of domestic terrorism: perpetrators and victims were Turkish citizens. Nonetheless, violence began to acquire a transnational character in the 1990s. The Turkish government became worried about Kurdish militants using neighbor states as bases of operation. Attention became directed toward neighboring states—particularly Syria and Lebanon—for sponsoring the PKK by providing bases of operation and financial support (San Akca 2009). These same states also supported other domestic terrorist organizations, both Armenian groups such as ASALA and leftist groups such as Dev-Sol. Unsurprisingly, concerns about militant infiltration from neighboring territories strained Turkey's relations with these states. In the 1990s, the PKK also managed to obtain international support and make strategic use of the Kurdish diaspora in Europe. Despite the fading relevance of state sponsorship of terrorism in the post–Cold War context, the PKK was unique in its ability to procure substantial state support: "In terms of enjoying international opportunities, the PKK should be cited as an exceptional case that has been tolerated almost as a legal entity" (Bacik and Coskun 2011, 261). In addition to leveraging bases of operation in neighboring states, the PKK drew on the transnational Kurdish diaspora in Europe. From 1984 on, at different times, the group enjoyed logistical and moral support from Greece, Bulgaria, Cyprus, Libya, the Soviet Union, and Cuba (Roth and Sever 2007).

Additionally, the foreign dimension of the PKK's campaign heightened threat perceptions. Prime Minister Özal emphasized the foreign dimension in his 1984 address to the Turkish National Assembly: "For the past 15 years, terrorist incidents have been used as a tool of worldwide strategy. The hot war was replaced by a cold war and the cold war was replaced by a war being waged by terrorist organizations. . . . In countries not armed against terrorism, professional terrorist groups can achieve surprising results in a short time" (TBMM 1984; translation mine). The recognition of the PKK as a terrorist group also complicated Turkey's diplomatic ties with other states. The Turkish state was quick to designate the group as a terrorist network. Not surprisingly, this designation became a stumbling block in Turkey's diplomatic relations with other states (Ciftci and Kula 2015a). The European Union, for example, did not ascribe the terrorist label to the PKK until 2002, a fact that cast a shadow on the European Union's relationship with Turkey.

In sum, the foreign policy ramifications of domestic terrorism coupled with mounting terrorist violence elevated security concerns in the 1980s and 1990s. Turkey followed a careful balancing act that showcases functional and geographic variation in the relative importance of trading and geopolitical interests. Security carried the day with regard to border control. In contrast, visa liberalization continued unperturbed and commerce played a fundamental role in visa controls.

## Explaining Policy Change

*1980s: Dominance of the Trading State Logic*

The post-1980 era laid the foundation for Turkey's flexible visa regime, which remains in effect today. The visa regime is based on a categorical system that allows Turkey to manage short-term migration. According to this regime, Turkey designates a category of countries as visa-waiver states whose nationals can stay in Turkey for ninety days. A second category comprises those whose nationals may obtain a visa at the border, dubbed the "sticker visa." This flexible approach dates back to the 1970s but was extended to apply to a wider group of countries throughout the 1980s and 1990s. The third group of countries constitutes those whose nationals are required to apply for a visa prior to arrival.[3]

Özal embraced the classical liberal belief that a liberal visa policy could be used as a tool of diplomatic rapprochement. As Özel observes, "Prime Minister Özal, like a good nineteenth-century liberal, had faith that extensive economic relations between nations would generate non-belligerence" (1995, 167). Parliamentary debates of the early 1980s underscored the principle of reciprocity. The primacy of economic ambitions was evident in liberal elites' staunch opposition to imposing restrictions against MENA countries. Traditionalists clung to the view that more restrictive visa policies could be leveraged as soft sanctions. For example, in 1984, in order to control border crossings from Hatay, Saudi Arabia imposed visa controls on Turkish nationals. While traditionalists such as Cüneyt Canver argued in favor of retaliation, members of ANAP, the ruling party, cautioned against retaliatory visa restrictions. Mesut Yilmaz, the leader of the ruling coalition, stressed that visas would hurt bilateral trade. The opportunity costs of trade losses precluded Turkey from imposing harder measures (TBMM 1985).[4]

Commerce shapes diplomatic relationships between states by inculcating trust at the individual level (Fordham and Kleinberg 2009). The Özal regime subscribed to a similar philosophy and emphasized the beneficial social effects of commerce (Hale 2000). In this spirit, Turkey signed a series of bilateral agreements with neighboring states that loosened restrictions on short-term travel. The visa-waiver agreement signed with Greece in 1988 is a case in point. Turkey used the visa waiver to bring about rapprochement with its long-time rival (Hale 2002). Relations with Greece had soured as a result of the conflict over Cyprus, and in 1964 both countries had suspended visa-free travel. The new visa-waiver program sought to ameliorate relations in order to bolster economic ties. The program was successful in increasing the volume of travel between the two countries, with the number of arrivals from Greece almost doubling within a decade. Also in this decade, Turkey signed a series of visa-waiver agreements with Eastern European countries. This was a continuation of the liberal policies that Turkey had pursued toward the Soviet Union and its satellite states.

Whereas policies toward Turkey's western neighbors exhibited continued liberalization in this decade, for a good part of the 1980s, security fears kept visa controls in place vis-à-vis Turkey's neighbors in the Middle East. Political turmoil—in particular, the 1979 Iranian Revolution and the 1980–1988 Iran-Iraq War—generated migratory pressures from the region. Furthermore, political elites pointed to the adverse effects of the ongoing Iran-Iraq War. Fearing transborder conflict spillover, political elites argued in favor of stricter border enforcement and monitoring. Additionally, Turkey's elites were suspicious of pan-Arab nationalism, which had swept the Middle East. Since the beginning of the Cold War, Turkey had responded to Arab nationalism by drawing closer to the West (Hale 2002). Compounding these fears was a widespread belief in foreign support for terrorism in Turkey. For instance, a speech by Prime Minister Özal on counterterrorism highlighted that various terrorist organizations operating in Syria and Lebanon exacerbated divisive terror in Turkey and sought to "take Turkey back to the dark ages" (TBMM 1984). These factors rendered Turkey reluctant to grant visa waivers to the states of the Middle East. Turkey also maintained the geographic restriction to the Geneva Convention for political migrants from these states (Kirişçi 1991).[5] The latter years of the decade, however, ushered in policy reversal, whereby Turkey loosened visa policies with regard to the states of the Middle East. This policy reversal was in part spurred on by Turkey's efforts to draw tourism and investment into the country (Kirişçi 2000). It was also closely tied to expanding trade with Arab countries. As a result, visa policies were relaxed with Gulf countries and Saudi Arabia, followed by similar agreements with Jordan, Tunisia, and Morocco.

Turkey's visa policies toward Western European countries present an interesting case. Turkey consciously shied away from retaliating against visa restrictions imposed on Turkish citizens. Pursuant to its application for associate membership in 1958, Turkey had also signed the Ankara Association Agreement with the European Economic Community (EEC) in 1963 (Aksoy 2007).[6] The 1970 Additional Protocol ratified by EEC member states in 1973 reiterated member states' commitment to freedom of movement between candidate and member countries. The Ankara agreement and its protocol indirectly implied mutual visa freedom with EEC states (Kirişçi 2007). However, following the 1980 coup d'état, fears over post-coup flight to Europe pushed EEC countries to enact visa restrictions. The Federal Republic of Germany and the United Kingdom spearheaded visa restrictions, and other EEC countries followed suit soon after. That Turkey did not respond in kind with visa restrictions against EEC nationals testifies to the dominance of economic interests. Instead of requiring visas, Turkey extended the sticker-visa program to these states, which permitted the nationals of EEC states to pay for a visa at border crossings.[7] Economic considerations and Turkey's dependence on tourism revenue from these states justified a liberal visa program toward Western European states.

While Turkey did not harden its visa policies in response to the threat of terrorism, border-control policies did reflect the threat of terrorism. Border control—especially along southeast Turkey—has typically been complicated by a range of factors, most importantly hard terrain and harsh climate (Sert 2013). Moreover, these border zones were poorly monitored and vulnerable to a raft of clandestine transnational actors: smugglers, traffickers, militants, and illegal migrants. Ethnic ties across borders further frustrate the state's efforts to effectively manage its borders. Turkey's security forces have thus been tasked with multiple challenges—preventing smuggling, mitigating unrest, protecting against terrorist infiltration—and often with little cooperation from neighbors, who possess limited resources and policing capabilities. The rugged terrain has typically inhibited the Turkish state's penetration into the border hinterlands in the southeast. The ability of terrorist groups—in particular the PKK—to exploit Turkey's mountainous terrain as hideouts played a significant role in amplifying the Turkish state's anxiety (Zehni 2008).

Border regions with Iran and Iraq in particular provided safe bases for terrorist groups to conduct hit-and-run attacks against Turkish forces. The PKK raided villages to forcibly recruit and draw material support from its ethnic brethren. In Chapter 1, I theorized that when states encounter asymmetric threats that are hard to deter or locate, preventing territorial access becomes crucial to security seeking. The Turkish case corroborates this argument. Unaccustomed to unconventional warfare and hindered by unwelcoming terrain, Turkish military forces opted at the outset for strictly military measures, declaring a state of emergency in the southeastern provinces. The government declared a state of emergency in eastern provinces, which replaced martial law in 1987 and stayed in place in thirteen provinces until 2002 (Mango 2005). Accompanying the state of emergency, the Turkish government cracked down on border control.

While the border zones had been susceptible to illegal crossings, terrorist infiltration garnered increasing attention in policy circles in the 1980s. In a 1984 address to the parliament, Prime Minister Özal drew attention to terrorism as a negative externality of the "authority vacuum resulting from the Iran-Iraq War," emphasizing that the onus of monitoring the border had fallen on the Turkish military forces. In the same speech, Özal alluded to the fact that other states were exploiting the threat of terrorism to undermine Turkey's liberalization and democratization (TBMM 1984, 396). This belief echoed among a wider range of political elites and compounded perceived security risks from terrorist infiltration. Parliamentary discussions centered on worries that Turkey's neighbors were harboring terrorist organizations in order to advance their own foreign policy agendas at the expense of Turkey. Elites believed that rival states were pursuing a divide-and-conquer strategy by fomenting militant activity on Turkish soil (TBMM 1984). Further, they were concerned that countries with unresolved territorial disputes with Turkey were sponsoring terrorist organizations to promote their agendas. For instance, Turkish politicians believed that Syria supported Kurdish militants to gain the upper hand with respect to the disputed Hatay province and maritime disputes over the Euphrates River, on Turkey's border with Syria.[8] These beliefs compelled Turkey to deploy troops and install land mines on segments of its border with Syria. Another example is the Turkey-

Greece border, which had become fortified in the late 1960s. As relations between the two countries deteriorated with Turkey's 1974 intervention in Cyprus, Turkey retaliated with harder migration- and border-control policies. Ankara revoked visa-waiver privileges and deployed troops to patrol its border. Even while Turkey relaxed visa controls for Greeks, the Turkey-Greece border remained tightly controlled throughout the 1980s. In short, traditional security concerns over regional dominance, territorial rivalry, and territorial claims and fears over nontraditional threats arising from terrorist activity, organized crime, and undocumented migration made for tightly controlled and militarized borders in the 1980s.

### 1990s: Resurgence of Geopolitics

The next decade ushered in new challenges, putting a strain on Özal's liberal project. The 1990s brought several setbacks: the banking crisis of 1994 and rampant inflation cast doubt on the success of the liberalization project. As the public grew increasingly disillusioned with unbridled capitalism, traditionalist policymakers regained leverage in foreign-policy decision making. Instability in Turkey's immediate neighbors further played into the hands of nationalist voices in policy circles. By the mid-1990s full-fledged liberalization capitulated to traditional interests (Özel 1995). Traditionalists emphasized national unity and territorial integrity and viewed regional states from the prism of geopolitical security. At the same time, however, the 1980s had created a well-entrenched and sizable liberal middle class, now able to act as a counterweight against the more traditionalist elements.

Despite the prominence of geopolitical interests, Turkey saw a liberal visa regime as a means of wielding soft power (Kirişçi 2005). Şükrü Elekdağ, then ambassador to the United States, championed a foreign policy predicated on diplomatic and economic strength rather than military might (Özel 1995, 168). These elements sustained the liberal project throughout the 1990s. Turkey's accession to the European Customs Union in 1995, followed by formal candidacy to the European Union at the Helsinki Summit in 1999, also strengthened the liberal project and ensured that grand strategy did not succumb fully to geopolitical considerations. The fall of the iron curtain further catalyzed liberalization in the post–Cold War environment. In the 1990s, Turkey granted visa waivers to the newly independent republics as well as a host of Latin American countries. It also widened the list of countries that qualified for the sticker visa and extended visa-free travel privileges to the specialty passport holders of a range of other states.

Economic interdependence had a pronounced impact on the expansion and sustenance of the liberal visa regime. By maintaining open borders, Turkey sought to nurture increased exchange and contact with regional powers (Kirişçi 2007).[9] These goals came to fruition in 1992 with the establishment of the Black Sea Economic Cooperation Area (BSEC). Another important milestone toward regional cooperation was Turkey's accession to the Economic Cooperation Organization (ECO) in 1995. ECO was a trade pact signed among Eurasian and Asian states and played a pivotal role in post–Cold War economic transitions.[10] Freedom of travel, especially for skilled labor, was fundamental to the success of ECO. The liberal visa regime was also pivotal to diplomatic opening and growth of social ties. Turkey maintained its liberal stance, even in the face of military tensions with its neighbors. The Kardak crisis of 1996 is a case in point: despite the maritime dispute, Turkey did not retaliate with visa controls. Continued interchange eased the public's mistrust toward Greece and to gradual rapprochement, especially after 1999 (Kirişçi 2007). Turkey also sought rapprochement with Armenia by supporting societal reconciliation. As a result of the Nagorno-Karabakh Conflict of 1993, Turkey's border with Armenia had been closed. However, in the 1990s, political entrepreneurs on both sides emphasized that interpersonal contact would be fundamental to building trust. Toward this goal, the Turkish-Armenian Reconciliation Commission (TARC) worked toward and facilitated liberalization of migration policies. These efforts paid off when finally, in 2003, Turkey included Armenian citizens in its sticker-visa program.

On the western frontier, economic interests gradually paved the way toward softer borders. Prior to the fall of the iron curtain, Turkey tightly monitored its borders with Bulgaria and with the Soviet Union. In the post–Cold War context, the government changed course. In the spirit of bridge building with the newly independent Turkic states, Turkey quickly moved to relax its border-control practices with these states. Concomitant with these efforts, Turkey demilitarized its borders with Georgia and Azerbaijan. Following the collapse of the communist regime in Bulgaria, it also loosened controls over the previously tightly sealed border. Nevertheless, fears over undocumented migration put a damper on full-scale liberalization. The post-communist transitions reinforced these fears as turbulent economic conditions drove undocumented migrants from the former Eastern bloc countries to Turkey (İçduygu 2004).

Territorial disputes also impeded liberalization. For instance, the Nagorno-Karabakh dispute escalated to full-scale conflict between Azerbaijan and Armenia in 1991. In express support for Azerbaijan and in retaliation against Armenia, Ankara sealed its border with Armenia and deployed troops at the frontier. Similarly, territorial disputes in the Middle East prevented open policies toward Turkey's neighbors in the region. Two other security concerns captured the limelight: the instability of the First Gulf War and, related to that, increasing irregular migrant inflows (Kaynak 1992). In tandem, these concerns meant that border liberalization trailed significantly behind the liberalization of visa policies.

### 2000s: Resurgence of the Trading State

The 2000s saw the return of economic liberalization, with deepening social acceptance of liberal ideas. Turkey's economic opening in the 2000s was qualitatively different compared to Özal's era in that it was firmly grounded in civil society. Though economic considerations became an important driving force of foreign policy in the 1980s, economic incentives gained primacy in the 2000s. While the government had almost single-handedly engineered liberalization in the previous decades, other types of actors—such as the military—began to back liberalization. Several other factors facilitated the dominance of economic interests in foreign policymaking. Turkey became a formal candidate country for full membership in the European Union at the December 1999 Helsinki Summit. Turkey's membership bid strengthened the dominance of economic interests. Candidacy also put pressure on Turkey to align its border and migration policies with the EU acquis (Kirişçi 2007). Concomitantly, a vibrant civil society had added new domestic actors to the scene. Powerful business associations such as the Turkish Exporters Assembly (TİM), the Foreign Economic Relations Board (DEİK), the International Transporters Association (UND), and the Turkish Contractors Association (TMD), as well as local organizations such as the Istanbul Chamber of Commerce (ISO), developed ties with businesses as trade partners. These interest groups not only lobbied various government agencies but also tried to influence public opinion to support trading interests.

Some scholars attribute the new liberalism to the policies and discourse of the Justice and Development Party (JDP), known by its Turkish acronym AKP (Kirişçi and Kaptanoğlu 2011; Öniş 2006). The AKP promoted the zero-problems policy as a means of acquiring new export markets. By inhibiting conflagrations with regional states in order to protect commercial ties, the AKP's foreign policy perspective went hand in hand with the idea of economic interdependence as constraint. The policy's chief architect, Ahmet Davutoğlu, placed a premium on using commerce to cement Turkey's regional dominance. He also trumpeted trade as a tool for resolving conflicts and building peace. The AKP government made a concerted push toward EU membership, which ultimately paid off. Between 2003 and 2008, exports to the European Union increased by over 300 percent and were a key ingredient in the AKP-led economic boom. The European Union became Turkey's greatest trading partner during this time period. Also during these years, Turkey enjoyed sustained export-led growth. Unlike the situation in earlier eras, the economy combined fiscal discipline with low interest rates. In a recent interview, Acemoğlu considers Turkey's economic growth in this time period remarkable: "You had economic growth that took place for about five years at rates that were pretty unusual for Turkey for such an extended period of time" (Canuto 2017). According to Eurostat, Turkey's GDP per capita increased from 36 to 54 percent of the EU average by 2012.

Economic interests regained importance in policymaking as terrorist violence declined in the 2000s. The capture of Abdullah Öcalan in Nairobi, Kenya, in 1999 was a turning point. Afterward, the PKK's strategic effectiveness plummeted. Shortly after, the group declared a ceasefire, which was to last until 2004. Another factor that contributed to the decrease in terrorist activity was the Adana Agreement, whereby Syria officially renounced its sponsorship of the group. Figure 10 illustrates the initial downturn in violence in Turkey. However, this downturn was not enduring. The figure also shows a sharp uptick in violence after 2011 and then again in 2013.

Figure 11 charts violent incidents perpetrated by the PKK from 2000 to 2015. It shows a drop in the incident rate from 2000 until 2002. In that year the PKK became more violent again, partly in response to the European Union's designation of the group as a terrorist actor. The group also exploited the power vacuum and turmoil left in the wake of the Second Gulf War. Nevertheless, the shift in Ankara's counterterrorism approach to a conciliatory

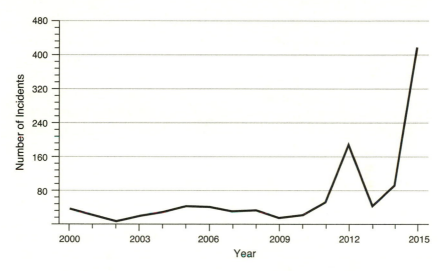

Figure 10. Total terrorist incidents in Turkey, 2000–2015.

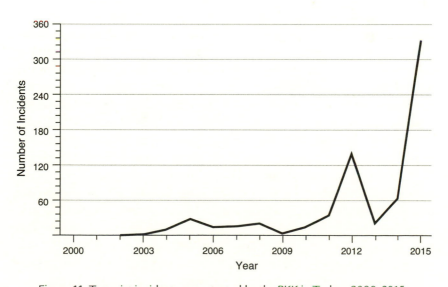

Figure 11. Terrorist incidents perpetrated by the PKK in Turkey, 2000–2015.

one stalled the PKK's resurgence (Ciftci and Kula 2015). The capture of the PKK leader meant that the state could abandon its strict approach. The country's candidacy for the European Union, which gained renewed steam under the AKP's first two terms, also motivated concessions to the Kurdish minority. Gradually Turkey eschewed the military approach for diplomacy, even going as far as attempting indirect negotiations with Öcalan (Çandar 2011). This is evidenced in Figure 11, which shows a low level of violent incidents until about 2011.

## Policies post-2000

The pivotal moment for Turkey's visa policies post-2000 was its acceptance as a candidate country to the European Union at the Helsinki Summit in December 1999. The status required Turkey to overhaul its migration system to conform to EU guidelines. The visa system in particular came under EU scrutiny, and the European Commission began publishing progress reports on Turkey's policy reforms. Turkey was required to adapt its policies to align with the Acquis Communitaire, which sets guidelines for common frontier policies. Moreover, growing economic interdependence, building upon the successful implementation of the 1995 Customs Union agreement, exerted a powerful liberalizing force. By 2000, the European Union's share in the country's overall trade balance had reached almost 50 percent. Since the post-1980 economic remake, Turkey's economy had been heavily dependent on trade, which magnified the policy salience of trade ties with the European Union.

The 2001 and 2003 Accession Partnership programs outlined the steps for the harmonization of Turkey's visa system with the Schengen criteria (COM 2001 [2003]). Specifically, the programs required Turkey to adopt the Schengen negative list and revoke its visa-waiver policies (Aygül 2013). In the 2001 National Action Program for Adoption of the Acquis (NPAA), Turkey committed to adopting the negative list. Although Ankara took some preliminary steps toward harmonization, the reform process was not smooth. Turkey initially harmonized some of its policies by imposing visas on Kazakhstan, Bosnia-Herzegovina, and Azerbaijan. It also lifted visas for countries on the European Union's white list: Guatemala, Paraguay, and Venezuela. In the latter half of the 2000s, however, the AKP government changed course and began to deviate from the European Union's criteria. In the latter part of the 2000s, Turkey resisted pressures to fully adopt the negative list. In fact, in direct contradiction to EU requirements, Ankara lifted visa restriction from some states that are on European Union's negative list: Azerbaijan, Mongolia, Tajikistan, Turkmenistan, and Uzbekistan (Özler 2003).

A stumbling block toward full harmonization was the incongruence of Turkey's categorical visa system with the Schengen system. The Schengen system is based on a hard distinction between negative and positive list (visa-waiver) countries and allows no room for the middle category of countries whose citizens are granted visas at border ports. As a candidate country, Turkey was required to terminate the sticker-visa program. Civil society groups and business interests objected to the termination of the sticker-visa program by stressing the transaction costs of eschewing it (Kavi 2007). Rather than eliminating the sticker visa, Turkey rebranded it as the e-visa. Political elites sold it as a tool for enhancing economic linkages. Minister of Foreign Affairs Davutoğlu praised the e-visa program on practical grounds, stating that it would facilitate business-related travel to Turkey. He also lauded the e-visa as "revolutionary" and noted that pragmatism, rather than security imperatives, played a role in devising this policy: "The e-visa . . . is also a reflection of the state's self-confidence and represents an approach which does not perceive everyone coming from outside a threat or risk element" ("Dışişleri" 2013; translation mine).

While the adoption of the negative list has been a thorn in the harmonization process, Turkey did undertake reforms to increase transparency in migration policies and provide avenues for appeal for migrants denied entry. In 2011, it instituted new biometric passports, more or less in line with EU standards. In 2014, it adopted the Law on Foreigners and International Protection (LFIP) to reform its procedures for visa issuance and processing.[11] Finally, in November 2015, Turkey agreed upon the Joint Action Plan to manage the migration crisis. With the migration deal, in exchange for fast-track visa liberalization and 3 billion EUR in aid for the support of refugees that Turkey hosts, Ankara pledged to take steps toward stanching the flow of illegal migration to Europe (Kirişçi 2016).

Table 23 catalogues the visa policy changes that Turkey has made in the 2000s. The divergence from EU policy is evident from the mid-2000s on. Turkey has drifted toward visa liberalization that suits its own interests and has added countries to the visa-waiver list that are on the European Union's negative list. The European Union has repeatedly reprimanded the Turkish government for its failure to adhere to uniform policies toward EU nationals

## Table 23. Turkey's Visa Policy Changes post-2000

| Year | Visa Policy Changes |
|------|---------------------|
| 2000 | EU demands alignment with acquis. |
| 2001 | Imposes visa restrictions on Kazakhstan and Bosnia-Herzegovina. |
| 2002 | Imposes visas for six states: Bahrain, Kuwait, Qatar, Oman, Saudi Arabia, and United Arab Emirates. Some headway made toward readmission agreements. |
| 2003 | Imposes visas for fourteen more countries: Azerbaijan, Bahamas, Barbados, Belize, Fiji Islands, Grenada, Indonesia, Jamaica, Kenya, Maldives, Mauritius, Saint Lucia, Seychelles, and South Africa. |
| 2004 | In line with the EU positive list, visas lifted for Brazil. Readmission agreement with Kyrgyzstan completed. Readmission talks begin with Bulgaria, Greece, Romania, Ukraine, and Uzbekistan. |
| 2005 | Visas imposed on two countries on EU negative list: Marshall Islands and Micronesia. In line with the positive list, visa exemption granted for Guatemala. Readmission agreements with Romania ratified. Readmission talks continue with Bulgaria, Ukraine, and Russia. Turkey opens further readmission talks with the European Union. |
| 2006 | Aligns policies with the EU positive list by lifting visas for Andorra, Colombia, Paraguay, and Venezuela. European Union demands replacement of Turkey's sticker visa. |
| 2007 | Adopts new visa-issuance guidelines and instructions distributed to consular and border officials. Turkey drifts from EU negative list by granting visa waivers to Azerbaijan, Mongolia, Tajikistan, Turkmenistan, and Uzbekistan. |
| 2008 | Stagnation on alignment with the negative list and in replacing the sticker visa. |
| 2009 | Turkey further drifts from EU negative list by granting waivers to Brunei and Kosovo. Receives criticism for failing to follow uniform policies vis-à-vis EU nationals and for failing to discontinue the sticker-visa program. |
| 2010 | Turkey signs visa liberalization agreements with Albania, Cameroon, Lebanon, Libya, Jordan, and Syria, the last five of which conflict with the EU negative list. |
| 2011 | In line with EU recommendations, biometric passports are put into circulation. Turkey agrees to visa waivers for Georgia, Serbia, and Russia and to waivers for specialty passport holders from Portugal, Sudan, and Yemen. These policies are not in agreement with EU negative lists. |

(continued)

Table 23 (continued)

| Year | Visa Policy Changes |
|------|---------------------|
| 2012 | European Union recommends that Turkey sign the readmission agreement. Turkey begins providing humanitarian assistance to Syrian refugees. |
| 2013 | Readmission agreement with the European Union signed at the end of the year. Instigates fast-track to visa liberalization. |
| 2014 | To conform to EU standards for transparency, Turkey enacts the Law on Foreigners and International Protection (LFIP). |
| 2015 | Joint Action Plan enacted to stem the flow of undocumented migration and to readmit transit migrants in exchange for fast-track visa liberalization for Turkish citizens. |

Source: Adapted from Aygül 2013.

(COM 2013).[12] Turkey has since adapted EU policies in a piecemeal fashion but has not fully harmonized its visa regime with EU protocols.

Interestingly, while EU candidacy generated pressure to adopt stricter visa policies, Turkey's economic ties with extra-EU states hindered full harmonization. Political elites could cite economic concerns and cultural ties to make a case for maintaining relaxed visa policies. Another factor that strengthened elites' lobbying against full harmonization was that while Turkey was required to adopt the EU/Schengen negative list, it itself was placed on the negative list. Hence political and business elites castigated the European Union for imposing a double standard (İçduygu 2009; İçduygu and Kirişçi 2009). Political elites pointed out that visa restrictions violated the standstill clause stipulated by the 1963 Ankara Association Agreement between the EEC and Turkey (Özler 2013). They also underlined that continued visa restrictions placed an undue burden on business transactions and had deleterious effects on par with non-tariff barriers to trade (Çağlayan 2005). Although the media widely disseminated these criticisms, Turkey did not backtrack from its liberal visa policies with regard to EU citizens. On the contrary, elite rhetoric hailed Turkey's liberal policy as an instrument of soft power and contrasted Turkey's regime with "fortress Europe" (Kirişçi 2005).

The EU accession reforms gathered pace during the first two terms (2002–2007 and 2007–2011) of the AKP. During this time, numerous other structural factors entrenched economic liberalism. Turkey became an exporter of capital, and Turkish firms funneled direct investments to neighboring counties. The AKP made a concerted effort to deepen economic cooperation with Middle Eastern states. In the 2000s, Turkey increased its exports to the Middle East sevenfold. Bilateral trade pacts, for example with Egypt, Israel, Morocco, and Tunisia, and then with the Gulf Cooperation Council, further stimulated trade. Construction companies in particular invested heavily in projects in the region. USAID estimated that the $2.8 billion construction market in northern Iraq was controlled by Turkish firms (USAID 2008). To provide another noteworthy example, a Turkish construction firm, TAV, built airports in numerous states in the Middle East, including Egypt, Israel, Morocco, and Tunisia ("Turkey in the Middle East" 2009). Turkey also pursued ambitious gas pipeline projects—for example, Nabucco—which sought to carry gas from the east to the west (Babali 2009).[13] Ankara made energetic efforts to establish freedom of travel pacts following on the heels of bilateral trade pacts. Visa liberalization for these countries was a direct result of growing economic interdependence. In September 2009, Turkey signed accords with Jordan, Lebanon, and Syria and affirmed intentions to grant reciprocal visa waivers (Kanbolat 2009). Turkey's status as a regional economic powerhouse also figured into its stance toward maintaining open visa policies with Middle Eastern states.

Turkey couched its liberal visa regime in ambitions for regional integration, in parallel fashion to the normative template EU liberals had trumpeted in past decades (International Crisis Group 2010, 11). Domestic interests—in particular the International Transporters Association—made a compelling case that hardening borders would be detrimental to the Turkish economy (Kirişçi 2014). Currently, out of 199 origin states, 80 enjoy visa-free travel.[14] Forty-five countries are on the visa-sticker program, which as of April 2013 has been labeled the e-visa program.[15] All told, Turkey has a fairly liberal visa policy with regard to 125 of 199 countries. Almost all of Turkey's neighbors' citizens qualify for the e-visa program and are able to secure territorial access for a nominal fee of approximately $25 at Turkey's border ports.

Border policies followed a parallel track in the 2000s in the sense of being guided by economic interests and the "zero problems with neighbors" philosophy. While territorial disputes had hampered cooperation with neighbors on border control, improving diplomatic relations with some neighboring states permitted joint border management. One clear example was Turkey's policies with respect to its border with Greece. Since the 1999 earthquake, the two rival states had experienced a thawing of relations. Labeled "earthquake diplomacy" by some, this broader process eased tensions at the Greece-Turkey border (Akcinaroglu, DiCicco, and Radziszewski 2010). During this decade, Turkey also relaxed its border policies with Syria. Turkey and Syria signed an agreement in 2004 whereby both states agreed to remove the mines that had been installed along the frontier.

Another notable policy change concerned the border with Armenia. The Turkey-Armenia border was a challenging case in the sense that several security concerns militated against liberalization. Although the border had remained shut in the prior decade, Turkey loosened visa policies for Armenian citizens, with the professed goal of stimulating trade. Witnessing a surge in trade, commercial interest groups clamored for further liberalization. Their efforts paid off, and in 2009 the two countries signed the Geneva accord, dismantling hard border controls ("Turkey, Armenia to Reopen Border" 2009). The accord was welcomed by the Turkish-Armenian Business Development Council (TABDC), an influential organization that aimed to bring together business circles. The TABDC praised the deal by noting the positive future effects on bilateral trade (Mumyakmaz 2009).

With Turkey's acceptance as a candidate country, its border management fell under the guidelines of the European Union. Member states were invested in Turkey's reforms because the country's eastern and southeastern borders were poised to become the European Union's external borders should Turkey attain full membership. Since the Amsterdam Treaty of 1999, candidate countries are required to align border-control policies with Schengen criteria. Instituted in 2001 and further refined in 2006, the EU guidelines for integrated border management cover criteria for border-control mechanisms and tools (Council of the European Union 2006). These criteria pertain to border checks at the European Union's external borders, interstate and interagency cooperation, surveillance, and risk analysis to combat irregular migration and crime (Sert 2013).

The European Union demanded changes along several dimensions. First, it advised streamlined collaboration and coordination among different units responsible for border management. Harmonization necessitated eliminating the multiagency border-control structure and installing a professional civilian unit for border management. In particular, the European Union admonished Turkey on the grounds that the simultaneous operation of the gendarmerie and the Turkish military forces created coordination problems (Akman and Kılınç 2010). Second, the European Commission advised that Turkey establish consistent and routine procedures for cooperation among border authorities and the Turkish national airline, THY. Toward that aim, it recommended training and exchanging information on pre-boarding and pre-arrival screening. Third, harmonization necessitated that Turkey reappraise its surveillance and border checks. In addition, the European Union demanded that Turkey cease installing minefields along the border and adopt safer procedures of control.

In a series of National Action Programs (NAPPs) published in the early 2000s, the Turkish government outlined the steps necessary to transition from military to civilian control over borders (COM 2001 [2003], 2013). One of the first steps was the establishment of a Task Force on Asylum, Immigration, and External Borders, which would identify the discrepancies between the EU acquis and Turkey's migration policies. The task force published the *Strategy Paper for the Protection of External Borders*, which reiterated the goal of setting up a civilian border-control unit (NAPP 2006). The Twinning Project, established in 2006, reiterated a series of concrete steps toward legislative and institutional reforms on border management (MOI 2006).

Although Turkey did take some steps toward harmonization, in its 2012 progress report for Turkey, the European Commission observed that Turkey had made limited progress in aligning its border control procedures with the Schengen criteria. Table 24 documents the adjustments in border-control policies enacted in the post-2000 period. Several developments are worth noting. Turkey established formal bodies, culminating in the Bureau of Border Management, that were charged with achieving integrated border management. It also began cooperating with the European Union's border monitoring agency, Frontex.

Despite committing to further reforms, Turkey was hesitant to disavow the military approach to border control. The reasons for stagnation are quite telling with regard to the enduring influence of security imperatives in Turkey's border management. The military was particularly recalcitrant in eschewing its command over Turkey's borders and argued that doing so would undermine security. In addition, anxieties over terrorist infiltration significantly hindered the transition to civilian control. In the aftermath of the Second Gulf War, the military found greater justification for holding onto the reins of border control by pointing to the postwar instability in Iraq. Smuggling across Turkey's porous southeastern borders with Iraq and Syria gave the European Union more reason to demand that Turkey modernize border management. However, Turkey's perspectives on the goals of border management were not in full agreement with those of the European Union (Kirişçi 2007). The European Union's main concern was stemming the flow of

## Table 24. Turkey's Border Policy Adjustments post-2000

| Year | Border Policy Changes |
|------|----------------------|
| 1999 | Turkey becomes a candidate country to the European Union at Helsinki Summit. |
| 2001 | NPAA programs published. Turkey's border-control policies come under the scrutiny of the European Union. |
| 2004 | Ministry of Interior establishes the Directorate for Project Implementation on Integrated Border Management (IBM) to plan and prepare projects on IBM. |
| 2006 | Task Force on Asylum, Immigration, and External Borders established. Task force publishes a strategy toward transforming border control policies. |
| 2008 | The Directorate for Project Implementation is replaced by the Agency for Development and Implementation of Legislation and Administrative Capacity for Border Management. |
| 2009 | IBM Phase I and II begin. IBM instigates technical capacity building for border control. The Capacity Enhancement of Border Surveillance and Mine Clearance Project commences, replacing mines with safer surveillance methods. Turkey begins receiving financial assistance from the European Union under the Instrument for Pre-Accession Assistance (IPA) program. |
| 2011 | The Agency for Development and Implementation of Legislation and Administrative Capacity for Border Management is replaced by the Bureau of Border Management. |
| 2012 | The progress report for Turkey states that there had been limited progress toward harmonization of border policies with Schengen criteria. |
| 2013 | Turkey begins cooperation with the European Union's border agency, Frontex. |
| 2014 | Turkey declares intention to fence its border with Syria. |
| 2015 | Turkey continues construction of the border fence with Syria and stepped-up policing. |

*Sources*: Akman and Kılınç 2010; Sert 2013; Afanasieva 2014.

undocumented migrants and, to a lesser extent, preventing smuggling. In contrast, Turkey focused primarily on thwarting terrorist infiltration and secondarily on preventing other types of illicit activity.

In the past few years, the trading state has faltered as the pendulum has swung back to the dominance of security imperatives. Post-2010, the ruling AKP began to encounter the harsh realities of foreign policy and its zero-problems approach began to disintegrate. As the violence in Syria has continued without an end in sight, as of 2015, the number of Syrian refugees in Turkey had reached three million, putting further resource strains on Ankara (Ferris and Kirişçi 2015). Consequently, liberal precepts have come under increasing strain in the past few years, in part owing to the diminishing prospects of full membership in the European Union. Trade with the European Union also slowed down, with exports growing by less than 7 percent in 2015, as the European Union reeled from economic recession. Declining tourism revenue, itself a partial consequence of the increasing specter of transnational terrorism, further eroded the liberal basis of open borders.

At the same time, the peace talks with the PKK collapsed in 2015, which in turn spurred the return to separatist-ethnic violence. There has been a rise in incidents perpetrated by the PKK and its offshoots, for example, the Kurdistan Freedom Hawks (TAK). As reconciliation with the Turkish government seemed out of reach, the PKK resumed its guerilla insurgency in the southeast. The ongoing civil war in Syria gave rise to ISIS. ISIS launched a campaign against Turkey in 2015 (Stein 2017). All told, Turkey has suffered over five hundred fatalities (Shaheen 2017). Toward the close of the decade and in the post-2010 period, expanding economic disparity between Turkey and Iraq has compounded instability in the region. This environment has led to a perfect storm whereby Turkish forces have become burdened with having to tackle multiple types of security challenges in the border zone ("Turkey's Fractious Politics" 2015).

The relaxed border policies that Ankara pursued between 2011 and 2014 led to a flow of foreign fighters, weapons, and cash to ISIS strongholds. Anecdotal evidence from former ISIS militants starkly illustrates this phenomenon (Bertrand 2016). After ISIS set its sights on European targets, Western states continued to try to convince Turkey to seal its border with Syria. The United States joined these calls, urging Turkey to close off the vulnerable sixty-mile stretch of its border between the Turkish city of Kilis and the Syrian city of Jarabulus. In 2015, the Obama administration upbraided Ankara, saying: "The game has changed. Enough is enough. The border needs to be sealed" (Entous and Lubold 2015).

While Turkey did not immediately respond to admonishments by Western states, the targeting of Turkish nationals and territory by ISIS touched off a shift in Ankara's approach to the border. Turkey witnessed the tragic consequences of loose border controls most starkly in 2013. On May 11, 2013, twin bombs went off in the normally tranquil border town of Reyhanlı, killing fifty-one people. The Reyhanlı terrorist attacks moved the government into action. Another trigger for policy change came when ISIS seized the border crossings at Karkamış and Akçakale along the Turkish side, which lie opposite the Cerablus and Tebyad border crossings on the Syrian side (Orhan 2014). Finally, in 2014, Turkey voiced its intention to fence its border with Syria (Afanasieva 2014; Avdan and Gelpi 2017). In 2015, Ankara stated that it intended to establish a twenty-five-kilometer buffer zone along the border whereby aerial bombardment would cut off funding and supplies to ISIS (Cole 2015).

After Ankara commenced construction of the border wall, a spate of terrorist violence aimed at Turkish nationals spurred further fencing. ISIS exploited the perforated border by networking across important demographic centers including Istanbul, Ankara, Konya, Adana, Izmir, Şanlıurfa, and Gaziantep. Stein (2016) writes that militants formed a Turkish cell of the Islamic State. My theoretical argument stated that when terrorist events affect the residents of a country or take place within its borders, security concerns predominate. In line with this expectation, it was when threats directly hurt Turkish nationals and occurred within the country that the government responded by hardening border controls.

While Turkey had initially resisted Europe's calls for tougher borders, a series of high-profile incidents perpetrated by foreigners triggered a shift in perspective. Evidence came to light that militants had exploited porous borders. For example, Şeyh Abdurrahman, who was responsible for the July 2015 Suruç bombing, and Yunus Emre, one of two suicide bombers who targeted the Ankara train station in October 2015, had crossed the border into Syria to train and plot the attacks and then crossed back into Turkey. Likewise, the January 1, 2017, attack at Reina was carried out by an Uzbek, raising doubts about Ankara's traditionally generous policies toward Turkic republics (Butler 2017). The Reina attack also illustrated the challenges of monitoring extremists after they make their way into the country. In response, Ankara deployed paramilitary forces in border towns, installed new checkpoints, and instituted new restrictions on refugees entering Turkey. It instituted twenty-four-hour field surveillance in Gaziantep and Şanlıurfa and increased military patrols along the 910-kilometer border. In 2015, Turkey imposed new visa limitations on Syrians. States targeted by terrorism also undertake visible and on-site controls as a show of force against non-state threats; Turkey's response fit this pattern. In January 2016, Prime Minister Davutoğlu reaffirmed that the government would institute more visible security measures in densely populated areas (Yeginsu and Homola 2016).

As of 2017, Turkey is in the process of sealing off other segments of the border. While Ankara officially terminated Turkey's open-border policies in the southeast in 2014, its border policies still remain inconsistent. Some border towns are patrolled by the paramilitary whereas others remain unmonitored. Moreover, Turkey has drawn fire from international audiences for bias in border control: border guards are tougher on suspected Kurdish militants than on Islamic State militants (Hubbard and Shoumali 2015). On the western front, Turkey's migration deal with the European Union has meant a crackdown on border controls. Monitoring maritime boundaries in the Mediterranean has become paramount to blunting the flow of undocumented migrants to the European continent. In accordance with the deal, Turkey significantly tightened up policing efforts. As a consequence, according to Frontex, there was a dramatic drop in 2016 in the flow of undocumented migrants to Europe from the Middle East (Pells 2016).[16]

### Turkey as the Modern Trading State

Rosecrance (1986) has acknowledged that the state will not fully neglect its territorial defense or base its grand strategy solely on trade. The evolution of Turkey's migration policies testifies to these insights. The weight of economic incentives varied not only by era but also by policy arena. While economic imperatives were predominant with regard to visa policies, they exerted a weaker impact on border-control policies. Geopolitical events including past territorial disputes and state sponsorship of terrorist groups affected border policies. Ironically, in the post-2000 environment, Turkey pursued soft border-control policies toward its neighbors in the Middle East despite pressures by the international community to crack down on border control.

Table 25. Changes in Economic Interdependence, Terrorism, and Policy

| | Independent Variables | | | Policy Change | |
|---|---|---|---|---|---|
| Decade | Trade Liberalization | Capital Liberalization | Terrorism | Visa Policies | Border-Control Policies |
| 1980s | Nascent liberalization | Limited liberalization | Nascent and increasing | Liberalization | Limited liberalization |
| 1990s | Moderate liberalization | Nascent liberalization | High and increasing | Liberalization | Limited liberalization |
| 2000s | Resurgent liberalization | Continued liberalization | Moderate/decreasing at first, then increasing | Mixed trends, then liberalization | Liberalization |
| Post-2010 | Continued liberalization | Continued liberalization | High/increasing | Mixed trends | Eventual tightening |

*Notes:* Coding of Interdependence: Nascent refers to novel policies. Limited means that liberalization was not full-fledged. Moderate means that liberalization continued but leveled off compared to the prior decade. Resurgent liberalization means that liberalization was revitalized. Continued liberalization means that trends paralleled the prior decade's levels.

Coding of Terrorism: Cells capture both levels and direction of change. The coding takes into account both threat perception and objective metrics of terrorism volume according to the Global Terrorism Database. Coding is relative to within-case variation, that is, with respect to other time periods. Threat perception refers to the extent of coverage of terrorism in the media and parliamentary debates.

Coding of policies: The coding of policies captures within-case variation. Liberalization and tightening are opposite ends of the spectrum of policy change. Limited means that there were aspects of the instrument that did not change much. Mixed entails countervailing trends.

Table 25 summarizes the chapter and chronicles the changes in visa and border policies across each of the eras. The table classifies policy changes substantively as "nascent," "limited," and "moderate." Economic globalization emerged in the post-1980 era; hence in this era, liberalization is marked as "nascent." Capital flows were gradually relaxed and capital interdependence somewhat lagged behind trade interdependence. In the 1990s, economic imperatives were put on the back burner but Turkey did not roll back liberalization. Hence the decade is typified by moderate liberalization. In the 2000s, especially after the AKP came to power, the liberalization project was revived. Finally, even though foreign policy has leaned toward hawkish politics based on geopolitical dominance, economic liberalization has continued apace since 2010.

Similarly, the table documents how the threat of terrorism varied each decade. The labels "high" and "moderate" refer to the levels of terrorism. These are loosely based on the number of incidents reported to the GTD. The categorization is also based on the coverage of the threat of terrorism in policy and media circles. The labels "nascent," "increasing," and "decreasing" refer to the change in the volume of terrorism. For instance, the PKK launched its insurgency against the Turkish government in the early 1980s and hence the threat was high but also rudimentary. In the next decade, the threat continued to climb as attention fixated on PKK activity and state sponsorship by neighbor countries and the PKK took its campaign to urban centers. In the 2000s, the threat is defined as moderate as violence oscillated: the capture of Öcalan stunted PKK activity until the mid-2000s when the PKK resumed action, in a bid to regain salience. Finally, during the past few years since the Arab Spring, Turkey has been besieged by terrorism on two fronts: the PKK and ISIS. Threat perception is defined as high owing to intensifying worries within the security establishment.

Strikingly, liberalization continued with little interruption. Economic factors were the primary drivers. However, this does not preclude foreign policy instrumentalism from guiding policies. For example, the post–Cold War environment, regional politics, and ideological flexibility propelled visa liberalization. Until the last time period under discussion here (post-2010), visa liberalization was almost impervious to concerns over terrorism. In congruence with my theoretical expectations, commerce overrode security fears. Border-control policies, in contrast, more readily bowed to security fears. The most recent and vivid example is the construction of the fence along the border with Syria. Traditional threats—past disputes over territory—had hardened Turkey's borders in decades past. However, once economic growth and globalization gained steam again under the AKP, Turkey purposefully pursued open-border policies to facilitate travel and trade with neighbors in the Middle East. In fact, until 2014, Turkey withstood pressures from the international community to toughen its border controls in the southeast.

Consonant with my argument, it was the directed and transnational nature of the threat from terrorism that prodded the government to clamp down on borders. Terrorist actors exploited loose controls when planning and carrying out fatal terrorist incidents in the country. Hence the linkage between open borders and violence was fairly evident. This element was not as overt when it came to visa policies: Turkey viewed visa waivers as an instrument of soft power and diplomatic rapprochement. It did not regard relaxed visa controls as heightening vulnerability to terrorist events. The porous nature of the borders, on the other hand, was a more evident obstacle to security seeking.

In sum, functional variation illustrates that economic and security interests influence pillars of migration control in different ways. Border and migration control are multifaceted. Securitization of policies is not uniform. And border tightening may be a misnomer.

CONCLUSION

# Improving Theory and Policy

The issue of border policies is one that has been critical in political discussions in Europe and the United States and one where there are complicated dynamics at play. On the one hand, countries need open borders for trade and a flow of workers. Companies structure their operations across borders with factories and offices in multiple countries. Open borders ease the flow of exports as well as individuals. Every year, the European Union sees 1.3 billion border crossings of people coupled with 57 million trucks transporting goods worth $3.7 million ("Putting up Barriers" 2016). Politicians recognize that the freedom of human mobility is inextricably linked to the flow of goods and capital. As Britain's prime minister stresses: "There cannot be freedom of movement of goods, free movement of capital, free movement of services if there isn't a free movement of people" ("May Gets Hollande Ultimatum" 2016). On the other hand, open borders have been heavily criticized for making countries vulnerable to terrorism. After attacks, there is pressure to close borders. This quandary is at the heart of the book. Border control is about striking a balance between these two concerns. Politicians use multiple tools to simultaneously achieve multiple "grand strategy" objectives when managing their borders. Two of these tools are border walls and visa policies.

Borders have always served as sites of exchange and projection of military power (Gavrilis 2008b). Traditionally, international borders are sites where states maximize territorial control and demonstrate authority. Borders also demarcate the reach of the state's jurisdiction and authority. As such, states should jealously guard their territory and vigilantly defend borders against intrusions from other states (Starr 2002, 2006; Vasquez 1993). Economic interdependence theory, in contrast, underscores that war stands to disrupt and degrade commerce (Oneal and Russett 1997; Oneal and Russett 1999; Russett and Oneal 2001). By extension, policies that exclusively emphasize the geomilitary functions of borders would not be conducive to efficacious economic exchange. Border disputes diminish trade because countries regard these borders as sites of power projection rather than sites of exchange (Simmons 2005). Thus states have faced the same dilemma in different forms. Traditionally they sought to balance the military and economic functions of borders. States now face the same dilemma where border control strives to reap the gains from economic globalization while insulating against globalized violence.

What stands out about modern border control is the significance of non-state threats. The September 11 attacks starkly illustrated that economic powerhouses could be vulnerable to destruction wielded by individuals. Coupled with the changing security landscape, border control is less about warding off the armies of other countries and increasingly about screening out non-state threats (Andreas 2000; Andreas and Nadelman 2006; Donaldson 2005). In 1986, Rosecrance wrote that the trading state would supplant the territorial state since economic prosperity would eliminate the necessity for territorial conquest. My book draws on this argument to then argue that trade and capital ties could overturn security fears as long as threats are diffuse. I also argue that the trading state does not preclude restrictionism. My theoretical framework illuminates why. It informs security fears may carry the day in spite of economic gains from globalization.

Migration policy is susceptible to politicization. Take the choice of the United Kingdom to exit the European Union. The U.K. Independence Party (UKIP) pitched restricting immigration as the carrot to push forward the Leave campaign. While migrants were perceived mostly as an economic threat—as a drain on the United Kingdom's resources—rather than as a security issue, concerns about transnational terrorism in Europe were embedded in restrictionist sentiment. The Leave campaign invited controversy by tying the freedom of movement to the vulnerability to "Orlando-style" terrorist events within the United Kingdom (Cowburn 2016). Yet Brexit does not showcase the return of the territorial state and the retreat of the trading state. Rather, as long as countries believe they can reap the economic gains from globalization while restricting migration, they may cater to restrictionist demands. Bearing testament to this, the Leave campaign underscored that the United Kingdom would retain the economic benefits without bearing the costs of remaining in the European Union.

In this final chapter, I consider the relevance of the book's theoretical framework for broad themes in international relations. Here, I survey how the findings speak to debates about territoriality, interdependence theory, and globalization and suggest directions for future research.

## Economic Globalization

While scholars have explored the connection between trade and conflict (Oneal and Russett 1997; Oneal and Russett 1999; Russett and Oneal 2001) and financial ties and conflict (Erik and Li 2003) at length, little heed is paid to how trade and capital ties relate to other types of state behavior. My book remedies this theoretical shortfall by applying the insights from the extant literature to migration and border policies. Stated differently, I interrogate how economic globalization shapes states' strategies for coping with non-state threats.

The book's findings strike a hopeful tone for interdependence theorists. Economic ties tend to result in more liberal migration policies and militate against fortified borders. However, the relative weight of security and economic incentives depends on how we measure transnational terrorism. I draw on the larger scholarship on economic interdependence theory to formulate hypotheses on the impact of trade and financial states on policy. Commerce functions as a counterweight to the effects of transnational terrorism. More broadly, while security concerns incentivize policy hardening, economic ties exert effects in the opposite direction. I show that trade and capital ties dampen the probability of visa restrictions. They also shape visa-issuance practices such that citizens of trade and finance partners encounter more lenient policies. Additionally, states are reluctant to fortify their borders with trade partners. Physical barriers are detrimental to trade ties insofar as they compound the inhibitory effects of borders on cross-border exchange. In addition to increasing the transaction costs of commerce, walls are often interpreted as hostile signals.

The case study chapter echoed the empirical findings. In Turkey, economic interdependence was the engine behind visa liberalization, starting Özal's ambitious reformation of Turkey's economy. Decades later, an incumbent with a very different political outlook, Erdoğan, advanced a similar rationale for liberalizing visas with southeastern and eastern neighbors, states that had up till then encountered stiffer controls. The AKP's neo-Ottoman vision of an economically integrated Middle East with Turkey as the regional hegemon fed into using visa relaxation to project cultural influence, or "soft power" (Özler and Toygür 2011). Nevertheless, the case study chapter also illustrated the limits of economic incentives. The trading-state logic had already begun waning in influence in the latter part of the 2000s, but security fears took over after a string of terrorist attacks convulsed Turkey when the PKK resumed its campaign and ISIS began targeting Turkey after 2015. Rising threat perception meant tougher border controls, and Turkey began building a wall along its border with Syria.

Nonetheless, I also show the limitations of the opportunity costs framework (Polachek 1980). The opportunity costs of economic exchange do not always override fears over security. These patterns also underscore the limits of economic interdependence on state behavior. Economic ties have liberalizing effects but only to the extent that terrorist events do not directly threaten the state's own territory or citizens. In addition, only a narrow subset of dyads enjoys interdependence levels high enough to override security concerns.

Up until recently, scholars have almost exclusively studied trade and financial flows in isolation from migration policies. Their work has thus overlooked the fact that dimensions of globalization may overlap. However, recently other scholars have recognized this by probing the question of why states restrict migration while opening borders to flows of goods and capital. Part of the answer lies in the sequencing of policies (Peters 2017). And part of the answer lies in whether trade and migration are complements or substitutes (Rudolph 2008). This literature has made headway in exploring the connection between labor and other factors of production. Yet it is almost exclusively focused on the economic consequences of labor mobility (Rudolph 2008). I depart from this exclusive focus by showing the circumstances in which security externalities outweigh material incentives. My book provides a different perspective on the question of why economically open states close their borders and restrict migration. My empirical focus is on transnational terrorism, but the implications potentially carry over to how states tackle other types of transnational threats. "Visas and Walls" is a step in the right direction in terms of exploring the fuller implications of interdependence for states' security-seeking behavior. Future scholarship should explore how economic interdependence influences states' policies vis-à-vis a diverse set of transnational actors, for example, human traffickers and arms smugglers.

The results also ask us to rethink globalization. Keohane (2002) has famously lamented that scholars have narrowly defined globalization as an economic issue. Transnational terrorist groups reap the gains from communication and transport technologies of globalization in similar ways that multinational corporations do (Kellner 2007). Consequently, the same technologies that assist benign flows across borders also facilitate flows of violence. My book explores this phenomenon by looking at transnational terrorism. Following Keohane (2002), I argue that globalization is not simply economic but also carries security externalities. Globalization scholars also expect economic exigencies to outweigh other state objectives, the implications of which are liberal border policies. But this may be an overly simplistic expectation. Rather, faced with globalization, states make bargains in their grand strategy, trading economic gain for security or vice versa (Rudolph 2003, 2006).

## Migration-Security Nexus

Policy leaders can leverage the migration-security nexus to advance their goals. Brexit shows that leaders can establish links between security and migration by playing up public anxieties. The Leave campaign sparked controversy and criticism for linking the referendum to terrorism in Europe and for stating that the freedom of movement enhanced vulnerability to terrorism. Yet, terrorism certainly weighed on voters' minds as they went to the polls, trailing behind larger-scale issues such as fears over virulent nationalism. Catering to this, the campaign simplified the vote for Brexit as a vote for securing the country's borders against Islamist terrorism (Robertson 2016). Leave advocates pointed to physically remote attacks such as the Orlando club bombing in the United States. They also drew attention to relatively proximate attacks on the European continent, such as the Paris and Brussels incidents. By doing so, these leaders further securitized migration by defining it as an existential threat to the United Kingdom.

My book asks scholars to think carefully about the securitization of migration. My theoretical framework expects that securitization is a function of how close to home threats strike. Events in the country's own backyard stimulate policy change. My framework thereby nuances our understanding of securitization by showing that it is not a uniform process and that it is contingent instead on the nature of threats. However, I also argue that elites are the gatekeepers through whom threats gain currency and carry weight in policymaking. For instance, Turkey had begun witnessing an increasing volume of political migration as early as the 1980s. However, it was not until the mid-1990s that political elites portrayed the phenomenon as a threat to Turkish interests. As İçduygu and Yükseker artfully put it, before then, "transit migration was ontologically present, but epistemologically absent" (2010, 562). Political elites also make the terrorist threat epistemologically present in order to spark policy change.

My work provides evidence that further qualifies the impact of security concerns. Threat perception is shaped by affinity. The results show that states harden their policies in response to attacks against proximate states. Chapter 3 showcases that European destination states tightened policies in response to attacks in Western Europe. This finding qualifies the modest effects of global terrorism. Attacks elsewhere do not exert as pronounced an impact as do attacks on the state's own soil. That said, incidents in geographically close countries approach the effect magnitude of targeted terrorism. Thus, as Chapter 5 discusses, the European Union zealously pressed Turkey to conform to Schengen standards for visa and border policies, not least because of the fact that Turkey bordered the European Union. What is more, with Turkey's possible EU membership, its borders were set to demarcate the European Union's periphery. Terrorist events in Turkey, a predominantly Muslim and non-Western country, may be culturally remote to European interests but they were poised to become physically proximate. Hence, events that had once seemed remote were now closer to the European Union's backyard. Proximity matters. This holds true even when the state's own nationals are not victimized. These findings are consistent with research on the psychology of risk perception that finds a positive relationship between proximity to attack sites and threat perception (Lowenstein et al. 2001). Proximity triggers fear and anxiety by warping risk assessments and creating a sense of imminent danger (Braithwaite 2013).

The findings also point to a complementary theoretical angle and a second research avenue: beyond physical proximity, cultural similarity shapes threat perception and, by extension, state responses. Thus European countries respond to attacks elsewhere in the region not just because these events are geographically proximate but also because of cultural affinity. On the one hand, countries might expect violence to spread from neighbor attack sites. On the other hand, they may perceive attacks against culturally similar states to be more salient. In fact, the spate of jihadi terrorist events in 2015 and 2016 sparked controversy in Western media and the blogosphere about the discrepancy in public reaction to terrorist assaults in Europe compared to elsewhere. For example, comparing the reactions to the attacks in Paris and Beirut, Graham captured the disparity in response in an article published in the *Atlantic*: "Every time there's a major terror attack in an American or European city—New York, Madrid, London, Paris, Paris again—it captures the attention and concern of Americans and Europeans in a way that similar atrocities elsewhere don't seem to do" (Graham 2015). He wrote that the response gap may be credited to familiarity with victims and venues in the case of attacks in Europe or North America and lack thereof in the case of events elsewhere. Another article published in the *Atlantic* remarked that "the discrepancy in attention and compassion may result from a variety of factors, including tourism patterns or cultural familiarity," as well as beliefs in the normalcy of violence in certain parts of the world (Ajaka 2015).

These findings point to fruitful future research pathways. Scholars can build on the findings here to study how cultural similarity and other measures of similarity among countries—shared language and religion, for instance—affect the policy impact of terrorist events. If similarity among states augments threat perception, we may expect border- and migration-control policies to spread rapidly across similar states. In "Visas and Walls", I show that policy tightening is dyad specific, but evidence of a rapid spread would refine this conclusion. The notion that cultural and geographic proximity guide states' responses ties in with symbolic motives that underpin border policies. Andreas surmises that by cracking down on border control, the government expresses its state-ness. And policies are symbolic in that by implementing them, the state strives to "project at least the appearance of control" (Andreas 2009, 152). We may imagine that violence against geographically and culturally proximate states should more easily activate symbolic motives. Symbolic policies have the citizenry as their audience. Insofar as familiarity and affinity condition public reaction, there would be an incentive for the government to subdue fears in the wake of attacks in proximate states, and we would expect it to do so through a highly visible tightening of border controls.

## Territoriality and Borders

This book makes inroads into conceptualizing the evolving role of territoriality and borders in world politics. A voluminous literature examines interstate conflicts over location of borders (Hensel 2000; Vasquez 1995). These studies look at the role that contiguity plays in militarized disputes. Yet the literature on border management strategies is rather thin. This oversight is significant not least because transnational threats have been gaining prominence in world politics (Shelley 2006). These actors can wield violence that was once the preserve of other states' militaries (Salehyan 2008b). In response to the rise of non-state actors, we are witnessing an ideological reconfiguration of what borders mean and what functions they perform. In this process, discourse emphasizes law enforcement and better policing of borders rather than their militarization (Andreas 2009). This book contributes to emerging work that explores how states maintain and manage their borders (Carter and Poast 2015; Gavrilis 2008a; Hassner and Wittenberg 2015). The theoretical focus shifts attention away from the role of borders in interstate conflict to their role in preventing territorial breach by non-state threats.

The book's findings contribute to the broader perspective of borders as institutions. Simmons (2005) finds that settled borders function effectively in stimulating economic exchange. In contrast, unresolved border disputes hamper dyadic trade. Little attention has been paid to how the management of borders affects their institutional makeup and functioning. There is anecdotal evidence, for example, that harsh border practices are perceived as a hostile signal by neighbors. As the narratives of emerging border walls showcase, walls antagonize neighbors. Norway's initiative to install a fence along its border with Russia has not gone unchallenged, eliciting rejoinders from Norwegian pro-migration and human rights lobbies. Linn Landro of the Refugees Welcome Group in Norway lamented that "the fence sends a very negative signal, including to Russia because it says that 'we don't trust you.'" ("Norway Will Build a Fence Along Its Border With Russia" 2016). Harder border strategies risk weakening cooperation among neighboring states and, according to Gavrilis (2008a), undermine the border regime. In this book, I focus on the trade-off between economic and security incentives. However, this discussion draws attention to a second trade-off between unilateral border measures and regional cooperation. Future research should explore how states manage the latter trade-off and what the implications are for the institutional robustness of international borders.

My book approaches border stability from the perspective of international cooperation. Gavrilis (2008b) argues that bilateral cooperation between neighbors is fundamental to keeping out unwanted actors. When neighboring states pool resources in monitoring and policing their borders, they are more likely to develop effective border management systems. Border stability depends on institutional design rather than state capacity. Going a step beyond Simmons's (2005) perspective, even settled borders may not necessarily be stable if the institutional design is weak. Gavrilis argues that bilateral cooperation is the product of evolution and that two rival states may cooperate in border management despite unresolved territorial disputes. Under what circumstances does bilateral cooperation evolve? My framework suggests that states that encounter targeted terrorism from the neighbor will be unwilling to cooperate and will instead adopt unilateral measures to secure the frontier.

Differences in threat perceptions may hamper cooperation. By extension, neighbor states must agree on which actors present security risks. Cooperation takes several forms: joint border exercises, joint task forces, dialogue between border guards, and the ability of border patrol agents to operate on the neighbor's territory to monitor the border zone. Gavrilis contends that these joint procedures are possible when states devolve authority to border agents. Discrepant threat perceptions can propel states toward unilateralism and also render governments unwilling to devolve authority to border agents. In other words, bilateral cooperation depends on concordant threat perceptions. Andreas (2009) similarly argues that the United States and Mexico disagree on what they perceive as threats to the border: they agree on the primacy of organized crime but the United States places a premium on illegal migration as a threat. According to my argument, if the state is highly vulnerable to terrorist attacks compared to its neighbor, it is likely to push for unilateral measures such as militarizing and fortifying the border. More generally, cooperation is less likely if neighbor states weigh economic and security incentives differently.

## Contributions to Policy Debates

### Securitization and Populism

To reiterate, my framework speaks to the securitization of migration and, in doing so, generates expectations about whether states will pursue restrictionist agendas. My book also provides a cautionary tale by drawing attention to threat perceptions and, concomitantly, to the influence of symbolic politics. In this respect, I echo the insights of earlier research (Andreas 2000, 2009), namely that border and migration control are prone to theater. States demonstrate authority by clamping down on border control. This fact by it-self is not problematic. However, the line between symbolic and populist politics may at times be thin. Populism pivots on public fear and political agitation. Widespread fears can cultivate populism. Politicians are also re-sponsible for spreading fears in order to gain an edge in elections (Müller 2016). On a cynical note, leaders of a certain stripe may point to a mélange of clandestine transnational threats to justify an agenda based on exclusionary politics—one that rests on hardening borders and excluding broad catego-ries of migrants. Bove and Bohmelt's (2015) research tells us that these blunt tools, far from attaining security in a globalized context, sooner or later backfire. Hence, a good dose of cynicism may be in order: publics should be discerning with regard to the securitization of migration.

The securitization of migration also has a second, darker side: it may fur-ther erode the humanitarianism at the heart of the international refugee regime. The 1951 Geneva accord and its 1967 protocol oblige host states to take into account origin-country human rights conditions when adjudicat-ing asylum outcomes. If tighter restrictions spill over into asylum policies, we may witness states further straying from humanitarianism. Avdan (2014b) finds that terrorism does not dictate asylum admissions and that humani-tarianism has so far withstood the rise of transnational terrorism. However, restrictionism is a broader migration policy posture. As such, it may cause states to ignore the connections between policy dimensions. Migration pol-icy is multifaceted, but multifaceted does not mean disconnected. Betts (2013) laments that the refugee regime is limited in its scope. The calls to strengthen the regime by including a larger set of migrants are likely to fall on deaf ears if the restrictive bent prevails. Dismissing connections among economic and political migration policies can spell deleterious and sometimes unintended consequences. Distinct types of migration flows are also interconnected. For example, strict visa policies can bleed into undocumented migration (Czaika and Hobolth 2016). Facing tough visa hurdles, migrants may overstay. Or strict visa regimes may propel prospective migrants into the hands of traf-fickers, thereby forcing them to seek irregular ways of gaining access to terr-ritory (Avdan 2012).

My book also questions the wisdom of selling border control as effective counterterrorism. Given how fractious this debate has become, my book asks policymakers, elites, and analysts to reconsider whether tighter policies are panacea against terrorism. Politicians may be willing to muster political capital by framing policies in this way. But is border control an effective counterterrorism tool? The answer is, not necessarily. Border policies are partially about demonstrating control. These policies are not necessarily conducive to curbing terrorism. Tighter policies may sometimes backfire by playing into terrorist groups' propaganda. Also, terrorists change tactics; Hamas, for example, resorted to firing rockets after Israel installed the West Bank barrier. Unchecked restrictionism fuels populism and loses sight of the unintended and pernicious policy consequences of exaggerated fears.

My book also speaks to debates over whether globalization can survive discontent. To date, the scholarly focus has been mostly on how the economic externalities of globalization—such as rising inequality and downward pressure on wages for some sectors—sap support for it. My framework illustrates how the security externalities also attenuate support for globalization. To the extent that politicians are able to cash in on fears over security, support for globalization is likely to wither further. Advocates of globalism have been concerned that the rise of populism and decline in support for the neoliberal project go hand in hand. Diminishing support has led to distrust in economic elites—the "establishment"—with significant political consequences. Additionally, the trend toward stringency showcases the fissures within the neoliberal economic consensus. These fears resonate with mounting discontent with globalization. The economic failures of globalization came into sharp relief with the 2008 global financial crisis. Erstwhile proponents of globalization have become cautious critics and acknowledged the negative externalities of unchecked globalization. For example, a former ardent supporter of free trade, Paul Krugman, confessed to a "guilty conscience" as the financial havoc of the 2008 crisis unspooled (Saval 2017). These views lead to polarization by eroding support for the center. On the one hand, the rise of leaders on the far right—such as Trump in the United States, Farage in the United Kingdom, and Le Pen in France—is a direct consequence of distrust in establishment elites. On the other hand, these views have also empowered the left, for example, Podemos in Spain and nonmainstream hybrid parties such as Italy's Five-Star Movement (Kirchgaessner 2017).

### Stability of Borders

My work addresses policy debates about optimal border management. IR scholarship is limited in terms of generating specific recommendations about border control because the bulk of scholarship grapples with conflicts over the locations of borders rather than on the question of border stability. It is difficult to overstate the importance of effective border management for regional stability. Not only do porous borders present a danger for the state in question, but they have ramifications for other states that can sometimes extend beyond the geographic neighborhood of the state and be cause for concern for states outside of the region. For instance, the global recruitment of jihadi fighters by the Islamic State to bases of operation in Syria and Iraq magnified the importance of stricter border control (Lang and Wari 2016). During the height of its power, ISIS recruited 40,000 fighters from 110 different countries (McCarthy 2017). Time and again, the international community has decried lax border systems of transit countries for funneling flows of foreign fighters. The civil war in Syria aided the transit of foreign fighters through Turkey, resulting in repeated calls for Turkey to seal off its sixty-mile stretch of border with Syria (Fitzgerald 2015). In addition, after the Islamic State claimed responsibility for the Brussels incident, there were calls in Europe for sweeping policy stringency. European states sounded the alarm that accepting refugees from war-torn regions could spell infiltration by jihadi militants.

Ineffective border management has longer-term consequences, with the potential to undermine stability in postconflict situations. As ISIL shrank and lost the key cities of Raqqa and Mosul in 2017, for example, states confronted a new problem: foreign fighters returning home. As of the fall of 2017, the European Union faced the prospect of 1,200 foreign fighters flooding back to the continent. Even after ISIL is dismantled, states will be tasked with deradicalizing and reintegrating ex-fighters. Regional countries' porous borders and European countries' insufficient surveillance systems permitted foreign fighters to flock to Syria and Iraq. The return migration of former fighters now presents a potential source of instability for source states. While European states seek the rehabilitation of former recruits, there are legitimate concerns that they will carry out future attacks. After all, the radicalized may act on their own as lone wolves, inspired by the ideology they fought for and exploiting the training they received in camps in Iraq and Syria. Counterterrorism and intelligence officials stress that it takes only a handful of militants to cross into Europe and carry out attacks. A risk analyst in New York echoed these concerns: "It only takes one or two fighters to slip through the cracks back to Europe—armed with militant knowledge or even instructions by their handlers—to wreak havoc and bring ISIS back to the TV screens"

(Schmitt 2017). While these concerns might seem far-fetched, some of these fighters may exploit loose border controls to make their way to elsewhere in MENA to regroup and rebrand under a different name. The CIA has been concerned that those who aren't caught or do not surrender may seek new battlegrounds in Libya or the Philippines (ibid.). Some analysts have remarked that the extremist ideas that ISIL espoused will survive the demise of the group. Unmonitored or poorly monitored borders can enable former recruits regrouping around these ideas to draw in new recruits and mobilize into off-shoot organizations.

Managing migration is at the heart of the modern security landscape. While terrorism certainly predates the 9/11 attacks, non-state actors as sources of instability assumed center stage after the attacks (Salehyan 2008a, 2008b). Since then, the international community has become increasingly vexed with transborder mobility as a transmitter of violence across borders. The United Nations Security Council Resolution 2178 placed a premium on developing best practices of border control, effective regulation of travel documents, and intelligence sharing in its recommendations to states in combating transnational terrorism (UNSC 2014). In response, forty-five states enacted and implemented new laws in line with these recommendations. On a related note, transnational migration networks may serve as a conduit for the transmission of violence at the international level (Bove and Bohmelt 2015). Terrorism is contagious locally and attacks tend to cluster in hot spots (Braithwaite and Li 2007). Migration reconfigures diffusion mechanisms and, by doing so, illustrates how terrorism can be contagious across borders.

States and international organizations should emphasize effective border and migration control as a key ingredient of counterterrorism. This policy recommendation is all the more important given territorial fixity in the international system (Atzili 2006). With normative consensus on the sanctity of territorial space, territorial expansion has receded as a means of power aggrandizement. As a consequence, states cannot easily change their geographic location. Thus geographic fixity boosts the importance of effective border management. In addition, it may not be politically salable to undertake policy changes to alter state characteristics that render states vulnerable to terrorism. The conventional scholarly wisdom holds that democratic states are more likely to confront terrorist attacks on their soil (Chenoweth 2010; Eubank and Weinberg 1994; Li 2005). It is impractical and normatively unacceptable to suggest democratic reversal. Other policy suggestions may not be as normatively taboo or dramatic but again infeasible. Democratic states are typically concerned about treading on civil liberties, which in turn limits the extent of counterterrorism tactics they can pursue (Crenshaw 2010). As another example, there is some evidence that economically open states may face a higher volume of terrorist attacks (Blomberg and Hess 2008). However, rather than advise states to cut off economic ties or pursue autarkic policies, recommendations should focus on balancing economic gains with maintaining security. Border management should reflect both objectives and seek to establish discerning borders that simultaneously facilitate benign flows and keep out threats.

### Effective Border Management

The existing literature is limited in providing a formula for optimal border management because it treats border control as a binary concept. According to my theoretical framework, border control is not simply about open or closed but rather about how well policies fit together. Policy design itself depends on the site of control and the border's functions. Thus border walls aim to thwart clandestine access and deter illicit flows. In contrast, visa policies govern short-term travel but also have secondary effects on asylum outcomes. To illustrate, border barriers are ineffective insofar as clandestine actors have alternate means of access (Hassner and Wittenberg 2015). Surveillance and policing boost the utility of barriers. For a state with difficult terrain that provides hideouts for clandestine actors, the border wall may not promise much in the way of denying territorial access. Geographic status also matters. For countries on transit routes, the border wall may do little to stymie transit refugee migration, which is propelled by push-and-pull dynamics. Refugees fleeing conflict use peripheral states of the European Union as transit routes to economically attractive destination states in Western Europe. For example, the European migration crisis spurred Bulgaria to erect a barrier on the frontier with Turkey. Hungary followed suit. Despite being touted as highly effective barriers, in both cases, migrants routinely circumvent the barrier, for example, by rerouting through Croatia and other neighboring countries (Kingsley 2015). For migrants, the decision to migrate, even if under duress in the case of forced migration, is a risky one. By the time migrants make it to the border, they have already undertaken significant costs and factored in risks. They are thus likely to seek other routes of access rather than be deterred by physical barriers. As long as push-and-pull dynamics are in force, the efficacy of border walls will be in question as migrants will seek alternate means of access.

## Organized Crime–Terrorism Nexus

Broadly speaking, this book advances our understanding of how globalization reshapes border control. The advent of globalization has presented new challenges for policymakers, one of which is the emerging crime-terrorism nexus. These concerns are more pronounced in some countries, such as Colombia and the Philippines, and regions of the world such as West and North Africa. The slackness of borders may help cultivate ties between criminal and violent organizations. Clandestine activity flourishes in poorly governed border zones, paving the way for alliances among terrorist and criminal groups. The simplest model is that perforated borders facilitate the formation of ties between terrorists and organized crime groups. Poorly monitored borders allow groups to more easily move back and forth across interstate boundaries. Both organized crime and terrorist groups are likely drawn to border zones that are beyond the reach of state authority. Afghanistan's Korengal Valley and Pakistan's turbulent Federally Administered Tribal Areas (FATA) are two such examples (Piazza 2012).

Border policies may affect the evolution and shape of the alliances of the crime-terrorism nexus. In some cases, these are ties of convenience. In other cases, terrorist groups undertake illicit smuggling. Some of the world's deadliest terrorist groups are also the world's wealthiest ones. ISIL amassed revenues from the illegal oil trade and from smuggling confiscated goods. By raising revenues through trafficking, ransom, kidnapping, extortion, and smuggling, it was able to maintain its army of recruits and hold territory. Terrorist actors' participation in the illicit economy can generate tremendous revenue, which organizations then funnel into recruiting, training, and paying new members, acquiring weapons and equipment, and building training camps. The income stream then feeds back into the illicit economy, whereby terrorist groups use the money to bribe border personnel and other officials to continue smuggling operations. In short, one type of organized crime—such as narcotrafficking—fuels other forms of illicit activities such as contraband smuggling and human trafficking.

I said earlier that border crackdowns can incite blowback by raising the ire of neighboring populations and thereby indirectly motivate violence down the line. Visa and asylum policies also have implications for the organized-crime nexus through unintended consequences. We know that strict visa regimes can force migrants into irregularity (Czaika and Hobolth 2016). These migrants are rendered vulnerable, despite having legal status at the outset. Some overstay their visa terms, fail to return to sending states, and resort to working in underground sectors to avoid being deported. In addition, strict policies may play into the hands of criminal networks that raise revenue by finding alternate and clandestine means of illegal access across interstate borders. Unilaterally tough measures such as militarization of the border, barricades, and fortifications also undermine cooperation with the neighbor state. These measures do not give local cooperative regimes the chance to develop. Bilateral cooperation is critical to effective border management, which encompasses the prevention of smuggling, illicit trade, and human trafficking (Gavrilis 2008b). Further, the crime-terrorism nexus can be particularly troubling if the formation of these alliances further weakens the state's ability to police its territory and impairs its projection of force to peripheral areas. The crime-terrorism nexus compounds corruption and detracts from good governance.

Recognizing the importance of border policies for the emerging organized crime-terrorism nexus should warn officials against viewing border management exclusively through the counterterrorism lens. Anecdotal and empirical evidence shows that organized crime correlates with terrorist violence (Piazza 2012). Thus lax borders can facilitate both criminal and terrorist activity. What we do not know is whether border and migration policies shape the formation of alliances between criminal and organized groups. The nexus can take different forms. In the Afghan case, militancy has thrived off drug trafficking. In contrast, kidnapping and ransom fuel terrorism in Nigeria. Porous borders enable these illicit activities but perhaps through different mechanisms. Do border policies shape these dynamics? Do lax borders render these alliances more permanent? Answering these questions would be a first step toward preventing the formation of dangerous alliances among clandestine transnational groups.

## Concluding Remarks

I have argued that states seek to screen out transnational threats while facilitating economic exchange. There may not be a one-size-fits-all set of policies that achieve this balance. Policy optimality will also vary across geographic contexts whereby states situated in terrorism hot spots and regions riven by conflict will be driven toward tighter policies. It will also vary according to states' grand strategies. Rudolph (2006) articulates that states differ in terms of the facets of grand strategy they prioritize; some countries place a premium on material gains, while others prize security more than economic gain. For states that are not directly affected by terrorist events, a flexible visa regime that grants short-term access to citizens of commercial partners emerges as the optimal option. Moreover, border barriers pay off for states confronting terrorist attacks from neighboring territory. For states enjoying sizable trade with neighbors, in contrast, border walls may be suboptimal. Similarly, unforgiving visa practices may hamper dyadic economic ties.

My theory speaks to the utility of border practices attuned to specific types of threats and tailored toward particular origin states. My work generates a straightforward piece of policy advice: policies should be discriminate. Discriminate is not simply a matter of the degree of policy stringency but also about how expansive these policies are. Bove and Bohmelt's (2015) research cautions that indiscriminate restrictions for citizens from terror-ridden and conflict-prone states may be counterproductive. Far from curbing terrorism, sweeping policy stringency may backfire, especially given inhospitable immigration integration systems in destination states. At the same time, however, the authors advocate easing migration control for citizens of countries that do not generate significant outflows of terrorism.

From that perspective, readers will take comfort from the book's conclusions about broader patterns in migration- and border-control practices. All-encompassing migration restrictions are not advisable. Empirical patterns presented in this book illustrate that countries behave in accord with this wisdom. States limit short-term migration from terror-exporting countries but do not impose wholesale restrictions. Moreover, states only restrict when their own interests are at stake. Additional findings that states also factor in geographic proximity with targeted states qualify this finding to some extent.

Finally, my findings suggest that investing in and sustaining economic ties proves crucial for a world with open borders. Globalization does not equate to the erasure of borders, as naïve globalists would prognosticate. Rather, by rendering harsh border practices more costly, commerce mitigates the fortification reflex. Thus, to some extent, the securitization of migration is exaggerated. To be sure, uncontrolled and clandestine human mobility poses very real dangers. It also increases anxiety over the perceived loss of territorial control. The impetus to expand border-control initiatives is inextricably tied to efforts to downplay these imagined dangers. My results inform us that economic interdependence can moderate this impetus. By inculcating trust and fostering dyadic ties, commerce can attenuate the deleterious impact of public fears on policy. If harder borders arise simply in response to public anxieties, then these policies do not make for optimal border design. To the degree that overblown fears dictate policy, decision making will gravitate away from strict cost-benefit analysis. Therefore, strong economic ties go a long way toward optimal border management. I conclude the book on a cautiously optimistic note for supporters of liberal economic theory and at the same time invite scholars to further explore how globalization reshapes states' pursuit of security in the face of transnational threats.

### Introduction

1. Throughout the book, I utilize the terms "fences" and "walls" interchangeably to refer to physical border barriers. There is considerable variation in the length, shape, and structure of barriers; thus some of these are tattered fences while others are solid walls with sophisticated surveillance technology. Discussion of the variation among these structures lies beyond the scope of this project.

2. This is not to say that border barriers are ineffective: Avdan and Gelpi (2017) find that fences effectively reduce the threat of transnational terrorist incidents.

3. Rudolph proposes threat perception as an intermediary factor between geopolitical and cultural security concerns and border policies.

4. Individual Passport Power Rank, *Passport Index*, https://www.passportindex.org /byIndividualRank.php.

### Chapter 1

1. This is not to suggest that clandestine actors necessarily weaken state control. As Andreas (2004) argues, the state has pushed back for example through increased monitoring and more sophisticated surveillance, resulting, ironically, in greater control. The loss of control theme also misses that the state has never wielded complete territorial control.

2. Some scholars argue that this reflects a loss of control. In this vein, Brown (2010) writes that the trend toward border fortification and militarization represents the last gasp of the territorial state and showcases the fact that state power is on the decline.

3. This is precisely one of the reasons why Sanchez-Cuenca and Calle critique the widely accepted empirical distinction between transnational and domestic incidents.

4. The authors' report finds that by measures of network connectivity, expressed in terms of the number of international ties among groups, terrorist groups are second only to narcotics traffickers.

5. Staniland's argument is about transnational insurgencies. He suggests that the defensive strategy he proposes to combat insurgencies may not necessarily be optimal when dealing with global terrorist networks such as Al-Qaeda. He notes that what makes insurgencies distinctive is the bid for territorial control. However, the argument applies insofar as the transnational element is concerned. Furthermore, transnational

terrorist groups also have territorial ambitions (Pape 2006). Piazza (2009) shows that even fundamentalist terrorist groups have moderate territorial goals. In addition, scholarship has not reached a consensus on how we should distinguish between an insurgency and a terrorist organization. According to Sanchez-Cuenca and Calle (2009), insurgent groups are typically more lethal (at least a thousand fatalities a year) and command more solid and expansive territorial control.

6. We might surmise that wealthier states can better reap the benefits of newer technologies. However, drones are surprisingly cost-effective and available for purchase online. I thank Roger Haydon for pointing this out.

7. Of course, the use of drones raises a host of ethical dilemmas. The use of drones to bolster border security is also controversial. See, for example, Elden 2013.

8. Lee, Enders, and Sandler (2009) show that the 9/11 attacks were not predictable with the information available beforehand.

9. I use the terms "nationals" and "citizens" interchangeably to refer to individuals who are citizens of the state. Thus permanent residents and legal aliens would be excluded from this category.

10. Victims here are included here according to the definition of the database of International Terrorism: Attributes of Terrorist Events (ITERATE): "those who are directly affected by the terrorist incident by the loss of property, lives, or liberty" (Mickolus et al. 2007). Technically, victims include those injured or killed. However, in the empirical analysis, I also utilize a narrower specification looking only at fatalities.

11. I create two measures that separately count the number of incidents that transpire on the state's own soil and incidents that involve its citizens. We might think that incidents that occur on a country's territory necessarily victimize its nationals. Empirically, however, there isn't as much overlap as we might think—when it comes to *transnational* terrorism. The ITERATE data, for 1968–2011, of incidents where the nationality of victims is known, report 628 of 3,140 transnational events where the nationalities of victims coincide with the nationality of the state where the event transpires. The rest are foreign victims or cases where the nationality of victims is unknown or unreported.

12. I use the term "targeted" to refer to incidents that affect state interests. Terrorism scholars acknowledge that the targets of terrorist events may not necessarily be the intended targets. Sanchez-Cuenca and Calle (2009) expand on this point to critique the demarcation between domestic and transnational terrorism. That said, what is theoretically relevant here is whether the event produces direct experience with terrorism, regardless of whether the victims were the intended targets. More concretely, in the Istanbul bombing, the victims might have been bystanders, but the events directly involved the United States and Israel.

## Chapter 2

1. Exit controls are an exception, but today only a handful of states restrict outflows. Among the few that do are Cuba, Russia, Belarus, Saudi Arabia, and Qatar.

Throughout the Cold War, communist autocratic regimes instituted exit controls as a means to keep populations in check, fearing that an outpouring of migrants would undermine the ideological appeal of communism.

2. A related issue is state sponsorship of terrorism, whereby rogue states are regarded as sponsors of terror networks. Sponsorship is empirically hard to trace and validate, however, in terms of identifying whether individual terrorist incidents are backed by sponsor states. See, for instance, Byman 2005.

3. Neumayer (2011) reports that visa restrictions are more damaging for developing states than for developed ones. He surmises that people travel to developed states despite visa requirements.

4. Kirişçi takes the argument further by suggesting that Schengen states' strict stance on visa policies undermines their soft power vis-à-vis nonmember states.

5. The nonmember political entities are mostly overseas dependencies of former colonial powers, the United Kingdom, France, the Netherlands, and the United States. These territorial units enjoy independent authority over their immigration policies.

6. To my knowledge, there is only one research project, Demig-visa, that strives to collect over-time data, which was not yet available as this book went to press. The data set will encompass policies for thirty-eight destination states. Demig-visa is part of a larger data collection effort on migration policies. See http://www.imi.ox.ac.uk/completed-projects/demig.

7. The website is searchable by region or by destination state. See http://www.projectvisa.com/.

8. The current release of ITERATE covers incidents up to and including 2011. The Boston bombing is given as an example and should be included in the newer release of the database.

9. The majority of incidents have only one nationality recorded. Scholars differ in how they operationalize directed counts. Using the first nationality discards information whereas summing across may lead to double counting, insofar as ITERATE has redundant information. In practice, however, these concerns do not affect the results because less than 2 percent of incidents have more than one nationality for perpetrators and victims. In the text, I use the terms "directed" and "targeted" interchangeably.

10. The sums do include self-referencing cases. In the case of the nationality-based measure of targeted terrorism, a self-referencing dyad would be where the nationalities of perpetrators and victims are the same (in the case of the nationality-based coding). This would be the case, for example, if an incident is carried out by Colombians and involves Colombian victims but transpires outside of Colombia. These are included in the analysis because they are transnational incidents by virtue of their location. A self-referencing dyad would be one in which the perpetrators' nationality matches that of the event location but the victims are foreign.

11. Note that the global count does not eliminate incidents by a country's nationals that transpire in the same country. These incidents might still be transnational because of the nationality of their victims. That is, these aren't necessarily incidents in

which the assailants have traveled abroad to conduct these attacks. Hence, the export of terrorism should not be taken to mean "exporting militants."

12. The countries are listed alphabetically in the text. Palestine (the West Bank and Gaza) is at the top in both counts. However, Palestine drops out of the analyses because it is missing information in all covariates. Here, it is given as an example to provide more insight into what the terrorism counts are tapping into.

13. I conducted additional analysis with visas and trade treated as endogenous variables in two-stage probit. The Hausman and Durbin-Wu-Hausman tests ruled against endogeneity. Further, the coefficients did not change sign, indicating that a single equation framework is appropriate.

14. The logged migrant stock represents total stock. The results survive the inclusion of bilateral migrant stock. However, the latter data are only available from the World Bank for 2010, or for years prior to 2000, not permitting a lagged specification consistent with other regressors. Furthermore, the total stock also accounts for the country's overall stance toward migration.

15. In sensitivity checks, I instead use a dummy variable for whether the state is a member of the twenty-six-nation Schengen zone. The Schengen Area comprises twenty-six states in total including twenty-two states of the European Union plus Switzerland, Norway, Liechtenstein, and Iceland.

16. Accordingly, Croatia, which joined the European Union in 2013, is not included. This is suitable because the dependent variable records policies for 2010. The alternative specification would be to include a joint EU membership dummy. However, because all EU dyads enjoy visa-free travel, this variable is invariant and would drop out of multivariate regression.

17. This is analogous to interacting the global and directed terrorism measures with the Polity IV score.

18. The mean bilateral trade value is 0.56 for autocratic regimes, compared to 0.59 for established democracies.

19. The authors' disaggregated data also include an unknown file, which includes all cases that the authors were not able to categorize as either a domestic or transnational incident.

20. I thank Todd Sandler for making the extended data available to me before the publication of his coauthored study.

21. Most famously, the GTD lost data for 1993, which prompted Enders, Sandler, and Gaibulloev (2011) to correct for missing data. It also overreports incidents from 1991 until 1997. Because I use the authors' corrected data, these issues should not bias my findings.

22. All these results are available from the author upon request.

### Chapter 3

1. Council Regulation (EC) N°539/2001 of March 15, 2001 provided a list of non-EU countries whose nationals must be in possession of visas when crossing external borders and those whose nationals are exempt from that requirement.

2. Membership in the European Union is defined by the year for which data is collected. Four of twenty-six members of the Schengen are partial members: Bulgaria, Romania, Cyprus, and Croatia are legally bound by the Schengen acquis and wish to join the area. The data set does cover these states as well. The database does not yet include information for Croatia.

3. The analysis extends to 2014; hence it treats the United Kingdom as an EU member state.

4. These are Austria, Belgium, Denmark, Finland, France, Germany, Greece, Ireland, Italy, Luxembourg, Netherlands, Portugal, Spain, Sweden, and the United Kingdom.

5. The full list includes states, special administrative regions of the People's Republic of China (Hong Kong, Macao), and territorial entities not recognized by at least one member state (the West Bank and Gaza). States that gained independence are added to reflect the current political landscape. Thus Montenegro and Kosovo are not among the list of origin countries before 2006 and 2008, respectively. Visa applications from embassies and consulates that are currently in Montenegro and Kosovo would be treated as applications originating from Serbia in years prior.

6. http://www.schengenvisainfo.com/schengen-visa-types/.

7. Hobolth used a different software tool by the company ABBYY to convert pdf files to Excel. To my knowledge, this is the only other effort to develop a database on EU and Schengen visa policies. EVD became available for use in 2014.

8. However, 100 can also mean that the applications were few in number: for example, Norway received 2 applications from Uzbekistan in 2015, both of which were issued.

9. There might be exceptions if, for one reason or another, countries have revoked a Schengen citizen's visa-waiver privileges. Such restrictions take the form of economic sanctions imposed against the individual. In addition, Schengen and EU nationals would still need a national (D) visa for longer-term stay. The EVD and my own data do not pool D visas together with short-term (A, B, C) visas.

10. I performed additional analysis with visas and trade treated as endogenous variables in two-stage probit. The Hausman and Durbin–Wu–Hausman tests ruled against endogeneity. Moreover, the coefficients were in the same direction, indicating that a single equation framework is appropriate.

11. Destination states in the sample all have Polity IV scores of 8 and above because these are all democratic countries. As Table 10 shows and to recap, Polity IV is a score ranging from −10 for a pure autocracy to 10 for a full democracy. As such, this obviates the need to control for destination states' democracy score.

12. http://www.mogenshobolth.dk/evd/ExploreConsularServices.aspx.

13. For regional categories, I use a modified version of the Central Intelligence Agency (CIA) Factbook, which records eleven regions as follows: Africa, Central Asia, East Asia, South Asia, Europe, Middle East, North America, Central America, South America, Oceania, and Antarctica. I use the first ten categories in this list but create a separate category for sub-Saharan Africa.

14. I use Stata's hetonly option to obtain PCSEs; this relaxes the assumption of panel homoscedasticity but assumes that no contemporaneous correlation is present. Lagrange multiplier (LM) tests for contemporaneous serial correlation were insignificant, which supports the choice of hetonly. The alternative is the independent option, which treats panel disturbances as homoscedastic instead. Results with the latter option are parallel. This is a reasonable constraint when estimating PCSEs given an unbalanced panel. Modeling both contemporaneous serial correlations at the same time proves too demanding if there are not sufficient numbers of panels with non-missing data. Piecewise deletion of panels drops too many cases and impedes convergence.

15. "Western Europe" is defined here as EU and Schengen members.

16. Including these variables does not change the findings; neither term emerges as significant.

17. The DPI's execrlc measures orientation on economic issues. Ideally we would like a more comprehensive measure of party orientation. However, the indicator is coded 1 if the party is conservative, Christian democratic, or right wing, which should also encompass orientation with respect to social issues.

### Chapter 4

1. I do not distinguish between types of barriers. The words "wall," "fence," and "barrier" are used interchangeably.

2. Hence the wall on Guantanamo Bay dividing U.S. territory from Cuba is not included; the U.S.-Cuba dyad has a COW Direct Contiguity score of 4, denoting a maritime boundary separated by 150 miles or less.

3. https://www.dur.ac.uk/ibru/publications/bulletin/.

4. http://en.wikipedia.org/wiki/Separation_barrier; http://nicolette.dk/borderbase.

5. A number of additional online pages proved informative. Among these were: a general commentary on the practice of fencing, http://subtopia.blogspot.co.uk/2007/04/border-to-border-wall-to-wall-fence-to.html. For the Greek-Turkish border, please see "Greece Finishes Border Fence" (2012); for the Pakistan-Afghanistan case, I consulted Ramesh 2005. For recent fences, including those imposed by European countries, I consulted recent news Batchelor 2015 and Witte 2016. For Russia's borders, see http://geocurrents.info/geopolitics/international-land-borders-hard-and-soft.

6. Most of these cases are motivated by the European migration crisis of 2015.

7. The original data include these cases and the chapter draws on the West Bank and Gaza cases as illustrative examples. ITERATE provides information on terrorists originating from these territorial units. Unfortunately, however, because of data unavailability on all other covariates for non-state territorial units, these cases drop out of my analysis. Hence, I acknowledge that the empirical analysis cannot speak specifically to the Israel-Palestine conflict.

8. The COW Bilateral Trade Data version 3.0 covers years up till 2009. Considering that the interstate fenced borders data extend to 2012, the lagged trade measure

would encompass the year 2010. I thus use the values for 2010 for the years 2011 and 2012.

9. The cubic polynomial cannot be included with fixed effects for the same reason that never-fenced cases are excluded.

10. All the supplementary checks discussed here are available from the author upon request.

11. Ideally, analysis would include bilateral FDI data. Previous chapters employ bilateral FDI data averaged from 2005 to 2008, sourced from Neumayer 2011. Given that the analysis in this chapter spans 1968 to 2012, utilizing this measure would not be appropriate because it would amount to using a forward lag of FDI on the right-hand side. The WDI measure is monadic and taps into capital openness of the builder rather than dyadic capital interdependence.

12. The technique is recommended by Keshk et al. (2004). I use the command cdsimeq in Stata, which is developed for simultaneous equations models in which one of the endogenous variables (terrorism) is continuous and the other endogenous variable (fences) is dichotomous. An alternative approach would be to fit a bivariate probit model, which is attuned to accommodating simultaneity bias. However, it is rather implausible that attacks will cause fence construction within the same border year, since it generally takes years after the initial policy decision to commence building.

## Chapter 5

1. Data come from UNCTAD statistics: "Inward and Outward Direct Investment Flows," http://unctadstat.unctad.org/ReportFolders/reportFolders.aspx.

2. Supplement to *Euromoney* (February 1982):5.

3. The list has been modified in stages over time. The current list of countries under each category is available from the Turkish General Directorate of Security (Emniyet Genel Müdürlügü [EGM]), www.egm.gov.tr.

4. At the time Cüneyt Canver was a member of Parliament from Adana for one of the opposition parties, Halkçı Parti, a nationalist party that later became known as the SHP, the Social Democratic People's Party.

5. The geographical limitation classified political migrants according to their countries of origin. The first tier—convention refugees—comprised migrants of European origin who enjoy all the rights granted by the Geneva Convention and are granted de jure refugee status, with the expectation that they will eventually be resettled or return to their countries of origin. Middle Eastern citizens were designated as non-convention refugees. This allowed Turkey to pursue a pragmatic policy of allowing citizens from this category to remain on Turkish soil without full refugee status.

6. The Ankara agreement ensured visa-free short-term travel not for all citizens but for specific categories of individuals: businesspeople, service providers, academics, and employers.

7. Visas at borders mostly serve a revenue rather than security maintenance function. See Neumayer 2006.

8. Hatay had been incorporated into Turkey in 1939 after first declaring its independence from French Syria in 1938 and then voting to join Turkey in 1939.

9. Özal was the prime minister from 1983 until 1989; from 1989 until his death in 1993, he served as Turkey's eighth president. Although the president as the head of state in Turkey mostly enjoys symbolic powers, Özal's ideas about liberalism continued to be influential in this period as well.

10. Signatory states are Afghanistan, Azerbaijan, Iran, Kazakhstan, Kyrgyzstan, Pakistan, Tajikistan, Turkey, Turkmenistan, and Uzbekistan.

11. The new system introduces two main categories of visas: the short-term visa for tourism, business, and family visits and the new airport-transit visa.

12. As of 2013, eleven EU states were on the e-visa list while sixteen EU members were exempted from visas. Since then, Turkey has instituted the new ninety-day-stay visa-at-the-border for EU nationals.

13. Nabucco wanted to carry gas across Turkey from Azerbaijan to the Middle East. Other important pipelines are Baku-Tblisi-Ceyhan (BTC), which transports oil, and Baku-Tblisi-Erzurum (BTE), which transport gas through the Black Sea and Caucasus region.

14. http://www.mfa.gov.tr/visa-information-for-foreigners.en.mfa.

15. For a current list of e-visa origin states, see https://www.evisa.gov.tr/en/info/who-is-eligible-for-e-visa/.

16. Of course, we should bear in mind the possibility that smugglers will find alternate routes.

# BIBLIOGRAPHY

Abrahms, Max. 2006. "Why Terrorism Does Not Work." *International Security* 31 (2):42–78.

———. 2012. "Does Terrorism Really Work? Evolution in the Conventional Wisdom Since 9/11." *Defence and Peace Economics* 22 (6):583–594.

———. 2013. "The Credibility Paradox: Violence as a Double-Edged Sword in International Politics." *International Studies Quarterly* 57:660–671.

Adamson, Fiona. 2006. "Crossing Borders: International Migration and National Security." *International Security* 31 (1):165–99.

Afanasieva, Dasha. 2014. "Turkey Builds Wall in Token Effort to Secure Border with Syria." Reuters, May 5. http://www.reuters.com/article/us-syria-crisis-turkey-wall -idUSBREA4409Z20140505.

Agnew, J. 1994. "The Territorial Trap: The Geographical Assumptions of International Relations Theory." *Review of International Political Economy* 1 (1):53–80.

Ahmad, F. 1993. *The Making of Modern Turkey.* London: Routledge.

Ahmed, Yasmin. 2016. "Downing Street Raises the Belgian Flag and We Tweet for Brussels—But Where Was This Sympathy After Ankara?" *Independent*, March 22, 2016.

Ai, Chunrong, and Edward C. Norton. 2003. "Interaction Terms in Logit and Probit Models." *Economics Letters* 80:123–129.

Ajaka, Nadine. 2015. "Paris, Beirut, and the Language Used to Describe Terrorism." *Atlantic*, November 17. http://www.theatlantic.com/international/archive/2015/11 /paris-beirut-media-coverage/416457/.

Akcinaroglu, Seden, Jonathan DiCicco, and Elizabeth Radziszewski. 2010. "Avalanches and Olive Branches: A Multimethod Analysis of Disasters and Peacemaking in Interstate Rivalries." *Political Research Quarterly* 64 (2):260–275.

Akman, Adem, and İsmail Kılınç. 2010. "AB'de Entegre Sınır Yönetiminin Gelişimi ve AB Sürecinde Türkiye'nin Entegre Sınır Yönetimine Geçiş Çalışmaları" [The Development of Integrated Border Management in the EU and the Works on Turkey's Transition into Integrated Border Management in the EU Process]. *Türk İdare Dergisi* [Turkish Administration Journal] 467 (June):9–28.

Aksoy, Murat U. 2007. "Avrupa Hukuku Açısıdan Türk Vatandaşlarına Uygulanan Vize Alma Mecburiyetinin Değerlendirilmesi Raporu." In *Iktisadi Kalkınma Yayınları 213*. Istanbul: IKV.

Aktan, C. Coşkun. 1991 (1993). "Turkey: From Inward-Oriented Etatism to Outward Looking Liberal Strategy." *Turkish Public Administration Annual* 17–19:55–85.

———. 1996. "Turgut Özal'ın Değişim Modeli ve Değişime Karşı Direnen Güçlerin Tahlili." *Türkiye Günlüğü Dergisi* 40 (5):15–31.

Albert, Mathias, David Jacobson, and Yosef Lapid. 2001. *Identities, Borders, Orders: Rethinking International Relations Theory*. Minneapolis: University of Minnesota Press.

Allison, Paul. 2009. *Fixed Effects Regression Models for Categorical Data, Quantitative Applications in the Social Sciences*. Thousand Oaks, Calif.: Sage Publications.

Allouche, J., and J. Lind. 2010. "Public Attitudes to Global Uncertainties: A Research Synthesis Exploring the Trends and Gaps in Knowledge." Institute of Development Studies. https://esrc.ukri.org/files/public-engagement/public-dialogues/full-report -public-attitudes-to-global-uncertainties/.

Altheide, D. 2006. "Terrorism and the Politics of Fear." *Cultural Studies* 6 (4):415–439.

Andreas, Peter. 2000. *Border Games*. Ithaca, N.Y.: Cornell University Press.

———. 2003a. "Redrawing the Line: Borders and Security in the Twenty-First Century." *International Security* 28 (2):78–111.

———. 2003b. "A Tale of Two Borders: The US-Canada and US-Mexico Lines After 9-11." In *The Rebordering of North America*, edited by Peter Andreas and Thomas J. Biersteker, 1–24. New York: Routledge.

———. 2004. "Illicit International Political Economy: The Clandestine Side of Globalization." *Review of International Political Economy* 11 (3):641–652.

———. 2009. *Border Games: Policing the US-Mexico Divide*. 2nd ed. Cornell Studies in Political Economy. Ithaca, N.Y.: Cornell University Press.

Andreas, Peter, and Ethan Nadelman. 2006. *Policing the Globe: Criminilization and Crime Control in International Relations*. New York: Oxford University Press.

Andreas, Peter, and Price Richard. 2001. "From War Fighting to Crime Fighting: Transforming the American National Security State." *International Studies Review* 3 (3):31–52.

Annual Surveys of Freedom Country Ratings 1972 to 2003. 2004. *Freedom House Index*. New York: Freedom House.

Arango, Tim. 2015. "Turkey Moves to Clamp Down on Border, Long a Revolving Door." *New York Times*, December 22. https://www.nytimes.com/2015/12/23/world /europe/turkey-border-refugees.html.

Arin, Tulay. 1998. *Financial Markets and Globalization in Turkey*. Istanbul: University of Istanbul Press.

Attanasio, Cedar. 2016. "Visa Overstays By The Numbers: 7 Things You Need to Know About a Festering Immigration Controversy." *Los Angeles Times*, January 21.

https://www.latintimes.com/visa-overstays-numbers-7-things-you-need-know
-about-festering-immigration-controversy-365355.

Atzili, Boaz. 2006. "When Good Fences Make Bad Neighbors: Fixed Borders, State
Weakness, and International Conflict." *International Security* 31 (3):139–173.

Avdan, Nazli. 2012. "Human Trafficking and Migration Control Policy: Vicious or Vir-
tuous Cycle." *Journal of Public Policy* 32 (2):1–35.

———. 2014a. "Controlling Access to Territory: Economic Interdependence, Transnational Terrorism, and Visa Policies." *Journal of Conflict Resolution* 58 (4):592–624.
doi: 10.1177/0022002713478795.

———. 2014b. "Do Asylum Recognition Rates in Europe Respond to Transnational
Terrorism? The Migration-Security Nexus Revisited." *European Union Politics* 15
(4):445–471.

Avdan, Nazli, and Christopher F. Gelpi. 2017. "Do Good Fences Make Good Neighbors? State Border Characteristics and the Transnational Flow of Terrorist Violence."
*International Studies Quarterly* 61 (1):14–27.

Aygül, Cenk. 2013. "Visa Regimes as Power: The Cases of the EU and Turkey." *Alternatives:
Global, Local, Political* 38 (4):321–337.

Babali, Tuncay. 2009. "Turkey at the Energy Crossroads." *Middle East Quarterly* 16
(2):25–33.

Bacik, Gokhan, and Bezen B. Coskun. 2011. "The PKK Problem: Explaining Turkey's
Failure to Develop a Political Solution." *Studies in Conflict and Terrorism* 34
(3):248–265. doi: 10.1080/1057610X.2011.545938.

Baker, Peter. 2017. "Trump Supports Plan to Cut Legal Immigration by Half." *New York
Times*, August 2. https://www.nytimes.com/2017/08/02/us/politics/trump-immigration
.html?mcubz=0.

Banco, Erin. 2014. "In Fight Against ISIS, US Needs Turkey to Stop Flow of Money,
Supplies, Foreign Fighters." *International Business Times*, September 14. http://
www.ibtimes.com/fight-against-isis-us-needs-turkey-stop-flow-money-supplies
-foreign-fighters-1688282.

Barbieri, Katherine, and Omar M. G. Keshk. 2012. Correlates of War Project Trade Data
Set Codebook.

Barbieri, Katherine, Omar M. G. Keshk, and Brian M. Pollins. 2009. "TRADING
DATA: Evaluating Our Assumptions and Coding Rules." *Conflict Management and
Peace Science* 26 (5):471–491.

Batchelor, Tom. 2015. "The New Iron Curtains: Where the Fences Are Going Up Across
Europe to Keep Migrants Out." *Sunday Express*, December 6. https://www.express
.co.uk/news/world/624488/Europe-border-fences-migrant-crisis.

Beck, Nathaniel. 2001. "Time Series Cross-Section Data: What Have We Learned in
the Past Years?" *Annual Review of Political Science* 4:271–93.

Beck, Nathaniel, and Jonathan N. Katz. 1995. "What to Do (and Not to Do) with Time-
Series Cross-Section Data." *American Political Science Review* 89:634–647.

Beck, Nathaniel, Jonathan N. Katz, and Richard Tucker. 1998. "Taking Time Seriously: Time-Series-Cross-Section Analysis with a Binary Dependent Variable." *American Journal of Political Science* 42 (4):1260–1288.

Beck, Thorsten, George Clarke, Alberto Groff, Philip Keefer, and Patrick Walsh. 2001. "New Tools in Comparative Political Economy: The Database of Political Institutions." *World Bank Economic Review* 15 (1):165–176.

Bennett, Andrew. 2010. "Process Tracing and Causal Inference." In *Rethinking Social Inquiry: Diverse Tools, Shared Standards*, edited by Henry E. Brady and David Collier. Lanham, Md.: Rowman and Littlefield.

Bensemra, Zohra. 2016. "After Islamist Attacks, Tunisia's Tourism Struggles." *Reuters*, June 25. https://www.reuters.com/article/us-tunisia-tourism/after-islamist-attacks -tunisias-tourism-struggles-idUSKCN0ZB0B8.

Bertrand, Natasha. 2016. "'Relax, They Are Our Friends': One Quote Shows Why Turkey's ISIS Problem Is Only Going to Get Worse." *Business Insider*, April 15. https:// www.businessinsider.com.au/turkey-isis-syria-border-problem-2016-4.

Betts, Alexander. 2013. *Survival Migration: Failed Governance and the Crisis of Displacement*. Ithaca, N.Y.: Cornell University Press.

Bever, Lindsey, Derek Hawkins, and Nick Miroff. 2017. "Slain Border Agent May Have Been Beaten to Death by Rocks in 'Grisly Scene,' Union Leader Says." *Washington Post*, November 20.

Biersteker, Thomas J. 2002. "State, Sovereignty, and Territory." In *Handbook of International Relations*, edited by Walter Carlsnaes, Thomas Risse, and Beth A. Simmons, 157–177. London: Sage Publications.

Bigo, Didier. 1997. "Security, Borders, and the State." In *Borders and Border Regions in Europe and North America*. San Diego: San Diego State University Press.

———. 2000. *Border Regimes and Security in an Enlarged European Community Police Cooperation with CEECs: Between Trust and Obligation*. Vol. 65, *EUI Working Papers*. San Domenico European University Institute.

———. 2005. "Frontier Controls in the European Union. Who Is in Control?" In *Controlling Frontiers. Free Movement into and Within Europe*, edited by Didier Bigo and E. Guild. London: Ashgate.

———. 2011. "Freedom and Speed in Enlarged Borderzones." In *The Contested Politics of Mobility: Borderzones and Irregularity*, edited by V. Squire, 31–50. New York: Routledge.

———. 2014. "The (In)securitization Practices of the Three Universes of EU Border Control: Military/Navy—Border Guards/Police—Database Analsyts." *Security Dialogue* 45:209–225.

Blomberg, S. Brock, and Gregory D. Hess. 2008. "The Lexus and the Olive Branch: Globalization, Democratization and Terrorism." In *Terrorism, Economic Development, and Political Openness*, edited by P. Keefer and N. Loayza, 116–147. New York: Cambridge University Press.

Boehmer, Charles R., and Sergio Peña. 2012. "The Determinants of Open and Closed Borders." *Journal of Borderlands Studies* 27 (3):273–285.

Bove, Vincenzo, and Tobias Bohmelt. 2015. "Does Immigration Induce Terrorism." *Journal of Politics*. doi: 10.1086/684679.

Brady, Henry E., and David Collier. 2004. *Rethinking Social Inquiry: Diverse Tools, Shared Standards*. Oxford: Rowman and Littlefield.

Braithwaite, Alex. 2013. "The Logic of Public Fear in Terrorism and Counter-terrorism." *Journal of Police and Criminal Psychology* 28:95–101.

Braithwaite, Alexander, and Quan Li. 2007. "Transnational Terrorism Hot Spots: Identification and Impact Evaluation." *Conflict Management and Peace Science* 24 (4):281–294.

Brambor, Thomas, William Roberts Clark, and Matt Golder. 2006. "Understanding Interaction Models: Improving Econometric Analyses." *Political Analysis* 14:63–82.

Brochmann, G., and T. Hammar. 1999. *Mechanisms of Immigration Control*. Oxford: Berg.

Brown, W. 2010. *Walled States, Waning Sovereignty*. New York: Zone Books.

Brubaker, Rogers. 1992. *Citizenship and Nationhood in France and Germany*. Cambridge, Mass.: Harvard University Press.

Bueno de Mesquita, Ethan. 2005. "Conciliation, Commitment, and Counterterrorism." *International Organization* 59:145–176.

Burke, Jason. 2017. "Salman Abedi: Why Manchester Bomber Fits Profile of Other Terrorists." *Guardian*, May 25.

Buthe, Tim. 2002. "Taking Temporality Seriously: Modeling History and the Use of Narratives as Evidence." *American Political Science Review* 96 (3):481–493.

Butler, Daren. 2017. "Turkey Captures Nightclub Attacker Who Acted for Islamic State." *Reuters*, January 17.

Button, S. H. 1995. "Turkey Struggles with Kurdish Separatism." *Military Review* 75:20.

Buzan, Barry, Waever Ole, and Jaap de Wilde. 1998. *Security: A New Framework for Analysis*. Boulder, Colo.: Rienner Publishers.

Byman, Daniel. 2005. *Deadly Connections: States That Sponsor Terrorism*. Cambridge: Cambridge University Press.

Çağlayan, Zafer. 2005. "AB Ülkelerinin Vize Engeli Türk İşadamının Onurunu Kırmıştır." *Asomedya*, 75.

Cakar, Bekir, Mahmut Cengiz, and Fatih Tombul. 2011. "The History of the PKK." In *The PKK: Financial Sources, Social and Political Dimensions*, edited by Charles Strozier and James Frank, 1–29. New York: Columbia University Press.

Callimachi, Rukmini, Alissa J. Rubin, and Laure Fourquet. 2016. "A View of ISIS's Evolution in New Details of Paris Attacks." *New York Times*, March 19. https://www.nytimes.com/2016/03/20/world/europe/a-view-of-isiss-evolution-in-new-details-of-paris-attacks.html?_r=0.

Çandar, Cengiz. 2011. "Dağdan İniş–PKK Nasıl Silah Bırakır?" TESEV Raporu. http://hakikatadalethafiza.org/wp-content/uploads/2015/01/TESEV-2011-Da%C4%9Fdan-%C4%B0ni%C5%9F_PKK-Nas%C4%B1l-Silah-B%C4%B1rak%C4%B1r.pdf.

Canuto, Otaviano. 2017. "Beyond the Ballot: Turkey's Economy at the Crossroads." April 2. https://seekingalpha.com/article/4059644-beyond-ballot-turkeys-economy -crossroads.

Caprioli, Mary, and Peter F. Trumbore. 2005. "Rhetoric Versus Reality: Rogue States in Interstate Conflict." *Journal of Conflict Resolution* 49 (5):770–791.

Carter, David B. and Curtis S. Signorino. 2010. "Back to the Future: Modeling Temporal Dependence in Binary Data." *Political Analysis* 18(3):271–292.

Carter, David B., and Paul Poast. 2015. "Why Do States Build Walls? Political Economy, Security, and Border Stability." *Journal of Conflict Resolution.* doi: 10.1177/0022002715596776.

Chenoweth, Erica. 2010. "Democratic Competition and Terrorist Activity." *Journal of Politics* 72 (1):16–30.

Ciftci, Irfan, and Sedat Kula. 2015. "The Evaluation of the Effectiveness of Counterterrorism Policies on the PKK-Inflicted Violence During the Democratization Process of Turkey." *Journal of Terrorism Research* 6 (1):27–42.

Clausewitz, C., Beatrice Heuser, Michael Howard, and Peter Paret. 2006. *On War.* Oxford: Oxford University Press.

Coelho, Carlos. 2017. Fencing off Europe." *Radio Free Europe*, February 10. https://www .rferl.org/a/fencing-off-europe/27562610.html.

Cole, Juan. 2015. *The Great Wall of Turkey? Ankara Imagines DMZ w/ Kurds, ISIL.* https://www.juancole.com/2015/06/turkey-ankara-imagines.html.

Collier, David. 2011. "Understanding Process Tracing." *PS: Political Science and Politics* 44 (4):823–830.

———. 2013. *Exodus: How Migration Is Changing Our World.* Oxford: Oxford University Press.

COM (European Commission). 2001 [2003]. "National Programme for the Adoption of the Acquis (NPAA)." ec.europa.eu/enlargement/pdf/turkey/summary_en.pdf. Brussels: Enlargement DG.

———. 2013a. "Overview of Schengen Visa Statistics, 2009–2012." http://ec.europa.eu/dgs /home-affairs/what-we-do/policies/borders-and-visas/visapolicy/index_en.htm.

———. 2013b. "Visa Statistics for 2010, 2011 and 2013." Brussels: European Commission. https://ec.europa.eu/home-affairs/what-we-do/policies/borders-and-visas /visa-policy_en.

———. 2015. "Complete Statistics on Short-Stay Visas Issued by the Schengen States." Brussels: European Commission.

Cornelius, Wayne A., Takeyuki Tsuda, Philip L. Martin, and James F. Hollifield, eds. 2004. *Controlling Immigration: A Global Perspective.* 2nd ed. Stanford, Calif.: Stanford University Press.

Council of the European Union. 2006. Council Conclusions of 4–5 December 2006 on Integrated Border Management. Press Release 15801/06. Brussels: Council of the European Union. https://www.consilium.europa.eu/ueDocs/cms_Data/docs /pressData/en/jha/91997.pdf.

———. 2009. Exchange of Statistical Information on Uniform Visas Issued by Member States' Diplomatic Missions and Consular Posts. Brussels: Council General Secretariat.

COW (Correlates of War). 2007. Correlates of War Project. Direct Contiguity Data, 1816–2006. Version 3.1. http://correlatesofwar.org.

———. 2013. World Religion Database Version 1.1. http://www.correlatesofwar.org /data-sets/world-religion-data.

Cowburn, Ashley. 2016. "EU Referendum: Fury as Leave Campaign Warns of 'Orlando-Style Atrocity' in UK Unless Brexit Wins." *Independent*, June 13. http://www .independent.co.uk/news/uk/politics/eu-referendum-brexit-leave-poster-orlando -shooting-free-movement-atrocity-a7079511.html.

Crenshaw, Martha. 2010. "The Consequences of Counterterrorism." In *The Consequences of Counterterrorism*, edited by Martha Crenshaw, 1–30. New York: Russell Sage Foundation.

Cronin, Audrey Kurth. 2002. "Behind the Curve: The Globalization of Terrorism." *International Security* 27 (3):30–58.

Czaika, Mathias, and Hein de Haas. 2013. "The Effectiveness of Immigration Policies." *Population and Development Review* 39 (3):487–508.

———. 2015. "The Globalization of Migration: Has the World Become More Migratory?" *International Migration Review* 48 (2):283–323.

Czaika, Mathias, and Mogens Hobolth. 2016. "Do Restrictive Asylum and Visa Policies Increase Irregular Migration into Europe?" *European Union Politics*. doi: 10.1177/1465116516633299.

Davis, Darren D., and Brian Silver. 2004. "Civil Liberties vs. Security in the Context of the Terrorist Attacks on America." *American Journal of Political Science* 48 (1):28–46.

Disdier, Anne-Célia, and Keith Head. 2008. "The Puzzling Persistence of the Distance Effect on Bilateral Trade." *Review of Economics and Statistics* 90 (1):37–48.

Dishman, Chris. 2005. "The Leaderless Nexus: When Crime and Terror Converge." *Studies in Conflict and Terrorism* 28:237–252.

"Dışişleri Bakanı Davutoğlu, 'e-Viza devrim mahiyetinde bir uygulamadir" [Foreign Minister Davutoğlu 'e-Visa is a revolutionary application]. 2013. Republic of Turkey Ministry of Foreign Affairs, April 24. http://www.mfa.gov.tr/disisleri-bakani -davutoglu-e-vize-devrim-mahiyetinde-bir-uygulamadir.tr.mfa.

Domke, William K. 1988. *War and the Changing Global System*. New Haven, Conn.: Yale University Press.

Donaldson, John W. 2005. "Fencing the Line: Analysis of the Recent Rise in Security Measures Along Disputed and Undisputed Boundaries." In *Global Surveillance and Policing: Borders, Security, Identity*, edited by Elia Zureik and Mark B. Salter. Portland, Ore.: Willan Publishing.

Doty, Roxanne Lyn. 1998. "Immigration and the Politics of Security." *Security Studies* 8 (2):71–95.

Doyle, Michael W. 1997. *Ways of War and Peace: Realism, Liberalism, and Socialism*. New York: W. W. Norton.

Eckstein, Harry. 1975. "Handbook of Political Science." In *Handbook of Political Science*, edited by Fred I. Greenstein and Nelson W. Polsby, 79–137. Reading, Mass.: Addison-Wesley.

Eddy, Melissa. 2016. "Germany Seeks Tunisian Tied to Berlin Christmas Market Attack." *New York Times*, December 21. https://www.nytimes.com/2016/12/21/world/europe/berlin-christmas-market-attack.html?mcubz=0.

Eder, Mine, A. Yakovlev, and Ali Çarkoğlu. 2003. "Suitcase Trade Between Turkey and Russia: Microeconomics and Institutional Structure." Working Paper WP4/2003/07. Moscow: Moscow State University.

Elden, S. 2013. "Secure the Volume: Vertical Geopolitics and the Depth of Power." *Political Geography* 34:35–51.

Enders, Walter, Gary A. Hoover, and Todd Sandler. 2016. "The Changing Nonlinear Relationship Between Income and Terrorism." *Journal of Conflict Resolution* 60 (2):195–225.

Enders, Walter, and Todd Sandler. 2005. "After 9/11: Is It All Different Now?" *Journal of Conflict Resolution* 49:259–267.

———. 2006a. "Distribution of Transnational Terrorism Among Countries by Income Class and Geography After 9/11." *International Studies Quarterly* 50 (2):367–393.

———. 2006b. *The Political Economy of Terrorism*. New York: Cambridge University Press.

Enders, Walter, Todd Sandler, and Khusrav Gaibulloev. 2011. "Domestic Versus Transnational Terrorism: Data, Decomposition, and Dynamics." *Journal of Peace Research* 48 (3):319–337.

Enders, Walter, and X. Su. 2007. "Rational Terrorists and Optimal Network Structure." *Journal of Conflict Resolution* 51 (1):33–57.

Entous, Adam, and Gordon Lubold. 2015. "U.S. Urges Turkey to Seal Border." *Wall Street Journal*, November 27. https://www.wsj.com/articles/u-s-urges-turkey-to-seal-syria-border-1448674401.

Epifanio, Mariaelisa. 2011. "Legislative Response to International Terrorism." *Journal of Peace Research* 48 (3):399–411.

Erik, Gartzke, and Quan Li. 2003. "War, Peace, and the Invisible Hand: Positive Political Externalities of Economic Globalization." *International Studies Quarterly* 47:561–586.

Erlanger, Steven. 2016. "Brussels Attacks Fuel Debate over Migrants in a Fractured Europe." *New York Times*, March 22. https://www.nytimes.com/2016/03/23/world/europe/belgium-attacks-migrants.html.

Eubank, W. L., and L. Weinberg. 1994. "Does Democracy Encourage Terrorism." *Terrorism and Political Violence* 6 (4):417–463.

"Europe's Response to the Paris Attacks Is Different This Time." 2015. *Economist*, November 14. https://www.economist.com/news/europe/21678514-je-suis-charlie-was-about-free-speech-time-issue-migrants-europe-sees-paris-attacks.

Feldman, S., and K. Stenner. 1997. "Perceived Threat and Authoritarianism." *Political Psychology* 18:741–770.

Ferris, Elizabeth, and Kemal Kirişçi. 2015. "What Turkey's Open Door Policy Means for Syrian Refugees." Washington, D.C.: Brookings Institution Press.

Finotelli, Claudia, and Giuseppe Sciortino. 2013. "Through the Gates of the Fortress: European Visa Policies and the Limits of Immigration Control." *Perspectives on European Politics and Society* 14 (1):80–101.

Fitzgerald, Jennifer, David A. Leblang, and Jessica Teets. 2014. "Defying the Law of Gravity: The Political Economy of International Migration." *World Politics* 66 (3):406–445.

Fitzgerald, Sandy. 2015. "Obama Administration Calls for Turkey to Seal Off Syrian Border." *Newsmax,* April 24. https://www.newsmax.com/Headline/turkey-seal -syria-border/2015/11/28/id/703738/.

Flynn, Stepher E. 2000. "Beyond Border Control." *Foreign Affairs* 79:57–68.

Flynn, Stephen E. 2003. "The False Conundrum: Continental Integration Versus Homeland Security." In *The Rebordering of North America*, edited by Peter Andreas and Thomas J. Biersteker, 110–128. New York: Routledge.

Fordham, Benjamin O., and Katja B. Kleinberg. 2010. "Trade and Foreign Policy Attitudes." *Journal of Conflict Resolution* 54 (5):687–714.

Franzese, Robert J. 1996. "A Gauss Procedure to Estimate Panel-Corrected-Standard-Errors with Non-rectangular and/or Missing Data." *Political Methodologist* 7 (2):2–3.

Freeman, Gary P. 1995. "Modes of Immigration Politics in Liberal Democratic States." *International Migration Review* 29 (4):881–902.

———. 1998. "The Decline of Sovereignty? Politics and Immigration Restriction in Liberal States." In *Challenge to the Nation-State: Immigration in Western Europe and the United States*, edited by Christian Joppke, 86–109. New York: Oxford University Press.

———. 2001. "Client Politics or Populism: Immigration Reform in the United States." In *Controlling a New Migration World*, edited by C. Joppke and V. Guiraudon. New York: Routledge.

Friedland, N., and A. Merari. 1985. "The Psychological Impact of Terrorism: A Double-Edged Sword." *Political Psychology* 6:591–604.

Friedman, Benjamin. 2011. "Managing Fear: The Politics of Homeland Security." *Political Science Quarterly* 126 (1):77–106.

Friedman, Thomas L. 1999. *The Lexus and the Olive Tree*. New York: Anchor Books.

Frontex. 2014. "Governance Documents." https://frontex.europa.eu/.

Gavrilis, George. 2008a. *The Dynamics of Interstate Boundaries*. Cambridge: Cambridge University Press.

———. 2008b. "The Greek-Ottoman Boundary as Institution, Locality, and Process, 1832–1882." *American Behavioral Scientist* 51 (10):1516–1537.

————. 2011. "Boundary Making and Boundary Disputes." In *International Encyclo-pedia of Political Science*, edited by Bertrand Badie, Dirk Berg-Schlosser, and Leon-ardo Morlino, 81–85. New York: CQ Press.

Gearson, John. 2002. "The Nature of Modern Terrorism." *Political Quarterly* 73 (1):7–24.

Geddes, Anthony. 2003. *The Politics of Migration and Immigration in Europe*. Thou-sand Oaks, Calif.: Sage Publications.

Gelpi, Christopher, and Nazli Avdan. 2015. "Democracies at Risk? A Forecasting Analysis of Regime Type and the Risk of Terrorist Attack." *Conflict Management and Peace Science* 35 (1):1–25. doi: 10.1177/0738894215608998.

Gelpi, Christopher, and Joseph Grieco. 2008. "Democracy, Trade, and the Nature of the Liberal Peace." *Journal of Peace Research* 45 (1):17–36.

Gibler, Douglas M. 2009. *International Military Alliances, 1648–2008*. Washington, D.C.: CQ Press.

Gleditsch, Kristian S. and Michael D. Ward. 2001. "Measuring Space: A Minimum-Distance Database and Applications to International Studies." *Journal of Peace Research* 38 (6):739–758.

Gleditsch, Nils Petter, Peter Wallensteen, Mikael Eriksson, Margareta Sollenberg, and Håvard Strand. 2002. "Armed Conflict 1946–2001: A New Dataset." *Journal of Peace Research* 39 (5):615–637.

Goertz, Gary, Jim Klein, and Paul Diehl. 2006. "The New Rivalry Data Set: Procedures and Patterns." *Journal of Peace Research* 43 (3):331–348.

Graham, David A. 2015. "The Empathy Gap Between Paris and Beirut." *Atlantic*, No-vember 16. http://www.theatlantic.com/international/archive/2015/11/paris-beirut -terrorism-empathy-gap/416121/.

"Greece Finishes Border Fence with Turkey." 2012. *Novinite*, December 17. http://www .novinite.com/view_news.php?id=146114.

Greene, William H. 1997. *Econometric Analysis*. 5th ed. Upper Saddle River, N.J.: Prentice Hall.

GTD (Global Terrorism Database). 2016. National Consortium for the Study of Ter-rorism and Responses to Terrorism (START). http://www.start.umd.edu/gtd/.

Guild, Elspelth. 2009. *Security and Migration in the 21st Century*. Cambridge: Polity.

Hale, William 2000. "Economic Issues in Turkish Foreign Policy." In *Turkey's New World: Changing Dynamics in Turkish Foreign Policy*, edited by Alan Makovsky and Sabri Sayarı. Washington, D.C.: Washington Institute for Near East Policy.

Hale, William. 2002. *Turkish Foreign Policy, 1774–2000*. London: Frank Cass Publishers.

Hassner, Ron, and Jason Wittenberg. 2015. "Barriers to Entry? Who Builds Fortified Boundaries and Why." *International Security* 40 (1):157–190.

Hegghammer, Thomas, and Petter Nesser. 2015. "Assessing the Islamic State's Com-mitment to Attacking the West." *Perspectives on Terrorism* 9 (4):14–29.

Helfstein, Scott, and John Solomon. 2014. *Risky Business: The Global Threat Network and the Politics of Contraband*. West Point, N.Y.: Combating Terrorism Center.

Hensel, Paul R. 2000. "Territory: Theory and Evidence on Geography and Conflict." In *What Do We Know About War?* edited by John A. Vasquez, 57–84. Lanham, Md.: Rowman and Littlefield.

Hiscox, M. 2006. "Through a Glass Darkly: Attitudes Towards International Trade and the Curious Effects of Issue Framing." *International Organization* 60 (3):755–80.

Hobolth, Mogens. 2012. *Border Control Cooperation in the European Union: The Schengen Visa Policy in Practice.* London: London School of Economics and Political Science.

———. 2013. "Researching Mobility Barriers: The European Visa Database." *Journal of Ethnic and Migration Studies* 40 (3):424–435.

Hoffman, Bruce. 1998. *Inside Terrorism.* New York: Columbia University Press.

Hollifield, J. F. 1992. *Immigrants, Markets, and States: The Political Economy of Postwar Europe.* Cambridge, Mass.: Harvard University Press.

———. 2000. "The Politics of International Migration: How Can We 'Bring the State Back in'?" In *Migration Theory: Talking Across the Disciplines*, edited by C. B. Brettell and J. F. Hollifield, 137–185. New York: Routledge.

Hollifield, J. F., and Gary Zuk. 1998. "Immigrants, Markets, and Rights." In *Immigration Citizenship and the Welfare State in Germany and the United States: Immigrant Incorporation*, edited by H. Kurthen, J. Fijalkowski, and Gert G. Wagner, 133–167. Stanford, Calif.: JAI Press.

Hope, Christopher, David Barrett, and Camilla Turner. 2016. "Security of Britain's Porous Borders Must Be Reviewed as Isil Threatens Summer of Tourist Massacres." *Telegraph*, April 20. https://www.telegraph.co.uk/news/2016/04/19/review-the-security-of-our-borders-to-keep-britain-safe-say-form/.

Horowitz, Michael C. 2010. "Nonstate Actors and the Diffusion of Innovations: The Case of Suicide Terrorism." *International Organization* 64 (1):33–64.

Høyland, B., I. Sircar, I. and S. Hix. 2009. "Forum Section: An Automated Database of the European Parliament." *European Union Politics* 10 (1):143–152.

Hubbard, Ben, and Karam Shoumali. 2015. "Fertilizer, Also Suited for Bombs, Flows to ISIS Territory from Turkey." *New York Times*, May 4.

Huddy, Leonie, Stanley Feldman, Theresa Capelos, and Colin Provost. 2002. "The Consequences of Terrorism: Disentangling the Effects of Personal and National Threat." *Political Psychology* 23:485–509.

Huddy, Leonie, Stanley Feldman, Charles Taber, and Gallya Lahav. 2005. "Threat, Anxiety, and Support for Antiterrorism Policies." *American Journal of Political Science* 49 (3):593–608.

Huth, Paul K. 1996. *Standing Your Ground.* Ann Arbor: University of Michigan Press.

Huysmans, Jef. 2006. *The Politics of Insecurity: Fear, Migration, and Asylum in the EU.* New York: Routledge.

IATA (International Air Transport Association). 2010. "Travel Information Manual." Edited by International Air Transport Association. Badhoevedorp.

İçduygu, Ahmet. 2004. "Demographic Mobility and Turkey: Migration Experiences and Government Responses." *Mediterranean Quarterly* 15 (4):88–99.

———. 2009. "International Migration and Human Development in Turkey." Munich: UNDP Human Development Research Paper 2009/52.

İçduygu, Ahmet, and Damla B. Aksel. 2013. "Turkish Migration Policies: A Critical Historical Perspective." *Perceptions* 18 (3):167–190.

İçduygu, Ahmet, and Kemal Kirişçi. 2009. "Turkey's International Migration in Transition." In *Land of Diverse Migrations: Challenges of Emigration and Immigration in Turkey*, edited by Ahmet İçduygu and Kemal Kirişçi, 1–25. Istanbul: Istanbul Bilgi University Press.

İçduygu, Ahmet, and Deniz Yükseker. 2010. "Rethinking the Transit Migration in Turkey: Reality and Re-presentation in the Creation of a Migratory Phenomenon." *Population, Space, and Place* 18 (November):441–456.

International Crisis Group. 2010. "Turkey and the Middle East: Ambitions and Constraints." Europe Report No. 203. April 7. https://www.crisisgroup.org/europe-central-asia/western-europemediterranean/turkey/turkey-and-middle-east-ambitions-and-constraints.

"Iran Constructing Fence on Pakistan Border." 2011. Tribune, April 16. https://tribune.com.pk/story/150669/iran-constructing-fence-on-pakistan-border/.

"Israel to Fortify Border Fence to Stop 'Forces of Radical Islam.'" 2014. NBC News, June 30. https://www.nbcnews.com/news/world/israel-fortify-border-fence-stop-forces-radical-islam-n144181.

Ivanovic, Tea. 2016. "Brussels as the Perfect Target: A Shock, but Not a Surprise." *SAIS Observer*, April 6. https://saisobserver.org/2016/04/06/brussels-as-the-perfect-target-a-shock-but-not-a-surprise-2/.

Jellissen, Susan M., and Fred M. Gottheil. 2013. "On the Utility of Security Fences Along International Borders." *Defense & Security Analysis*. doi: 10.1080/14751798.2013.842707.

John, Tara. 2015. "This Is Why Border Fences Don't Work." *Time*, October 22. http://time.com/4080637/this-is-why-border-fences-dont-work/.

Jones, Reece. 2012a. *Border Walls: Security and the War on Terror in the United States, India, and Israel.* London: Zed Books Ltd.

———. 2012b. "Something There Is That Doesn't Love a Wall." *New York Times*, August 27. http://www.nytimes.com/2012/08/28/opinion/Border-Fences-in-United-States-Israel-and-India.html.

Jones, Reece, and Corey Johnson. 2016. "Border Militarization and the Re-articulation of Sovereignty." *Transactions of the Institute of British Geographers* 41:187–200.

Joonghoon Lee. 2008. "Exploring Global Terrorism Data." *ACM Crossroads* 15 (2):7–16.

Joppke, Christian. 1998. "Asylum and State Sovereignty: A Comparison of the United States, Germany, and Britain." In *Challenge to the Nation-State: Immigration in Western Europe and the United States*, edited by Christian Joppke. New York: Oxford University Press.

Jordan, B., and F. Düvell. 2002. *Irregular Migration: The Dilemmas of Transnational Mobility*. Cheltenham: Edward Elgar Publishing.

Joslyn, Mark, and Donald Haider-Markel. 2007. "Sociotropic Concerns and Support for Counterterrorism Policies." *Social Science Quarterly* 88 (2):306–319.

Juergensmeyer, Mark. 1997. "Terror Mandated by God." *Terrorism and Political Violence* 9:16–23.

———. 2003. *Terror in the Mind of God: The Global Rise of Terrorist Violence*. 3rd ed. Berkeley: University of California Press.

Kanbolat, Hasan. 2009. "Cumhurbaşkanı Gül'ün Ürdün Ziyareti: Vize Kalktı, Serbest Ticaret Antlasması Imzalandı" [President Abdullah Gul's Visit to Jordan:Visa Requirements Abolished, Free Trade Agreement Signed]. *Ortadoğu Analiz*, 56–60.

Kanter, James. 2016. "E.U. Delays Decision on Requiring Visas of Americans and Canadians." *New York Times*, April 12.

Karanja, Stephen Kabera. 2008. *Transparency and Proportionality in the Schengen Information System and Border Control Co-Operation*. Boston: Martinus Nijhoff Publishers.

Kavi, Hüsamettin. 2007. "Vize Uygulamasi Gümrük Birliği'nin de Ruhuna Aykırıdır" [Visa Restrictions Are Against the Spirit of the Customs Union]. *Işveren* (April):45–49.

Kaynak, Muhteşem, ed. 1992. *The Iraqi Asylum Seekers and Türkiye*. Ankara: Tanmak Publications.

Keiger, J., and M. Alexander. 2002. "Special Issue on France and the Algerian War, 1954–62: Strategy, Operations, and Diplomacy." *Journal of Strategic Studies* 25 (2):206–210.

Kellner, Douglas. 2007. "Globalization, Terrorism, and Democracy: 9/11 and Its Aftermath." In *Frontiers of Globalization Research: Theoretical and Methodological Approaches*, edited by Ino Rossi, 243–271. New York: Springer.

Kennedy, Paul. 1987. *The Rise and Fall of the Great Powers: Economic Change and Military Conflict from 1500 to 2000*. Lexington, Mass.: Lexington Books.

Kennedy, Peter. 2003. *A Guide to Econometrics*. 5th ed. Malden, Mass.: Blackwell Publications.

Keohane, Robert O 2002. "The Globalization of Informal Violence, Theories of World Politics, and the 'Liberalism of Fear.'" *Dialogue IO* (Spring):29–43.

Keshk, Omar M. G., Brian M. Pollins, and Rafael Reuveny. 2004. "Trade Still Follows the Flag: The Primacy of Politics in a Simultaneous Model of Interdependence and Armed Conflict." *Journal of Politics* 66 (4):1155–1179.

Khalil, L. 2006. "Public Perceptions and Homeland Security." In *Homeland Security: Protecting America's Targets*, edited by J. F. Forest. Westport, Conn.: Praeger Security International.

Kim, Soo. 2015. "Tunisia Sees a Million Fewer Tourists After Terror Attacks." *Telegraph*, September 22. https://www.telegraph.co.uk/travel/destinations/africa/tunisia/articles/Tunisia-sees-a-million-less-tourists-after-terror-attacks/.

King, Gary, and Langche Zeng. 2001. Logistic Regression in Rare Events Data. *Society for Political Analysis* 9 (2):137–163.

Kingsley, Patrick. 2015. "Hungary's Migrant Fence Is Simply a Pointless PR Exercise." *Guardian*, August 25.

Kirchgaessner, Stephanie. 2017. "Italy's Five Star Movement Part of Growing Club of Putin Sympathisers in West." *Guardian*, January 5.

Kirişçi, Kemal. 1991. "The Legal Status of Asylum Seekers in Turkey: Problems and Prospects." *International Journal of Refugee Law* 3 (3):510–528.

———. 2000. "Disaggregating Turkish Citizenship and Immigration Practices." *Middle Eastern Studies* 36 (3).

———. 2006. "A Friendlier Schengen Visa System as a Tool of 'Soft Power': The Experience of Turkey." *European Journal of Migration and Law* 7 (4):343–346.

———. 2007. "Border Management and EU-Turkish Relations: Convergence or Deadlock." CARIM-Research Reports-2007/03. Florence: Robert Schuman Centre for Advanced Studies, San Domenico di Fiesole (FI), European University Institute.

———. 2009. "The Transformation of Turkish Foreign Policy: The Rise of the Trading State." *New Perspectives on Turkey* 40:29–57.

———. 2014. "Will the Readmission Agreement Bring the EU and Turkey Together or Pull Them Apart?" *CEPS Commentary*, February 4, 1–4. https://www.ceps.eu /publications/will-readmission-agreement-bring-eu-and-turkey-together-or-pull -them-apart.

———. 2016. "Europe's Refugee/Migrant Crisis: Can 'Illiberal' Turkey Save 'Liberal Europe' While Helping Syrian Refugees?" February 19, 1–30. https://www .brookings.edu/articles/europes-refugeemigrant-crisis-can-illiberal-turkey-save -liberal-europe-while-helping-syrian-refugees/.

Kirişçi, Kemal, and Neslihan Kaptanoğlu. 2011. "The Politics of Trade and Turkish Foreign Policy." *Middle Eastern Studies* 47 (5):705–724.

Kopan, Tal. 2017. "Trump Administration Adding Extra Hurdle for Green Cards." *CNN Politics*, August 29. http://www.cnn.com/2017/08/28/politics/trump-administration -green-cards-interviews/index.html.

Koslowski, Rey. 2009. "Global Mobility Regimes: A Conceptual Reframing." Paper presented at the Annual Meeting of the International Studies Association. New York.

Kovacks, Peter. 2002. "The Schengen Challenge and Its Balkan Dimensions." CEPS Policy Brief No. 17. Brussels.

Kraska, P. B. 2001. *Militarizing the American Criminal Justice System: The Changing Roles of the Armed Forces and the Police.* Boston: Northeastern University Press.

Krasner, Stephen. 1999. *Organized Hypocrisy.* Princeton, N.J.: Princeton University Press.

Kunreuther, H. 2002. "Risk Analysis and Risk Management in an Uncertain World." *Risk Analysis* 22:655–664.

Lacqueur, Walter. 1999. *The New Terrorism: Fanaticism and the Arms of Mass Destruction.* New York: Oxford University Press.

Lahav, Gallya. 2004. *Immigration and Politics in New Europe: Reinventing Borders.* Cambridge: Cambridge University Press.

Lang, Hardin, and Muath Al Wari. 2016. "The Flow of Foreign Fighters to the Islamic State: Assessing the Challenge and the Response." Center for American Progress.

Lavenex, Sandra. 2001. "Migration and the EU's New Eastern Border: Between Realism and Liberalism." *Journal of European Public Policy* 8 (1):24–42.

———. 2010. "Shifting Up and Out: The Foreign Policy of European Immigration Control." *Western European Politics* 29 (2):329–350.

Lee, Beom S., Walter Enders, and Todd Sandler. 2009. "What Did We Know and When Did We Know It?" *Defense and Peace Economics* 20 (2):79–93.

Leiken, Robert S. 2004. *Bearers of Global Jihad?: Immigration and National Security After 9/11.* Washington, D.C.: Nixon Center.

Li, Quan. 2005. "Does Democracy Promote or Reduce Transnational Terrorist Incidents?" *Journal of Conflict Resolution* 49 (2):278–297.

Lowenstein, George F., Elke U. Weber, Christopher K. Hsee, and Ned Welch. 2001. "Risk as Feelings." *Psychological Bulletin* 127 (2):267–286.

Lutterbeck, D. 2004. "Between Police and Military: The New Security Agenda and the Rise of Gendarmeries." *Cooperation and Conflict* 39:45–68.

Lyman, Rick. 2015. "Bulgaria Puts Up a New Wall, but This One Keeps People Out." *New York Times*, April 5. https://www.nytimes.com/2015/04/06/world/europe /bulgaria-puts-up-a-new-wall-but-this-one-keeps-people-out.html.

Mango, Andrew. 2005. *Turkey and the War on Terror: For Forty Years We Fought Alone.* New York: Routledge.

Mansfield, Edward, and Jon Pevehouse. 2000. "Trade Blocs, Trade Flows, and International Conflict." *International Organization* 54:775–808.

Mansfield, Edward, and Brian Pollins, eds. 2003. *Economic Interdependence and International Conflict: New Perspectives on an Enduring Debate.* Michigan Studies in International Political Economy. Ann Arbor: University of Michigan Press.

Maoz, Zeev, and Errol A. Henderson. 2013. "The World Religion Dataset, 1945–2010: Logic, Estimates, and Trends." *International Interactions* 39:265–291.

Marshall, Monty G., and Keith Jaggers. 2013. Polity IV Project: Political Regime Characteristics and Transitions, 1800–2013. http://www.systemicpeace.org/polity/polity4.htm.

Mau, S., L. Laube, C. Roos, and S. Wrobel. 2008. "Borders in a Globalized World: Selectivity, Internationalization, and Extraterritorialization." *Leviathan* 36 (1):123–148.

Mau, Steffen. 2010. "Mobility Citizenship, Inequality, and the Liberal State: The Case of Visa Policies." *International Political Sociology* 4 (4):339–361.

Mau, Steffen, Fabian Gulzau, Lena Laube, and Natascha Zaun. 2015. "The Global Mobility Divide: How Visa Policies Have Evolved over Time." *Journal of Ethnic and Migration Studies* 41 (8):1192–1213.

"May Gets Hollande Ultimatum: Free Trade Depends on Free Movement." 2016. *Guardian*, July 21. https://www.theguardian.com/politics/2016/jul/21/may-gets-hollande -ultimatum-free-trade-depends-on-free-movement.

McCallum, John. 1995. "National Borders Matter: Canada-US Regional Trade Patterns." *American Economic Review* 85 (3):615–623.

McCarthy, Niall. 2017. "Scores of ISIS Fighters Have Returned Home." *Forbes*, October 25.

Meyers, Eytan. 2000. "Theories of International Immigration Policy: A Comparative Analysis." Paper presented at the Annual Meeting of the International Studies Association, Los Angeles.

"Mexican Anger over US 'Trespass.'" 2007. *BBC News*, February 23. http://news.bbc.co.uk/2/hi/6390291.stm.

Mickolus, E., Todd Sandler, J. Murdock, and P. Flemming. 2012. *International Terrorism: Attributes of Terrorist Events (ITERATE)*. Dunn Loring, Va.: Vinyard Software.

Midlarsky, Manus I., Martha Crenshaw, and Fumihiko Yoshida. 1980. "Why Violence Spreads: The Contagion of International Terrorism." *International Studies Quarterly* 24:262–298.

Milton, Daniel, Megan Spencer, and Michael Findley. 2013. "Radicalism of the Hopeless: Refugee Flows and Transnational Terrorism." *International Interactions* 39 (5):621–645.

Miroff, Nick and Erica Werner. 2018. "First Phase of Trump Border Wall Gets $18 Billion Price Tag, in New Request to Lawmakers." *Washington Post*, January 5. https://www.washingtonpost.com/world/national-security/trump-border-wall-gets-18-billion-price-tag-in-new-request-to-lawmakers/2018/01/05/34e3c47e-f264-11e7-b3bf-ab90a706e175_story.html?undefined=&utm_term=.9f0cd4bb6fb5&wpisrc=nl_most&wpmm=1.

MOI (Ministry of the Interior). 2006. "Final Report of the Integrated Border Management Twinning Project." Ankara: Ministry of the Interior.

Monar, J. 2001. "The Dynamics of Justice and Home Affairs: Laboratories, Driving Factors and Costs." *Journal of Common Market Studies* 39 (4):747–764.

Morgenthau, Hans. 1978. *Politics Among Nations: The Struggle for Power and Peace.* 5th ed. New York: Alfred A. Knopf.

Mueller, John. 2005. "Simplicity and Spook: Terrorism and the Dynamics of Threat Exaggeration." *International Studies Perspectives* 6:208–234.

———. 2006. *Overblown: How Politicians and the Terrorism Industry Inflate National Security Threats, and Why We Believe Them.* New York: Free Press.

Muller, Benjamin. 2010. "Unsafe at Any Speed? Borders, Mobility, and 'Safe Citizenship.'" *Citizenship Studies* 14 (1):75–88.

Müller, Jan-Werner. 2016. *What Is Populism?* Philadelphia: University of Pennsylvania Press.

Mumyakmaz, Barış. 2009. "Turkey and Armenia Draw Nearer Via Trade." http://bianet.org/english/print/117997-turkey-and-armenia-draw-nearer-vi.

Naim, Moises. 2005. "Broken Borders." *Newsweek*, October 23. http://www.newsweek.com/broken-borders-120937.

Naim, Moises. 2006. "Outlook: Fluid Borders Pose Security Challenge" *Washington Post,* May 30. http://www.washingtonpost.com/wp-dyn/content/discussion/2006/05/25/DI2006052501565.html.

NAPP (National Action Plan for the Application of Turkey's Integrated Border Management Strategy). 2006. *Türkiye'nin Entegre Sınır Yönetimi Stratejisinin Uygulanmasına Yönelik Ulusal Eylem Planı* [National Action Plan for the Application of Turkey's Integrated Border Management Strategy]. https://ec.europa.eu/neighbour hood-enlargement/sites/near/files/pdf/turkey/ipa/2008/tr080210_action_plan _on_ibm_phase_ii-revised_final_en.pdf.

National Commission on Terrorist Attacks upon the United States. 2002. Complete 9/11 Commission Report. 361-383. Washington, D.C. http://govinfo.library.unt.edu/911 /report/.

National Consortium for the Study of Terrorism and Responses to Terrorism (START). (2017). Global Terrorism Database [Data file]. Retrieved from https://www.start .umd.edu/gtd.

"Netanyahu: Israel Will Support Jordan in the Face of ISIS." 2014. *Middle East Monitor*, June 30.

"Netanyahu: Israel Won't Dismantle West Bank Fence." 2009. Haaretz Service and News Agencies, July 22. https://www.haaretz.com/1.5080518.

Neumayer, Eric. 2006. "Unequal Access to Foreign Spaces: How States Use Visa Restrictions to Regulate Mobility in a Globalized World." *Transactions of the Institute of British Geographers* 31 (1):72–84.

———. 2010. "Visa Restrictions and Bilateral Travel." *Professional Geographer* 62 (2):171–181.

———. 2011. "On the Detrimental Impact of Visa Restrictions on Bilateral Trade and Foreign Direct Investment." *Applied Geography* 31 (3):901–907.

Newman, David. 2000. "Boundaries, Territory, and Postmodernity: Towards Shared or Separate Spaces?" In *Borderlands Under Stress*, edited by Martin Pratt and Janet Brown. Durham, UK: Kluwer Law International.

———. 2006. "The Lines That Continue to Separate Us: Borders in Our 'Borderless' World." *Progress in Human Geography* 30 (2):143–161.

Nixon, Ron. 2017. "U.S. Moves to Build Prototypes for Mexican Border Wall." *New York Times*, August 31. https://www.nytimes.com/2017/08/31/us/mexico-wall-prototypes -trump.html?mcubz=0.

Nordstrom, Louise. 2015. "Hungary to Fend Off 'Terrorist Migrants' with 175-Kilometre -Long Border Fence." France 24, June 19. http://www.france24.com/en/20150618 -hungary-fence-immigrants-border-terrorists.

Norris, Pippa. 2009. Democracy Time-series Data Release 3.0. January 2009.

"Norway Will Build a Fence Along Its Border with Russia." 2016. *New York Times*, August 24. https://www.nytimes.com/2016/08/25/world/europe/russia-norway-border -fence-refugees.html?.

Nuseibeh, Ghanem. 2009. Saudi Government Awards Border Fence Contract. *Risk and Forecast*, July 15. www.riskandforecast.com/post/saudi-arabia/saudi-govern ment-awards-border-fence-contract_50html.

O'Bryne, D. J. 2001. "On Passports and Border Controls." *Annals of Tourism Research* 28:399–416.

OECD (Organisation for Economic Co-operation and Development). 2009. International Direct Investment Statistics. Edited by Organization for Economic Cooperation and Development. Paris.

Ohmae, Kenichi. 1990. *The Borderless World*. New York: Oxford University Press.

Oneal, John R., and Bruce Russett. 1997. "The Classical Liberals Were Right: Democracy, Interdependence, and Conflict, 1950–1985." *International Studies Quarterly* 41:267–294.

———. 1999. "The Kantian Peace: The Pacific Benefits of Democracy, Interdependence, and International Organizations, 1885–1992." *International Organization* 52 (1):1–37.

Öniş, Ziya. 2006. "Globalization and Party Transformation: Turkey's Justice and Development Party in Perspective." In *Globalizing Democracy: Party Politics in Emerging Democracies*, edited by Peter Burnell, 122–141. London: Routledge.

Orhan, Oytun. 2014. "Struggle Against ISIS, Border Crossings, and Turkey." *Orsam Review of Regional Affairs* 11 (September):1–12.

"Ottawa Shooting Sparks Fears Border Clampdown Will Slow Trade with U.S." 2014. *Financial Post*, October 23. http://business.financialpost.com/news/economy/ottawa-shooting-rampage-raises-fears-border-clampdown-will-slow-trade-with-u-s.

Özal, Turgut. 1983. *Genel Ekonomi Sorunları, Turgut Özal'ın Görüşleri*. Ankara: Türkiye Cumhuriyeti.

Özel, S. 1995. "Of Not Being a Lone Wolf: Geography, Domestic Plays, and Turkish Foreign Policy in the Middle East." In *Powder Keg in the Middle East: The Struggle for Gulf Security*, edited by Geoffrey Kemp and Janice G. Stein. Lanham, Md.: Rowman and Littlefield.

Özler, Zeynep. 2003. "Visa Politics Under AKP Rule with Respect to EU Visa Policies." *Perceptions: Journal of International Affairs* 18 (3):33–61.

———. 2013. "Breaking the Vicious Circle in EU-Turkey Relations: Visa Negotiations." *Turkish Policy Quarterly* 11 (1):121–131.

Özler, Zeynep, and Ilke Toygür. 2011. "Visa-Free Travel: Is It Working as an EU Foreign Policy Tool?" FRIDE Policy Brief. http://fride.org/download/PB_73_Visa_Free_Travel_Eng.pdf.

Palmer, Glenn, Vito D'Orazio, Michael Kenwick, and Matthew Lane. 2015. "The MID4 Data Set: Procedures, Coding Rules, and Description." *Conflict Management and Peace Science* 32 (2):222–242.

Pape, Robert A. 2003. "The Strategic Logic of Suicide Terrorism." *American Political Science Review* 97 (3):343–361.

Pape, Robert A. 2006. *Dying to Win: The Strategic Logic of Suicide Terrorism*. New York: Random House.

Paul, T. V. 2005. "The National Security State and Global Terrorism." In *Globalization, Security, and the Nation State*, edited by Ersel Aydinli and James N. Rosenau, 49–67. New York: State University of New York Press.

Peffley, Mark, Marc L. Hutchison, and Michal Shamir. 2015. "The Impact of Persistent Terrorism on Political Tolerance: Israel, 1980 to 2011." *American Political Science Review* 109 (4):1–16.

Pells, Rachel. 2016. "Refugees and Migrants Arriving in Greece Down 90 Percent, Says Border Agency." *Independent*, May 13.

Peters, Margaret E. 2017. *Trading Barriers: Immigration and the Remaking of Globalization*. Princeton, N.J.: Princeton University Press.

Pettersson, Therése, and Peter Wallensteen. 2015. "Armed Conflicts, 1946–2014." *Journal of Peace Research* 52 (4):536–550.

Piazza, James A. 2006. "Rooted In Poverty? Terrorism, Poor Economic Development and Social Cleavages." *Terrorism and Political Violence* 18:159–177.

Piazza, James A. 2009. "Is Islamist Terrorism More Dangerous?: An Empirical Study of Group Ideology, Organization, and Goal Structure." *Terrorism and Political Violence* 21 (1):62–88.

———. 2012. "The Opium Trade and Patterns of Terrorism in the Provinces of Afghanistan: An Empirical Analysis." *Terrorism and Political Violence* 24 (2):213–234.

———. 2015. "Terrorist Suspect Religious Identity and Public Support for Harsh Interrogation and Detention Practices." *Political Psychology* 36 (6):667–690.

Pitel, Laura. 2016. "Turkey in Crisis: 'Ripple Effect' from Syria and Iraq Sees Worst Flare-up in Kurdish Conflict in 20 Years." *Independent*, January 17. https://www .independent.co.uk/news/world/middle-east/turkey-in-crisis-ripple-effect-from -syria-and-iraq-sees-worst-flare-up-in-kurdish-conflict-in-20-a6818331.html.

Polachek, Solomon W. 1980. "Conflict and Trade." *Journal of Conflict Resolution* 24:55–78.

"Putting up Barriers." 2016. *Economist*, February 6. http://www.economist.com/news /briefing/21690065-permanent-reintroduction-border-controls-would-harm -trade-europe-putting-up-barriers.

Ramesh, Randeep. 2005. "US Backs Pakistani-Afghan Border Fence." *Guardian*, September 13. https://www.theguardian.com/world/2005/sep/14/pakistan.afghanistan.

Rapoport, David C. 2001. "The Fourth Wave: September 11 in the History of Terrorism." *Current History* 100 (650):419–425.

Robertson, Nic. 2016. "Safer in or out of the EU? Why Security Is Key to Brexit Vote." CNN, June 21. https://www.cnn.com/2016/06/21/europe/brexit-security-debate -robertson/index.html.

Rodrik, D. 1998. "Why Do More Open Economies Have Bigger Governments?" *Journal of Political Economy* 106 (5):997–1032.

Romanov, D., A. Zussman, and N. Zussman. 2010. "Does Terrorism Demoralize? Evidence from Israel." *Economica* 2:1–16.

Rosecrance, Richard N. 1986. *The Rise of the Trading State: Commerce and Conquest in the Modern World*. New York: Basic Books.

———. 1996. "The Rise of the Virtual State." *Foreign Affairs* 75 (4):45–61.

Rosiere, S., and Reece Jones. 2012. "Teichopolitics: Re-considering Globalization Through the Role of Walls and Fences." *Geopolitics* 17:217–234.

Roth, Mitchel P., and Murat Sever. 2007. "The Kurdish Workers Party (PKK) as Criminal Syndicate: Funding Terrorism Through Organized Crime: A Case Study." *Studies in Conflict and Terrorism* 30 (10). doi:10.1080/10576100701558620.

Roy, Olivier. 2017. "Who Are the New Jihadis?" *Guardian*, April 13.

Rudolph, Christopher. 2003. "Security and the Political Economy of International Migration." *American Political Science Review* 97 (4):603–620.

———. 2005. "Sovereignty and Territorial Borders in a Global Age." *International Studies Review* 7:1–20.

———. 2006. *National Security and Immigration: Policy Development in the United States and Western Europe Since 1945.* Stanford, Calif.: Stanford University Press.

———. 2008. "Refuting Mundell's Theorem: Why Trade and Migration Are Not Substitutes." Paper presented at the annual meeting of the American Political Science Association, Boston, August 28. http://www.allacademic.com/meta/p278837_index.html.

Russett, Bruce, and John R. Oneal. 2001. *Triangulating Peace: Democracy, Interdependence, and International Organization.* New York: W. W. Norton.

Sageman, Marc. 2004. *Understanding Terror Networks.* Philadelphia: University of Pennsylvania Press.

Sais, Samantha. 2013. "Price Tag for 700 Miles of Border Fencing: High and Hard to Pin Down." NBC News, June 21. http://usnews.nbcnews.com/_news/2013/06/21/19062298-price-tag-for-700-miles-of-border-fencing-high-and-hard-to-pin-down?lite.

Salehyan, Idean. 2006. "Rebels Without Borders: State Boundaries, Transnational Opposition, and Civil Conflict." PhD thesis, Department of Political Science, University of California–San Diego.

———. 2008a. "US Asylum and Refugee Policy Towards Muslim Nations Since 9/11." In *Immigration Policy and Security: U.S., European, and Commonwealth Perspectives*, edited by Terri Givens, Gary P. Freeman, and David L. Leal. London: Routledge.

———. 2008b. "US Refugee and Asylum Policy: Has Anything Changed After 9/11?" Paper presented at International Studies Association annual meeting, March 26–30, San Francisco.

Salter, Mark B. 2003. *Rights of Passage: The Passport in International Relations.* London: Lynne Rienner Publishers.

San Akca, Belgin. 2009. "Supporting Non-State Armed Groups: A Resort to Illegality?" *Journal of Strategic Studies* 32 (4):589–590. doi: 10.1080/01402390902987012.

Sanchez-Cuenca, Ignacio, and Luis de La Calle. 2009. "Domestic Terrorism: The Hidden Side of Political Violence." *Annual Review of Political Science* 12:31–49.

Sandler, Todd, Daniel G. Arce, and Walter Enders. 2009. "Transnational Terrorism." Copenhagen Consensus 2008: Copenhagen Consensus Center.

Sassen, Saskia. 1996. *Losing Control? Sovereignty in an Age of Globalization.* New York: Columbia University Press.

———. 1998. *Globalization and Its Discontents: Essays on the New Mobility of People and Money.* New York: New Press.

———. 2006. *Territory, Authority, Rights: From Medieval to Global Assemblages.* Princeton, N.J.: Princeton University Press.

Saval, Nikil. 2017. "Globalisation: The Rise and Fall of an Idea That Swept the World." *Guardian*, July 14. https://www.theguardian.com/world/2017/jul/14/globalisation-the-rise-and-fall-of-an-idea-that-swept-the-world.

Scheve, K. F., and M. J. Slaughter. 2001. "Labor Market Competition and Individual Preferences over Immigration Policy." *Review of Economics and Statistics* 88 (1):133–145.

Schmid, Alex P. and A. Jongman. 1988. *Political Terrorism: A New Guide to Actors, Authors, Concepts, Data Bases, Theories, and Literature.* Amsterdam: North-Holland Publishing Company.

Schmitt, Eric. 2017. "ISIS Fighters Are Not Flooding Back Home to Wreak Havoc as Feared." *New York Times*, October 22.

Schuster, M.A., B. D. Stein, L. H. Jaycox, R. L. Collins, G. N. Marshall, M. N. Elliott, A. J. Zhou, D. E. Kanouse, J. L. Morrison, S. H. Berry. 2001. "National Survey of Stress Reactions After the September 11, 2001 Terrorist Attacks." *New England Journal of Medicine* 345:1507–1512.

Sert, Deniz. 2013. "Turkey's Integrated Border Management Strategy." *Turkish Policy Quarterly* 12 (1):173–180.

Shaheen, Kareem. 2017. "The Turkish Referendum: All You Need to Know." *Guardian*, April 10.

Shelley, Louise. 2006. "Border Issues: Transnational Crime and Terrorism." In *Borders and Security Governance: Managing Borders in a Globalised World*, edited by Alan Bryden, Marina Caparini, and Otwin Marenin. Berlin: LIT Verlag.

Simmons, Beth. 2005. "Rules over Real Estate: Trade, Territorial Conflict, and Borders as Institution." *Journal of Conflict Resolution* 49 (6):823–848.

Smith, Myles G. 2012. "Borders Hardening Throughout Central Asia in Anticipation of NATO Pullout." *Global Research and Analysis*.

Solingen, Etel. 1998. *Regional Orders at Century's Dawn: Global and Domestic Influences on Grand Strategy.* Princeton, N.J.: Princeton University Press.

Staniland, Paul. 2006. "Defeating Transnational Insurgencies: The Best Offense Is a Good Fence." *Washington Quarterly* 29 (1):21–40.

Starr, Harvey. 2002. "Opportunity, Willingness, and Geographic Information Systems: Reconceptualizing Borders in International Relations." *Political Geography* 21:243–261.

———. 2006. "International Borders: What They Are, What They Mean, and Why We Should Care." *SAIS Review* 26 (1):1–8.

Stein, Aaron. 2016. "The Islamic State in Turkey: A Deep Dive into a Dark Place." *War on the Rocks.* https://warontherocks.com/2016/04/the-islamic-state-in-turkey-a-deep-dive-into-a-dark-place/.

Stein, Aaron. 2017. "Turkey Is Tangled up in Terrorism." *War on the Rocks*, January 11. https://warontherocks.com/2017/01/turkey-is-tangled-up-in-terrorism/.

Sterling, Brent L. 2009. *Do Good Fences Make Good Neighbors?: What History Teaches Us About Strategic Barriers and International Security*. Washington, D.C.: Georgetown University Press.

Steves, Rick. 2013. "The Security Fence, the Anti-Terrorism Barrier, the Wall." *Huffington Post*, November 18. https://www.huffingtonpost.com/rick-steves/the-security-fence-the-an_b_4296601.html.

Stinnett, Douglas M., Jaroslav Tir, Paul F. Diehl, Philip Schafer, and Charles Gochman. 2002. "The Correlates of War (Cow) Project Direct Contiguity Data, Version 3.0." *Conflict Management and Peace Science* 19 (2):59–67.

Strand, H., L. Wilhelmsen and N. P. Gleditsch. 2004. "Armed Conflict Dataset Codebook." Oslo: International Peace Research Institute.

Strange, Susan. 1996. *The Retreat of the State: The Diffusion of Power in the World Economy*. New York: Cambridge University Press.

———. 1997. "The Erosion of the State." *Current History* 96:365–369.

TBMM (Türkiye Büyük Millet Meclisi). 1984. Türkiye Büyük Millet Meclisi Tutanak Dergisi. 17. Dönem, 2. Yasama Yılı, 16.12. In *Türkiye Büyük Millet Meclisi Tutanak Dergisi*. Ankara.

———. 1985. Türkiye Büyük Millet Meclisi Tutanakları. *Hatay Milletvekili Abdurrahman Demirtaş'ın, Hatay'ın Anavatana ilhakından sonra toprakları Suriye'de kalan vatandaşlarımıza dağıtılan topraklara ilişkin Maliye ve Gümrük Bakanından sözlü soru önergesi*. 17. Dönem, 2. Yasama Yılı, 13.2. Ankara.

Teitelbaum, M. S., and M. Weiner, eds. 1995. *Threatened Peoples, Threatened Borders: World Migration and U.S. Policy*. New York: W. W. Norton.

Torpey, John. 1998. "Coming and Going: On the State Monopolization of the Legitimate 'Means of Movement.'" *Sociological Theory* 16:239–259.

———. 2000a. *The Invention of the Passport: Surveillance, Citizenship, and the State*. Cambridge: Cambridge University Press.

———. 2000b. "States and the Regulation of Migration in the Twentieth-Century North Atlantic World." In *The Wall Around the West*, edited by Peter Andreas, 31–55. Oxford: Rowman and Littlefield.

Troianovski, Anton and Marcus Walker. 2015. "Paris Terror Attacks Transform Debate over Europe's Migration Crisis." *Wall Street Journal*, November 16. https://www.wsj.com/articles/paris-terror-attacks-transform-debate-over-europes-migration-crisis-1447608944.

"Travel Visas: Sticker Shock." 2015. *Economist*, December 30. https://www.economist.com/news/leaders/21684782-they-have-their-uses-burden-visas-impose-travellers-and-recipient-countries-too.

Traynor, Ian. 2016. "Is the Schengen Dream of Europe Without Borders Becoming a Thing of the Past?" *Guardian*, January 5. https://www.theguardian.com/world/2015/nov/18/eu-travellers-tighter-id-checks-french-clampdown-borders-paris-attacks.

"Turkey, Armenia, to Reopen Border." 2009. *Wall Street Journal*, October 11. https://www.wsj.com/articles/SB125518039736978131.

"Turkey in the Middle East: Looking East and South." 2009. *Economist*, October 29. https://www.economist.com/node/14753776.

"Turkey's Fractious Politics: Fighting on Two Fronts" 2015. *Economist*, August 6. https://www.economist.com/news/europe/21660585-caretaker-government-attacks-kurds-abroad-and-home-fighting-two-fronts.

UNHCR (United Nations High Commissioner for Refugees). 2014." Global Trends 2013." Edited by UN High Commissioner for Refugees. http://www.unhcr.org/en-us/statistics/country/5399a14f9/unhcr-global-trends-2013.htm.

USAID (United States Agency International Development). 2008. "Kurdistan Region Economic Development Assessment." USAID Report, December. http://www.mop.gov.krd/resources/MoP%20Files/PDF%20Files/DCC/Studies/EDA%20Report_English.pdf.

UNSC (United Nations Security Council). 2014. United Nations Security Council Resolution 2178. https://www.un.org/sc/ctc/wp-content/uploads/2016/09/FTF-Report-1-3_English.pdf.

United States. 2011. *National Strategy for Counterterrorism*. [Washington, D.C.]: [Executive Office of the President]. http://purl.fdlp.gov/GPO/gpo9627.

Ünver, Can. 2013. "Changing Diaspora Politics of Turkey and Public Diplomacy." *Turkish Policy Quarterly* 12 (1):181–189.

Vallet, Elisabeth. 2016. *Borders, Fences, and Walls: State of Insecurity?* Border Regions Series. London: Routledge.

Vasquez, John A. 1993. *The War Puzzle*. Cambridge: Cambridge University Press.

———. 1995. "Why Do Neighbors Fight? Proximity, Interaction, or Territoriality." *Journal of Peace Research* 32 (3):277–293.

Viner, Jacob. 1951. *International Economics*. Glencoe, Ill.: Free Press.

Waever, Ole, Barry Buzan, Morten Kelstrup, and Pierre Lemaitre. 1993. *Identity, Migration and the New Security Agenda in Europe*. New York: St. Martin's Press.

Wang, Christine. 2016. "Brussels Attacks: Can Europe Keep Its Open Borders?" CNBC, March 22. https://www.cnbc.com/2016/03/22/brussels-attacks-can-europe-keep-its-open-borders.html.

Whitaker, Brian. 2004. "Saudi Security Barrier Stirs Anger in Yemen." *Guardian*, February 16. https://www.theguardian.com/world/2004/feb/17/saudiarabia.yemen.

WDI (World Development Indicators). 2015. Washington, D.C.: World Bank.

Weiken, Oliver. 2013. "Israel Becomes a Fortress Nation as It Walls Itself off from the Arab Spring." *New York Times*, March 20.

Witte, Griff. 2016. "Europe's New Border Fences Are Derailing Migrants, but Not Stopping Them." *Washington Post*, March 9. https://www.washingtonpost.com/world/europe/europes-new-border-fences-are-derailing-migrants-but-not-stopping-them/2016/03/09/2a932c9e-dfc9-11e5-8c00-8aa03741dced_story.html?utm_term=.508f5dccd18a.

Wyne, Ali. 2005. "Suicide Terrorism as Strategy: Case Studies of Hamas and the Kurd-
    istan Workers Party." *Strategic Insights* 4(7). Resource document. Center for Con-
    temporary Conflict. https://www.hsdl.org/?view&did=455140.
Yalpat, Alpan. 1984. "Turkey's Economy Under the Generals." *Middle East Informa-
    tion and Research Project* 122:16–24.
Yeginsu, Ceylan, and Victor Homola. 2016. "Istanbul Bomber Entered as a Refugee,
    Turks Say." *New York Times*, January 13. https://www.nytimes.com/2016/01/14
    /world/europe/istanbul-explosion.html.
Young, Joseph, and Michael Findley. 2011. "Promise and Pitfalls of Terrorism Research."
    *International Studies Review* 13 (3):411–431.
Yu, Roger. 2010. "Companies Criticize U.S. Business Visa Process." ABC News, Sep-
    tember 5. http://abcnews.go.com/Business/companies-criticize-us-business-visa
    -process/story?id=11555728.
Zacher, Mark W. 2001. "The Territorial Integrity Norm: International Boundaries and
    the Use of Force." *International Organization* 55 (2):215–250.
Zechmeister, Elizabeth, and Jennifer Merolla. 2009. *Democracies at Risk: How Terrorist
    Threats Affect the Public.* Chicago: University of Chicago Press.
Zehni, Tevfik. 2008. "Turkey and PKK Terrorism." Thesis, Naval Postgraduate School, San
    Jose, Calif.
Zolberg, Aristide R. 1987. "Wanted but Not Welcome: Alien Labor in Western Develop-
    ment." In *Population in an Interacting World*, edited by William Alonso. Cambridge,
    Mass.: Harvard University Press.
Zureik, Elia, and Mark B. Salter. 2005. "Global Surveillance and Policing: Borders,
    Security, Identity-Introduction." In *Global Surveillance and Policing: Borders,
    Security, Identity*, edited by Elia Zureik and Mark B. Salter, 1–11. Portland, Ore.:
    Willan Publishing.

# INDEX

Abedi, Salman, and homegrown terrorism, 110

Afghanistan: and global terrorism, 53; Korengal Valley, 196; migration from into Turkey, 151; and organized crime, 196

Agnew, John, 15

airport security, 20

airport transit visas, in the EU and Schengen, 84

AKP (Adalet ve Kalkinma Partisi) (Turkey): border policies of, 181; and economic cooperation with MENA, 172; and EU accession reforms, 171; foreign policy of, 166, 176; and Kurdish minority rights, 168; and liberalization, 180; and neo-Ottomanism, 184; and zero-problems policy, 166. *See also* Justice and Development Party (JDP)

Al-Qaeda, 118; and border fences, 118

Amri, Anis, and Berlin Christmas market attack, 2

Amsterdam Treaty of 1999, and the EU, 80

Anavatan Partisi (ANAP) (Turkey). *See* Motherland Party

Andreas, Peter, 4

Annex I, and the EU negative list, 80

Annex II, and the EU white list, 80

anti-drug trafficking, 24

anti-immigrant sentiment, 2, 112

anti-immigration lobbies, 12, 13

antiterrorism, 28, 31; in democracies, 64; in Israel, 118, 123; and policy toughness, 32; post–September 11 attacks, 21; in response to the Madrid and London attacks, 20

Arab Spring: consequences of, 118; effects on Turkey's border policies of, 180

Armenian Secret Army for Liberation Armenia (ASALA), 156

asylum policies: effects on irregular migration, 197; and relationship with visa controls, 191

asylum seekers and visa policies, 41

asymmetric threats, 20. *See also* non-state actors

atypical threats, 20, 26; and cooperation among states, 28

autarkic policies, 195

authoritarian leaders, and hardline policies, 113

authoritarianism, and illiberalism, 32

autocracies: impact of terrorism on policies of, 67; measurement of, 67

barriers, demonstrative function and symbolic value of, 4

Belgium: and policy stringency, 193; and Schengen area, 80

Berlin Wall, 121

bias, in measuring visa rejection rates, 91. *See also* endogeneity bias

Bigo, Didier, 21

bilateral cooperation, in border management, 190

bilateral trade: and economic interdependence, 13, 24; impact of visas on, 7, 46; measurement of and data sources on, 87. *See also* Correlates of War (COW) Bilateral Trade Data

biometric identity, 41

biometric passports: and mobility regime, 41; Turkey's adoption of, 169

Boaz, Atzili, 28, 194

border agents: and bribing of, 196; and devolution of authority, 190; functions in border regimes, 189

border barriers, historical examples of, 121

# ACKNOWLEDGMENTS

The book took shape at several different institutions: beginning at Duke, continuing at University College, Oxford, and finally at the University of Kansas (KU). At each institution, I met colleagues and friends who left their imprint on the book through spontaneous dialogue, detailed email correspondence, or blunt critique.

Without the meticulous guidance of Peter Agree, my editor at Penn Press, the editorial board, and anonymous reviewers, this book would not have come to fruition. It goes without saying that I am very grateful to Peter above all for believing in the project. He diligently answered all my questions, provided excellent feedback, and took me through the stages of book review and publishing in a professional and candid manner. I would also like to thank the anonymous reviewers Peter solicited.

I thank my colleague Christopher F. Gelpi for critical feedback and for continued collaborative mentorship through the years. In addition, I am indebted to several scholars at Duke for their indispensable mentorship and support. Joseph M. Grieco motivated me to find a dependent variable to fall in love with, leading me to study migration and border policies. I thank Michael Munger for excellent feedback and suggestions, particularly for encouraging me to explore my ideas through the political economy lens. Bahar Leventoğlu's support and optimism renewed my confidence each time I had doubts about the project.

At Oxford, suggestions from Duncan Snidal, Alex Betts, and David Sylvan contributed independently to the project. I am fortunate that at KU I found myself surrounded by supportive, productive, and collegial colleagues. I would like to thank Robert Rohrschneider for his mentorship and confidence in me. Mariya Omelicheva provided friendship and keen advice on how to market the proposal. Last but not least, Michael Wuthrich walked me through the steps of book publishing, conversing fluently in both English and Turkish. Outside of KU, I was fortunate enough to encounter other excellent scholars. I am thankful to Amanda Murdie for excellent feedback on the book proposal and for taking the time to read through early drafts of the introduction and theory chapters. Victor Asal's mentorship and guidance have proved invaluable, and I thank him for reading early drafts of chapters. I am also indebted to Roger Haydon at Cornell University Press for reading early drafts of some of the chapters and providing helpful suggestions on how to polish and streamline my writing.

The acknowledgments section would be incomplete if I did not extend thanks to all my friends in Lawrence. Time with them provided a pick-me-up when I needed it. Most important of all, I am grateful to my family members and for their unwavering support. A special thank you goes out to the furry companion who accompanied me while I wrote the concluding chapter; may your beautiful soul rest in peace. Each of them has contributed to this book in a unique way. Most valuable to me has been their conviction that the book would one day be published. Without further ado, this book is for you.